Achieving Education for All through public–private partnerships?

Concern for achieving Millennium Development Goals (MDGs) by 2015 has led to a focus on the role that non-state providers (NSPs) can offer in extending access and improving quality of basic services. While NSPs can help to fill a gap in provision to those excluded from state provision, recent growth in both for-profit and not-for-profit providers in developing countries has sometimes resulted in fragmentation of service delivery. To address this, attention is increasingly given in the education sector to developing 'partnerships' between governments and NSPs. Partnerships are further driven by the expectation that the state has the moral, social, and legal responsibility for overall education service delivery and so should play a role in facilitating and regulating NSPs.

Even where the ultimate aim of both non-state providers and the state is to provide education of acceptable quality to all children, this book provides evidence from diverse contexts across Africa, South Asia, and Latin America to highlight the challenges in them partnering to achieve this.

This book was published as a special issue of *Development in Practice*.

Pauline Rose was Reader in International Education at the University of Sussex at the time of editing this book. She has subsequently been working as Senior Policy Analyst for the Education for All Global Monitoring Report based at UNESCO in Paris. She has published widely on issues related to educational policy and practice from a variety of perspectives – including financing and governance, non-state provision, democratisation, and the role of international aid in shaping the education agenda.

Development in Practice
Series Editor: Deborah Eade

Each title in the *Development in Practice Books* series offers a focused overview of practice-relevant analysis, experience, and research on key topics in development.

Participatory Research and Gender Analysis
New Approaches
Edited by Nina Lilja, John Dixon, and Deborah Eade

Achieving Education for All through public–private partnerships?
Non-state provision of education in developing countries
Edited by Pauline Rose

Achieving Education for All through public–private partnerships?
Non-state provision of education in developing countries

Edited by

Pauline Rose

LONDON AND NEW YORK

First published 2011
by Routledge
2 Park Square, Milton Park, Abingdon, Oxon, OX14 4RN

Simultaneously published in the USA and Canada
by Routledge
711 Third Avenue, New York, NY 10017

Routledge is an imprint of the Taylor & Francis Group, an informa business

First issued in paperback 2013

© 2011 Oxfam GB
Preface is the copyright of Deborah Eade

This book is a reproduction of *Development in Practice*, vol. 20, issue 4&5. The Publisher requests to those authors who may be citing this book to state, also, the bibliographical details of the special issue on which the book was based.

Typeset in Times New Roman by Taylor & Francis Books

All rights reserved. No part of this book may be reprinted or reproduced or utilised in any form or by any electronic, mechanical, or other means, now known or hereafter invented, including photocopying and recording, or in any information storage or retrieval system, without permission in writing from the publishers.

Achieving Education for All through public–private partnerships?: Non-state provision of education in developing countries is based on Development in Practice Volume 20, Numbers 4&5 (June 2010), published by Routledge, Taylor & Francis Group Ltd. We gratefully acknowledge generous financial support for the journal from affiliates of Oxfam International, in particular Oxfam GB. The views expressed in this volume are those of the named individual contributors and not necessarily those of the Series Editor or Publisher.

A summary of each chapter is available in French, Portuguese, and Spanish on the journal's website. To view these and other development resources, please visit: www.developmentinpractice.org

British Library Cataloguing in Publication Data
A catalogue record for this book is available from the British Library

ISBN13: 978-0-415-58371-8 (hbk)
ISBN13: 978-0-415-84582-3 (pbk)

Disclaimer
The publisher would like to make readers aware that the chapters in this book are referred to as articles as they had been in the special issue. The publisher accepts responsibility for any inconsistencies that may have arisen in the course of preparing this volume for print.

Contents

Previously published Development in Practice Readers   vii
Notes on Contributors   ix

Preface
   Deborah Eade   xii

Introduction
   Pauline Rose   1

1. Civil society, basic education, and sector-wide aid: insights from Sub-Saharan Africa
   Karen Mundy, with Megan Haggerty, Malini Sivasubramaniam, Suzanne Cherry, and Richard Maclure   12

2. Marching to different rhythms: international NGO collaboration with the state in Tanzania
   Sheila Aikman   26

3. The roles of non-state providers in ten complementary education programmes
   Joseph DeStefano and Audrey-marie Schuh Moore   39

4. Reaching the underserved with complementary education: lessons from Ghana's state and non-state sectors
   Leslie Casely-Hayford and Ash Hartwell   55

5. Public–private partnerships or privatisation? Questioning the state's role in education in India
   Prachi Srivastava   68

6. *Madrasas* as partners in education provision: the South Asian experience
   Masooda Bano   82

7. Struggles for memory and social-justice education in Latin America
   Lauren Ila Jones and Carlos Alberto Torres   95

8. Collaboration in delivering education: relations between governments and NGOs in South Asia
   Richard Batley and Pauline Rose   107

CONTENTS

9. Working effectively with non-state actors to deliver education in fragile states
    Chris Berry — 114

10. Non-state providers, the state, and health in post-conflict fragile states
    Stephen Commins — 122

11. Free primary education still excludes the poorest of the poor in urban Kenya
    Moses Oketch and Moses Ngware — 131

12. The evolution of NGO–government relations in education: ActionAid 1972–2009
    David Archer — 139

Index — 147

Previous titles from *Development in Practice*
Series Editor: Deborah Eade

Practical Action Publishing, Rugby

Deconstructing Development Discourse: Buzzwords and Fuzzwords (2010)
Edited by Andrea Cornwall and Deborah Eade

Kumarian Press, Bloomfield, CT

Development and Humanitarianism: Practical Issues (2007)
Edited by Deborah Eade and Tony Vaux

Development and the Private Sector: Consuming Interests (2006)
Edited by Deborah Eade and John Sayer

Development NGOs and Labor Unions: Terms of Engagement (2005)
Edited by Deborah Eade and Alan Leather

Oxfam GB, Oxford

Development, Women, and War: Feminist Perspectives (2004)
Edited by Haleh Afshar and Deborah Eade

Development Methods and Approaches: Critical Reflections (2003)
Edited by Deborah Eade

Development and the Learning Organisation (2003) (in association with the Institute of Development Studies and Oxfam America)
Edited by Laura Roper, Jethro Pettit, and Deborah Eade

Development and Culture (2002) (in association with World Faiths Dialogue on Development)
Edited by Deborah Eade

Development and Cities (2002) (in association with UNRISD)
Edited by David Westendorff and Deborah Eade

Development and Agroforestry: Scaling Up the Impact of Research (2002) (in association with the World Forestry Centre, CGIAR)
Edited by Steven Franzel, Peter Cooper, Glenn L. Denning, and Deborah Eade

PREVIOUS TITLES FROM DEVELOPMENT IN PRACTICE

Development and Advocacy (2002)
Edited by Deborah Eade

Debating Development: NGOs in the Future (2001) (in association with Oxfam International)*
Edited by Deborah Eade and Ernst Ligteringen

Development, NGOs, and Civil Society (2000)*
Edited by Deborah Eade

Development and Management: Experiences of Value-Based Conflict (2000) (in association with The Open University)
Edited by Deborah Eade, Tom Hewitt, and Hazel Johnson

Development and Social Action (1999)
Edited by Deborah Eade

Development with Women (1999)
Edited by Deborah Eade

Development and Rights (1998)*
Edited by Deborah Eade

Development for Health (1997)
Edited by Deborah Eade

Development and Patronage (1997)*
Edited by Deborah Eade

Development and Social Diversity (1996)*
Edited by Deborah Eade

Development in States of War (1996)*
Edited by Deborah Eade

* Also published in Spanish translation by Intermón, Barcelona.

Notes on Contributors

Sheila Aikman is senior lecturer in Education and Development in the School of International Development at the University of East Anglia. She has worked extensively in Latin America, particularly in the Amazon region, with indigenous peoples and intercultural education. Between 2001 and 2008, she held the position of Global Education Advisor for Oxfam GB. During that time she co-managed the research project Beyond Access: Gender, Education and Development, with Oxfam GB and Prof. Elaine Unterhalter at the Institute of Education.

David Archer is Head of Education at ActionAid.

Masooda Bano is Economic and Social Research Council (ESRC)/Arts and Humanities Research Council (AHRC) Research Fellow at Oxford Department of International Development (ODID) and Wolfson College, University of Oxford.

Richard Batley is Emeritus Professor of Development Administration at the International Development Department, School of Government and Society, University of Birmingham. His research interests are in government, regulation, urban policy, service delivery, non-state service provision, public–private partnership, and aid management. He is also Director of the DFID Governance and Social Development Resource Centre (www.gsdrc.org).

Chris Berry is the education adviser for DFID in Ethiopia.

Leslie Casely-Hayford is Director of Associates for Change, a research and consulting firm based in Ghana.

Suzanne Cherry was a graduate student at OISE/University of Toronto, Canada at the time of writing. She is currently Research and Publications Manager in the Advocacy and Education department of World Vision Canada.

Stephen Commins is Strategy Manager, Fragile States, International Medical Corps and a Lecturer in the Department of Urban Planning, University of California, Los Angeles.

Joseph DeStefano is a Senior Education Research Analyst with the Research Triangle Institute (RTI) International. He provides policy, planning and reform advice to international development projects and governments around the world. He served as the principal investigator on the EQUIP2 research on complementary education in

NOTES ON CONTRIBUTORS

ten countries. He has over 20 years experience researching and supporting education reform.

Megan Haggerty is a research consultant specializing in education advocacy through networking and social movements at the national and transnational level. At the time of writing, she was a graduate student at OISE/University of Toronto, Canada.

Ash Hartwell is Adjunct Professor at the Center of International Education, University of Massachusetts.

Lauren Ila Jones is the Program Officer of the Paulo Freire Institute, Graduate School of Education and Information Studies, University of California – Los Angeles.

Richard Maclure is an Associate Professor at the University of Ottawa, Canada.

Karen Mundy is the principal investigator for the research study on 'Civil Society, Basic Education and Sector-Wide Aid: Insights from Sub-Saharan Africa.' She is an Associate Professor and the Director of the Comparative, International and Development Education Research Centre at the Ontario Institute for the Studies in Education (OISE) at the University of Toronto, Canada.

Moses Ngware is Associate Research Scientist at African Population and Health Research Center (APHRC)

Moses Oketch is Senior Lecturer at the Institute of Education, University of London, and also Senior Research Scientist at African Population and Health Research Center (APHRC).

Pauline Rose was Reader in International Education at the University of Sussex at the time of editing this book. She has subsequently been working as Senior Policy Analyst for the Education for All Global Monitoring Report based at UNESCO in Paris. She has published widely on issues related to educational policy and practice from a variety of perspectives – including financing and governance, non-state provision, democratisation, and the role of international aid in shaping the education agenda.

Audrey-marie Schuh Moore is Deputy Director of EQUIP2 of the Academy for Educational Development. She has extensive experience in educational development, evaluation, economic analysis, microfinance, and secondary education in Latin America, Africa, the Middle East, and the USA.

Malini Sivasubramaniam is a graduate student at OISE/University of Toronto, Canada. Her doctoral research examines parental decision making structures and social capital within low-cost private schools in Kenya.

Prachi Srivastava is Assistant Professor at the School of International Development and Global Studies, University of Ottawa. Her research interests include the privatisation of schooling in South Asia, low-fee private schooling in India, and the role of private actors in education delivery.

Carlos Alberto Torres is Professor of Social Science and Comparative Education in the Graduate School of Education and Information Studies at the University of California – Los Angeles (UCLA), Division Head of Social Sciences and Comparative Education and the Founder and Director of the Paulo Freire Institute, UCLA, as

NOTES ON CONTRIBUTORS

well as the Founder and Director of the Paulo Freire Institute, Brazil. Most recently he has accepted the ad-honorem responsibility to be International co-Director of the Paulo Freire Institute, Roehampton University. He is the author of more than 300 research articles and 62 books.

Preface

Deborah Eade

This Development in Practice Book, based on *Development in Practice* 20(4&5), guest-edited by Pauline Rose, focuses on contemporary experiences of non-state provision of essential education.

Historically, of course, the provision of formal education long pre-dates the modern state. There is evidence of formal schooling in several of the ancient civilisations. Universities existed in what are now China, India, Iran, Korea, and Turkey long before the earliest mediaeval European universities of Bologna, Montpellier, Naples, Oxford, Padua, Paris, and Salamanca. Much education, both basic and advanced, was – and in many cases remains – closely connected to religious institutions, along with the associated masculine bias. Despite occasional philanthropic efforts to enable young men from modest backgrounds to attend university, in the main these institutions served to enable the privileged to consolidate their position rather than promoting social mobility, let alone gender equity.

It is relatively recent that the provision of universal primary education (also called basic education) has been predominantly recognised as an obligation of the state. Education was proclaimed as a fundamental human right in the 1948 Universal Declaration of Human Rights (UDHR), a commitment reinforced and made binding on signatories to the December 1966 International Covenant on Economic, Social and Cultural Rights. In 1990, delegates from 155 countries and representatives from as many organisations agreed at the World Conference on Education for All: Meeting Basic Learning Needs, to universalise primary education and massively reduce illiteracy before the end of the decade.

Despite these declarations, advances in the 1990s and 2000s were in many cases reversed as governments were encouraged to cut public spending – school attendance declined, teachers left the profession or were retrenched, and existing disparities became more pronounced between girls and boys, rural and urban, rich and poor, North and South. Some governments have succeeded in withstanding this trend, and maintained their commitment to universal education despite the worsening economic context. Dharam Ghai's (1999) fascinating study shows that countries with very different histories, economies, and political ideologies – Chile, China, Costa Rica, the Indian state of Kerala, Sri Lanka, and Viet Nam – continue to have impressive records on health and education. Ghai concludes that 'a social policy that accords priority to maternal and child care, prevention of insect-borne and infectious diseases, and improvement, without gender discrimination, of health education, adult literacy, basic education and sanitary and hygienic conditions, can have a quick and powerful impact on social indicators'. In other words, even cash-strapped governments have some room

PREFACE

to exercise political will in favour of universal provision of the most essential services. But these are the exceptions that prove the rule.

In the meantime, however, in many parts of the world generations of children – particularly girls – are growing up to be adults who are unable to read or write, which in turn deprives them of the 'means of acquiring the printed knowledge, new skills, and technologies that could help them improve the quality of their lives and help them to shape, and adapt to, social and cultural change' (from the Preamble to the World Declaration on Education for All: Meeting Basic Learning Needs: Jomtien, Thailand, 5–9 March 1990, cited in Eade and Williams 1995: 354). In the so-called Information Age, the exclusion of the non-literate assumes multiple dimensions at a time when many previous boundaries are being eroded.

Until the 1990s, Northern NGOs were reluctant to get involved in funding formal education systems for two principal reasons. First, there was still the widespread belief that the provision of basic education is properly the duty of governments and that to take this on was either allowing them to abdicate responsibility, or colluding with the neo-liberal agenda of rolling back the state. Second, almost all NGOs are themselves dependent on back-donors, and cannot therefore assume any major or long-term financial burden since they cannot guarantee their continuing support. Donors pay lip service to the long-term nature of interventions intended to bring about sustainable social and policy change, but in practice few commit funds for more than three to five years at a time, which is far too short for real transformations to take root. Contributing to one-off costs such as building a village classroom or paying for a batch of notebooks and pencils is one thing; paying the salary for a qualified teacher (and ensuring that they actually show up) is quite another. A further factor was NGOs' unwillingness to be associated with inferior or inappropriate formal education, especially when this sometimes involved crude nation-building ambitions that involved erasing the cultural and linguistic characteristics of minority or oppressed population groups. It is no accident that since the end of Guatemala's 37-year war one of the first things that the Maya have asserted is their right to sustain their own educational traditions while at the same time pressing for a reform the national education system to reflect the country's majority indigenous population. (1)

Thus from the 1970s to the mid-1990s, secular NGOs tended to support non-formal or popular education, often provided for their members by labour or peasant farmers' unions. In Latin America and beyond, such programmes were deeply influenced by the Brazilian educationalist, Paulo Freire and by Liberation Theology, and were explicitly linked to wider struggles for civil and political, as well as for economic, social, and cultural, rights. The prevailing logic was to equip poor and marginalised people to press for their rights, including the right to universal education, and to avoid at all costs either displacing a legitimate but underperforming government, or appearing to prop up an undemocratic one.

Since then public–private partnerships, which have been presented as the acceptable face of inevitable privatisation, have been zealously promoted in both the North and the South. Even in relatively strong economies, it has come to be viewed as being mired in the past or simply naïve to express concerns about for-profits being brought into public services that were previously ring-fenced as being quintessentially not-for-profit, whether managing prisons or providing care for the terminally ill. At the same time, there is today a far greater awareness than in the past that the semi-voluntary 'care economy' has a female, usually underpaid and undervalued, face. Women lose both the

PREFACE

benefits of redistributive social policies, and are disproportionately expected to darn the increasingly frayed social fabric.

This collection tackles some of these issues head-on, in particular the question of how non-state provision of social services – in this case, education – should be paid for: in what circumstances is it acceptable for governments to subcontract NGOs or private companies to provide such services? And in the case of subcontracting, what is the proper regulatory role of the state, such as in setting standards of universal access and not, for example, of elite league-table achievements – although donors or shareholders may demand such tangible evidence of the 'effectiveness' of their grantee or company? How can discrepancies between different providers be reconciled, particularly when they do not share the same ethos or systems of internal accountability, or are working in very different settings?

As Pauline Rose concludes in her Introduction, non-state education providers do need various forms of state support, in particular a clear policy framework within which all relevant parties must operate. In reality, all non-state providers are residually dependent on public services of some kind or another, be it roads, telecommunications, judicial systems, government ministries, a civil service, trained professionals in many fields. Should for-profit providers also contribute to these services via taxation? On the other hand, governments are hesitant to let non-state providers into the policy process, where doing so 'could be seen as them relinquishing control to these providers, and so could undermine their legitimacy to provide services, weaken their hold over the content of education programmes, and perhaps even threaten national security'. The danger, as Rose points out, is that relationships risk becoming confrontational rather than collaborative, at the expense of achieving the Millennium Development Goal of ensuring that children everywhere, boys and girls alike, can complete a full course of primary schooling – Education for All by 2015.

Notes

1 Mother-tongue teaching remains an issue of debate. A report entitled 'Language and Education: The Missing Link', published in November 2009 by Save the Children Fund-UK (SCF-UK) and the Centre for British Teachers (CfBT), argues that the failure to teach children in their first language is a major cause of school drop-outs and poor performance (de Lotbinière 2009). The standard arguments against doing so are that children are disadvantaged if they cannot function in the national language and/or in a major international language, and that governments of multilingual nations cannot afford books and materials for every minority language.

References

de Lotbinière, Max (2009) 'Stark lessons in mother tongues', *The Guardian Weekly* 11 December.

Eade, Deborah and Suzanne Williams (1995) *The Oxfam Handbook of Development and Relief* (3 vols.), Oxford: Oxfam UK and Ireland.

Ghai, Dharam (1999) *Social Development and Public Policy: A Study of Some Successful Experiences*, Basingstoke: Palgrave.

Achieving Education for All through public–private partnerships?

Pauline Rose

Education is commonly regarded as a state responsibility. Non-state provision is, however, increasingly prevalent in many developing countries in response to the inaccessibility and poor quality of state provision. Its unplanned growth has led to proposals for developing 'public–private partnerships'. However, as a number of the papers in this collection indicate, such partnerships are insufficiently developed in national planning, with potentially adverse consequences for equity. More often, non-state providers are attempting to develop relationships with the state, both to strengthen their own service delivery as well as to put pressure on government to improve the quality of its own provision.

Parvenir à l'Éducation pour tous à travers les partenariats publics-privés ?
L'éducation est généralement perçue comme la responsabilité de l'État. Cependant, la prestation de services d'éducation par des entités ne relevant pas de l'État est de plus en plus fréquente dans de nombreux pays en développement, conséquence logique du caractère inaccessible et de la qualité médiocre des services de l'État. La croissance non planifiée de ce secteur a donné lieu à des propositions de développement de « partenariats publics-privés ». Cependant, comme l'indiquent plusieurs des contributions à ce recueil, les partenariats de ce type sont insuffisamment développés dans la planification nationale, ce qui a des conséquences potentiellement négatives pour l'équité. Les prestataires non publics tentent, plus fréquemment, de développer des relations avec l'État, à la fois pour renforcer leur propre prestation de services et pour exercer une pression sur le gouvernement pour le pousser à améliorer ses propres services.

Alcançando Educação para Todos através de parcerias público-privadas?
A educação é normalmente vista como uma responsabilidade do estado. A provisão não-estatal, porém, cada vez mais predomina em vários países em desenvolvimento em resposta à inacessibilidade e má-qualidade da provisão estatal. Seu crescimento não-planejado tem levado a propostas para desenvolver "parcerias público-privadas". Porém, como vários dos artigos desta coleção indicam, tais parcerias são insuficientemente desenvolvidas no planejamento nacional, com consequências potencialmente adversas para a equidade. Mais frequentemente, provedores não-estatais estão tentando desenvolver relações com o estado, tanto para fortalecer a implementação de seu próprio serviço como também para pressionar o governo para que melhore a qualidade de sua própria provisão.

ACHIEVING EDUCATION FOR ALL THROUGH PUBLIC-PRIVATE PARTNERSHIPS?

¿Lograr la Educación para Todos a través de alianzas público-privadas?

Comúnmente se piensa que la educación es responsabilidad del Estado. Sin embargo, cada día se amplía más la oferta educativa privada en muchos países en desarrollo dada la baja calidad del servicio estatal y las dificultades para acceder a él. Esta sorprendente expansión ha dado lugar a iniciativas como la creación de "alianzas público-privadas". Varios ensayos del presente volumen señalan que estas alianzas no se han incorporado al proceso de planeación nacional, lo cual puede derivar en consecuencias negativas para la equidad. En la mayoría de los casos, los proveedores no estatales desean establecer convenios con el Estado para mejorar su propia oferta, pero también para presionarlo a fin de que mejore la calidad de su servicio.

Introduction

Non-state provision is changing the education landscape in many developing countries. Basic education is often regarded in international agreements and national constitutions as being a state responsibility, and increasingly expected to be fee-free for government provision. At the same time, concern for achieving Millennium Development Goals and Education for All by 2015 has led to a focus on the role that non-state providers can play in extending education access and improving its quality. While non-state providers can help to fill a gap by extending access to those excluded from state provision, unplanned growth in both for-profit and not-for-profit provision has resulted in fragmentation of service delivery. In response, attention is increasingly given to developing 'partnerships' between governments and non-state providers. Such partnerships are being developed in contexts where the state continues to be viewed as having the moral, social, and legal responsibility for overall education-service delivery, and so is expected to play a role in facilitating and regulating non-state providers. However, as contributions in this collection highlight, there are benefits as well as tensions in the state partnering with non-state providers to achieve education of acceptable quality to all children.

State–non-state relationships in development have been extensively researched since the 1980s in particular – and have been the subject of numerous articles in *Development in Practice*. As Volume 17 Issue 4 & 5 of the journal highlights, the term 'partnership' is one of the 'buzzwords' that has gained growing prominence in development discourse, but has often remained an empty rhetoric (Cornwall 2007). Understanding the experience of formal and informal relationships has emerged as an area of concern particularly since the 1980s, as NGOs began to play a more prominent role in development programmes with the support of international aid agencies (Farrington and Bebbington 1993; Hulme and Edwards 1997; Lewis and Kanji 2009). Since the 1990s, the role of the for-profit private sector has also come to prominence in development debates in the context of an international neo-liberal agenda advocating a reduced role for the state. This has led to proposals about whether and how these private providers should partner with public institutions.

Within the education sector more specifically, the role of non-state providers and the ways in which they can and should partner with the state is one of the most contentious areas of policy debate. Questions have arisen over whether it is always necessary for government to fulfil its commitment to education-service delivery directly through its own provision; who should pay for education delivered by other providers (so, even where access to government schooling is fee-free, should vouchers be provided to allow parents to choose alternative providers, and should governments finance provision by NGOs given they extend access to hard-to-reach areas); and whether promoting choice and competition is beneficial to reducing costs, or whether this has adverse consequences for equity.

Despite these active policy debates, there has been very limited documentation of the experiences of state–non-state relationships in practice – a gap that this collection aims to fill. Relationships within the education sector are likely to be distinctive from other sectors for a number of reasons. First, education-service delivery is a highly political process. Since education plays a key role in national identity formation, there are implications for the way in which the state might choose to engage with non-state providers in this sector. Governments may be more reluctant to promote non-state provision of education compared with health, for example. To the extent that non-state providers are emerging by default in many situations, governments either refuse to acknowledge their existence or see their own role as controlling and regulating non-state activities, rather than actively supporting them (Rose 2009).

Second, education is a lifelong activity, with certificates gained at different levels in the system providing an entry point to the next level of education or into the labour market. Where children access non-state provision at some stage in their schooling, there is a need for the qualifications gained to be recognised by government schools and by employers to enable students to make a successful transition. Third, education potentially plays an important role in social mobility, and is an instrument that can be used by governments to promote greater equity. Where different providers are involved in service delivery, there are dangers that government ability to promote equity through education is weakened. One option is, therefore, for government to play a role in regulating and monitoring non-state provision to ensure that choice and competition do not undermine equity objectives.

As the contributions in this collection highlight, there is a range of providers involved in supporting education to poor and disadvantaged households – including non-government and other civil-society organisations (see papers by Archer, Batley and Rose, Casely-Hayford and Hartwell, DeStefano and Moore, Jones and Torres, and Mundy *et al.*), private providers with profit-making motives (Oketch and Ngware, and Srivastava), and religious providers (Bano). The nature of their relationship with the state depends on the motives of the provider. Distinguishing between them is not, however, always straightforward. NGOs are often contrasted with private providers on the grounds of their philanthropic aims rather than being driven by profit. As Bano (2008) notes, however, the growing availability of development aid to NGOs is leading to the term 'NGO' becoming synonymous with non-profit making, and philanthropic aims being highly contested. At the same time, while NGOs are commonly viewed as playing a key role in addressing the educational needs of the most 'hard to reach', low-cost for-profit private providers are now (contentiously) viewed by some as reaching poor households who are underserved by the state system (Rose 2009; Tooley and Dixon 2006). Despite the blurring of boundaries between different providers, distinctions can be made on the basis of whether profits are primarily used to further support development activities of the organisation (as with NGOs), or are distributed to owners and shareholders (as with private providers).

Balancing advocacy and service-delivery roles of civil-society organisations influences their relationship with the state

Relationships can take a variety of forms – including with respect to policy dialogue, contracting, facilitation (including through financing), and registration and regulation (Batley 2006;

Rose 2006). The nature of formal relationships depends both on the type of non-state provider, and on whether they are primarily involved in service delivery or advocacy. In this collection, Jones and Torres, and Mundy *et al.* focus in particular on the role of civil-society organisations in advocacy, while DeStefano and Moore, and Casely-Hayford and Hartwell take NGO service provision as their starting point. Aikman, Archer, and Batley and Rose all look at the interplay between the roles of NGOs in service provision and advocacy, showing how their service provision can influence advocacy roles with a mixture of outcomes.

As Batley and Rose show, experience with formal relationships can range from confrontation and conflict to collaboration, with the outcome in part determined by the ways in which non-state providers engage informally. More successful formal relationships are often built on the investment of considerable time and energy by non-state providers in fostering collaborative informal relationships. This not only has the potential of strengthening the quality of education that children accessing non-state provision receive, but can also enable non-state providers to advocate for improvements in government provision more broadly – an issue also highlighted by Aikman in relation to Oxfam GB's role in Tanzania, and Casely-Hayford and Hartwell in the context of Ghana's School for Life programme.

Focusing on civil-society organisations' role in advocacy, Mundy *et al.* highlight their growing importance in policy dialogue. On the basis of analysis of four African countries (Burkina Faso, Kenya, Mali, and Tanzania), the authors find that civil-society organisations, and NGOs in particular, are 'increasingly expected to be partners in the formulation, implementation, and monitoring of national education-sector plans – and in this sense have a growing policy voice. However, capacity and coordination among these actors vary substantially by country, as do the formal opportunities available for their participation' (p. 485). Opportunities for real, ongoing dialogue are, therefore, often severely restricted. Research summarised in their contribution also finds that, even though donor organisations are their main funders, they also lack a well-informed and coordinated strategy for supporting the involvement of civil-society organisations in the education sector.

The implications of the dual role that some NGOs play in service delivery and advocacy for improving government provision is identified by both Aikman and Archer in relation to two major international NGOs – Oxfam GB and ActionAid. They highlight the attention that each of these NGOs has given to balancing service-delivery and advocacy objectives in their planning. In both cases, this has been occurring in the context of a move towards decentralised approaches within the organisations, aimed at enabling their programmes to be more tailored towards local circumstances. The shift from centralised (international and national-led) campaigns to local initiatives is an issue that Mundy *et al.* also raise, noting that many national civil-society organisations indicate the valuable role played by international initiatives, such as the Global Campaign for Education and the Commonwealth Education Fund (with which both ActionAid and Oxfam GB are associated), in supporting their efforts to establish a new policy presence. However, most nationally based organisations argue for the need for a strong locally led effort whose features emerge from the distinct features of civil society in each national context, rather than an externally led campaign which could deflect from the need for the development of national capacities. Aikman focuses on such experiences in Tanzania. According to Mundy *et al.*, Tanzania provides more positive experience of a case where aid donors have been particularly supportive towards national civil-society organizations to enable them to engage in sustained programmes of research or advocacy.

More specifically, Aikman shows the ways in which Oxfam GB's programmes in Tanzania have aimed at supporting improvement of formal basic education through pedagogical innovation, as well as empowering pastoralist peoples through education. Both of these approaches are designed to feed into and provide a direct source of evidence for education-policy advocacy (including research, lobbying, and campaigning). Some aspects of their activities have involved NGO and government officials working alongside each other in delivering the services. In some areas – such as supply of educational materials, and supporting access to flexible modes of educational delivery – the relationship was found to be collaborative, while a lack of shared understanding was apparent in politically sensitive areas such as control over curriculum content and language policy. Aikman argues that, for the NGO's advocacy role to be effective, it should not be 'something bolted on'. Rather, it needs to be 'gently nourished through actions which at times may have more of a "service delivery" flavour to them' (p. 508).

Drawing a somewhat different conclusion, Archer provides a historical account of ActionAid's transition from being primarily focused on service delivery in the early 1990s to playing a mainly advocacy role in the 2000s. This change was based on a critical self-reflection of the organisation. As with other NGO programmes, ActionAid considered its non-formal education to have benefits in reaching more remote and poor communities, and being cost-effective by using low-cost improvised buildings put up by parents themselves. Local parents became actively involved in decision making, including on the annual calendar of the school year so that holidays coincided with the peak periods where children needed to work, for example during harvesting. They could also set the daily timetable so that working children could learn in the morning, in the afternoon, or the evening. As with other NGO programmes, centres aimed to use a child-friendly approach to learning. Despite their success, by the mid-1990s ActionAid decided that it should minimise its direct engagement in service provision.

A key concern for many NGOs is the sustainability of their provision where they rely on short-term financing primarily from international aid agencies (an issue also raised by DeStefano and Moore, and Casely-Hayford and Hartwell). Based on its self-evaluation, ActionAid discovered that, not only would governments be reluctant to take on the costs of running the non-formal education centres (as often unrealistically anticipated), but also they were unable to do so because the centres did not comply with government regulations. The recruitment of teachers was one important element of this, as those teaching in non-formal centres did not possess the official qualifications needed to teach in formal schools. Archer states that, through its analysis, 'it became clear that, unintentionally, ActionAid was absolving governments of their responsibility and was becoming an agent in the privatisation of education for poor children. ... [L]ocal people ... had no sense of the government having responsibility to provide education and no established relationships that could help them to demand this effectively' (p. 614). Working with coalitions and campaigns at local, national, and international levels, ActionAid now focuses its energies on making government schools and government education systems work more effectively for the poorest people, rather than delivering those services through its own programmes.

Government financing of NGO provision: relationships built on collaboration or control?

In terms of the role of civil-society organisations as service providers, their provision is commonly seen by international agencies as being more cost-effective than that of government, at the same time as being able to offer more appropriate, flexible provision to hard-to-reach children most likely to be excluded from formal government schooling (including child labourers, those living in remote rural areas, and girls). This is taken up by Casely-Hayford and Hartwell, and DeStefano and Moore. On the basis of evidence from ten countries, and a more in-depth investigation in Ghana, both sets of authors conclude that there are distinct advantages to NGO provision for extending access to the hard-to-reach. However, they point to the need for governments to provide support, particularly in terms of financing, to ensure sustainability of NGO provision.

From their thorough review of ten complementary education programmes run by NGOs, DeStefano and Moore show that, in seven of the cases, the interaction between these providers and the government was limited – government simply allowed the non-state actors to provide education. However, in most of these cases, government interaction with non-state providers was evolving to include more government promotion of non-state provision, but not direct funding. The authors present a two-dimensional model showing that, in the majority of cases, there is limited flow of government resources to these providers, with their relationship varying between one of 'benign neglect' to that of principal–agent. Egypt represents a case at the midpoint – both in terms of shared funding and collaboration between the partners. Where government funding is more readily available (as in Guatemala and Honduras), the relationship is more likely to be controlled by government.

The correlation between sources of funding and extent of collaboration is also highlighted in the Research Round-Up by Batley and Rose. In their summary of a research project on state–non-state relationships in South Asia, they show that the influence of the relationship on service delivery and advocacy roles of NGOs depends on the motives of NGO leaders, as well as the extent of the organisation's financial independence from government. Where NGOs are directly contracted through government and so are financially dependent, there is greater likelihood that the relationship could become antagonistic, which is potentially damaging for the sustainability of the NGO's provision. Alternatively, where NGOs can choose between different funding sources, with government funding being one among these, there are benefits for NGOs to invest in building collaborative relationships to ensure their graduates can re-enter the formal government system, with tensions between the 'partners' being less likely.

Looking in more detail at one of the programmes covered by DeStefano and Moore, Casely-Hayford and Hartwell highlight the benefits of Ghana's School for Life programme in reaching large numbers of children who would otherwise be out of school in the north of the country. Approximately 40 per cent of school-age children are not in formal government schooling across the northern region, the majority of whom are girls. School for Life offers a nine-month programme, including tuition in local languages with more flexible hours and centres located closer to homes. The benefits have extended to providing opportunities for many of these children to enter the formal government education system, where they go on to perform at least as well as their counterparts.

An important finding of Casely-Hayford and Hartwell's contribution is that, not only has School for Life had positive outcomes for those learning through its programme, but it has also had a multiplier effect as a consequence of its influence on state provision. By demonstrating what flexible approaches can achieve, along with building a constructive relationship with government officials, the programme has both become integrated it into national planning, and provided lessons for government's own provision. Although there have been challenges, the experience from Ghana pushes collaboration far beyond what has happened in many other countries. It also makes the Ghana case relatively unique in DeStefano and Moore's two-dimensional model as, next to Egypt, Ghana is closest to achieving a collaborative relationship even though (unlike in the Egypt case) there is no financial responsibility on the part of government. Even so, Casely-Hayford and Hartwell propose a need for government to play a more active role in supporting financing of the programme to ensure its sustainability. On the basis of Batley and Rose's findings, for the programme to maintain its collaborative relationship with government, it could, however, be important for it not to rely on government as its core source of finance.

Partnering with for-profit private providers to improve choice and quality of provision for all, or at the expense of equity?

Debates on partnerships are particularly controversial with regard to profit-motivated private provision. There is some evidence of growth in commercially oriented private schools charging relatively modest fees in many developing countries, giving rise to a lively debate about the quality of such provision, its cost, and the implications that this has for choices for the poor (see Rose 2009). On the one hand, the unprecedented growth in low-fee private provision is proposed by some to extend choice to the poor, who previously only had recourse to government provision. Through increased competition, it is also seen as a means to improve the quality of education. These commentators advocate building partnerships with the intention that the state could play a greater financial role in supporting the development of such private provision (Patrinos *et al.* 2009). On the other hand, other commentators argue that the prominence of private providers primarily highlights problems with government schooling which remains the only form of provision for the poorest who have no choice, and so government financing needs to focus on strengthening its own provision (see UNESCO 2009).

This debate, if anything, intensified in the light of the global economic crisis from 2008 onwards. Notably, the World Bank is playing a more active role in promoting private provision through proposals to give fellowships for students in private schools as a means of 'averting a human crisis'. The reason given for this proposal is that an exodus of students to government schools in the context of the economic downturn would 'entail overcrowding in the public sector and loss of revenue in the private sector – with potentially lower quality in both' (World Bank 2009: 13). The 2009 Education for All Global Monitoring Report presents evidence which cautions against this approach (UNESCO 2009). It raises the concern that when poor households pay for education they divert income from other areas, including nutrition, health, shelter, and savings for emergencies. Paying for education at low-fee private schools can, therefore, either be viewed as a market preference freely expressed – or as an act imposed by policy failures that leave poor households with two stark options: paying for education through severe sacrifices in other areas, or accepting that their children have no opportunity for an education meeting minimum quality standards. These sacrifices are even more severe for vulnerable households suffering most from the global downturn.

The concerns raised in the 2009 Education for All Global Monitoring Report are supported by evidence from Kenya presented by Oketch and Ngware. They highlight serious equity concerns in using public resources to support private provision. An alternative response that is put forward is for support to be directed at improvements in the quality of government provision. This solution would address the root of the problem, rather than the symptom. As such, to avert a human crisis in the face of global downturn, what matters is for governments to focus their energies and resources on public provision of good-quality basic education for everyone, and for aid donors to focus their energies in supporting governments to this end.

India has been at the forefront of these debates on low-fee private schools, where the scale of their provision has been recognised since at least the early 1990s. Srivastava critically examines the development of the government's public–private partnership approach in relation to education, particularly since 2000. She finds that recent government plans adopt the rhetoric of partnership, but fail to specify what this means. As a result, the plans appear to present a contradiction between the government promoting itself as playing a central role in service provision, while also putting forward a public–private partnership agenda. In practice, this agenda is essentially reduced to strategies for privatised delivery with a diminished role for the state in financing, management, and regulation. Thus, government plans are doing little to provide clear guidance on its response to the mushrooming of private providers, which is seen to be occurring due to public dissatisfaction with the quality of public provision.

Governments need to view *madrasas* as partners in achieving Education for All, not as threats

One area that has received more limited research attention relates to the relationship between religious providers and the state. Since the terrorist attack on the World Trade Center on 11 September 2001, there have been numerous (mainly unsubstantiated) claims that *madrasas* play a role in fostering religious extremism. These claims have given rise to international and national concerns for ensuring greater state control of *madrasas* given they are identified with posing a global security threat. However, as Bano points out, this focus inappropriately diverts attention away from the role that many *madrasas* play in extending education to poor and disadvantaged communities that are underserved by state provision. Rather than seeing them as a threat, Bano argues that governments need to build collaborative relationships with the religious elite. Using a comparative analysis of Bangladesh, India, and Pakistan, she shows that, by providing financial support to *madrasas* and investing in building the trust of religious elites, governments can work together with *madrasas* to ensure that they provide appropriate religious education together with an education in secular subjects, and so can contribute towards the achievement of international development goals in education.

In fragile contexts, relationships with non-state providers need to balance immediate service delivery with building state capacity and legitimacy

Two shorter pieces in the collection focus on non-state provision in fragile states. While the term itself is contentious (Osaghae 2007), countries identified as having weak political will and capacity to deliver basic services (many of which are affected by conflict) are particularly significant for the debate on relationships between the state and non-state providers, given the latter are often the main provider of education in such situations. As the capacity and willingness of these states begins to strengthen, issues arise on the role that non-state providers play – should their service provision be taken over by the state, or are there advantages to them continuing to provide education while ensuring that their activities are integrated within a national planning system?

The role of aid donors in promoting non-state provision is particularly striking in fragile situations. As Berry argues, typical donor engagement in such environments tends to lead to the development of parallel, fragmented systems, which can weaken state authority and visibility and make it difficult to rebuild a coherent education system when conditions become more favourable. Berry highlights lessons from three fragile contexts – Aghanistan, Nepal, and Yemen – each of which has experience of different aid approaches, with different degrees of emphasis on coordination and state building. The examples highlight the importance of supporting community initiatives while recognising state capacity constraints in realising community demands for education which remain resilient throughout conflict. Afghanistan is a striking example (as also highlighted by DeStefano and Moore): NGOs began providing education in defiance of government restrictions on who could attend school, placing a ban on girls' schooling in particular. As the political situation in Afghanistan evolved, NGOs built more formal relationships with a government that was increasingly concerned with absorbing schools previously run by non-state providers. The Afghan government promotes NGO support of community-based schooling in regions it still has trouble serving, but sees that as a temporary measure. In recognising the role of non-state providers in planning education systems for fragile countries, Berry concludes that there is a need for careful analysis of the role of different stakeholders to ensure that donor-driven development programmes working with non-state providers not only 'do no harm', but in fact contribute to peace and security.

Commins, also focusing on fragile states, presents lessons from the health sector. In many ways, the aid architecture in health is further advanced in thinking about how to work with non-state providers in fragile states. However, many of the challenges are similar to those in the education sector. As countries emerge from conflict, Commins identifies a 'two track' challenge of balancing the urgent need for delivering services with the long-term process of building effective and accountable public institutions. This challenge poses questions of the way in which states that are beginning to regain their legitimacy post-conflict choose to engage with non-state providers. Drawing on experience of contracting health services in Afghanistan and the Multi-Donor Trust Fund in Southern Sudan, Commins suggests that the greater problem is not non-state providers acting without any relationship with the state, but rather the lack of any overall policy or coordination framework, both between donors, and between donors, governments, and non-state providers – an issue that resonates with other contributions in this collection. The lack of such a framework is even more critical in fragile situations given the danger that efforts to rebuild legitimacy can be undermined where the state is not playing a visible role in service delivery. Commins highlights how a number of factors, including the political settlement dynamics, donor aid instruments, and roles that non-state providers play, all affect how well the two tracks of service delivery and building state capacity can be connected and that, provided there is appropriate planning, a trade-off between the two tracks can be avoided.

The role of social movements in influencing governments from below

Jones and Torres take a somewhat different perspective from the other contributions, using 'popular education' as the focal point. They look at the role of social movements in Latin America in 'educationally challenging "neo-liberal" educational standardisation' (p. 567). They give particular attention to radical political models of education building on Paulo Freire's experiences in Brazil in the 1970s. Unlike other contributions on civil-society organisations in this collection, where aid donors are key sources of their financing and so often play a mediating role in the relationship between the state and non-state providers, Jones and Torres focus on the role that social movements can play in challenging what is seen as a reductionist international political agenda promoted by the World Bank and IMF. This agenda is associated with neo-liberalism, which has become closely linked with privatisation in education and attempts to reduce public costs of schooling. Jones and Torres highlight the role of a range of Latin American social movements in resisting these trends in education. While the aims of the movements differ (including ones with a feminist agenda, for example), they have a common theme of transformation, with the aim of challenging the neo-liberal model of globalisation.

Conclusion

In conclusion, the contributions in this collection highlight the various ways in which state and non-state actors engage in delivering education. These relationships are not straightforward and can take many different forms. They are shaped by the type of non-state provider (ranging from for-profit private providers to civil-society organisations and religious providers), the activities in which they are engaged (whether advocacy or service delivery), and contexts in which they are operating. Despite international attention to the role of non-state providers in supporting the move towards Education for All and the desire for developing partnerships with government, many of the contributions highlight the lack of clarity in national policy and planning. In some cases, this is due to concerns by governments that giving more explicit recognition to non-state providers could be seen as them relinquishing control to these providers, and so could undermine their legitimacy to provide services, weaken their hold over the content of education programmes, and perhaps even threaten national security. However, as non-state provision has been growing by default in many countries, failure to provide a clear policy framework leaves unanswered questions of the conditions under which the state intends to support such provision, or whether and how it will be regulated. The lack of such a framework has potential adverse consequences for equity – for example, where access to different providers is constrained by who is able to pay.

In practice, 'partnerships' are often driven by non-state providers, either seeking to gain recognition for their provision, or as a means to put pressure on government to improve the quality of its provision. The desire by non-state providers to gain recognition from government in order to receive its financial support as a means of ensuring sustainability of provision is also apparent. While this is driving some non-state providers to engage more directly with government, it also raises a danger of leading to relationships that are more confrontational rather than collaborative. At the same time, there is a failure on the part of the state to show how it is responding to the underlying problems in its own provision that have given rise to the growth of non-state provision in the first place. These are all issues that require more urgent attention if governments are to show their commitments to achieving Education for All by 2015.

Acknowledgement

I am extremely grateful to Frances Hunt for her support to this volume.

References

Bano, Masooda (2008) 'Non-profit education providers *vis-à-vis* the private sector: comparative analysis of NGOs and Traditional Voluntary Organisations in Pakistan', *Compare* 38 (4): 471–82.
Batley, Richard (2006) 'Engaged or divorced? Cross-service findings on government relations with non-state service-providers', *Public Administration and Development* 26 (3): 241–51.
Cornwall, Andrea (2007) 'Buzzwords and fuzzwords: deconstructing development discourse', *Development in Practice* 17 (4&5): 471–84.
Farrington, J. and A. Bebbington (1993) *Reluctant Partners? Non-governmental Organisations, the State and Sustainable Agricultural Development*, London: Routledge.
Hulme, David and Edwards Michael (eds.) (1997) *NGOs, State and Donors: Too Close for Comfort*, New York, NY: Palgrave Macmillan.
Lewis, David and Nazneen Kanji (2009) *Non-governmental Organisations and Development*, London: Routledge.
Osaghae, Eghosa E. (2007) 'Fragile states', *Development in Practice* 17 (4&5): 691–9.
Patrinos, Harry Anthony, Felipe Barrera-Osorio, and Juliana Guáqueta (2009) *The Role and Impact of Public–Private Partnerships in Education*, Washington, DC: The World Bank.
Rose, Pauline (2006) 'Collaborating in Education for All? Experiences of government support for non-state provision of basic education in South Asia and Sub-Saharan Africa', *Public Administration and Development* 26 (3): 219–30.
Rose, Pauline (2009) 'Non-state provision of education: evidence from Africa and South Asia', *Compare* 39 (2): 127–34.

ACHIEVING EDUCATION FOR ALL THROUGH PUBLIC-PRIVATE PARTNERSHIPS?

Tooley, James and Pauline Dixon (2006) '"De facto" privatisation of education and the poor: implications of a study from Sub-Saharan Africa and India', *Compare* 36 (4): 443–62.
UNESCO (2009) *Education for All Global Monitoring Report. Overcoming Inequality: Why Governance Matters*, Oxford: Oxford University Press.
World Bank (2009) 'Averting a Human Crisis during the Global Downturn. Policy Options from the World Bank's Human Development Network', Washington, DC: The World Bank.

Civil society, basic education, and sector-wide aid: insights from Sub-Saharan Africa

Karen Mundy, with Megan Haggerty, Malini Sivasubramaniam, Suzanne Cherry, and Richard Maclure

Emerging trends in reforms of education-sector plans indicate a shift not only in how foreign aid is disbursed, but also in how civil-society actors engage in new policy and advocacy roles. This contribution examines these changing civil-society roles in four countries: Burkina Faso, Kenya, Mali, and Tanzania. While sector-wide approaches have created new opportunities for civil-society participation at the national level, this research suggests that sector reforms have also presented significant challenges for engagement with government and donors. This research emphasises the need for a transparent, regularised, and democratic process for the inclusion of civil-society organisations at the policy table.

Société civile, éducation de base et aide pour tout le secteur : nouvelles idées émanant d'Afrique subsaharienne
Les tendances émergentes des réformes des plans du secteur de l'éducation indiquent une évolution non seulement de la manière dont l'aide étrangère est versée, mais aussi de la façon dont les acteurs de la société civile assument de nouveaux rôles ayant trait aux politiques générales et au plaidoyer. Cette contribution examine ces rôles en mutation de la société civile dans quatre pays : le Burkina Faso, le Kenya, le Mali et la Tanzanie. Si les approches sectorielles ont effectivement créé de nouvelles occasions de participation de la société civile au niveau national, ces recherches suggèrent que les réformes du secteur ont également soulevé des défis considérables pour le dialogue avec les pouvoirs publics et les bailleurs de fonds. Ces recherches mettent l'accent sur la nécessité d'un processus transparent, réglementé et démocratique pour l'inclusion des organisations de la société civile dans les débats portant sur les politiques.

Sociedade civil, educação básica e ajuda setorial ampla: ideias da África Subsaariana
Tendências emergentes nas reformas de planos do setor da educação indicam uma mudança não apenas em como a ajuda estrangeira é desembolsada, mas também em como os agentes da sociedade civil engajam-se em novas funções de políticas e advocacy. Esta contribuição examina essas funções da sociedade civil que estão em transformação em quatro países: Burkina Faso, Quênia, Mali e Tanzânia. Embora as abordagens setoriais amplas tenham criado novas oportunidades para a participação da sociedade civil em nível nacional, esta pesquisa sugere que as reformas

setoriais também têm apresentado desafios significativos ao engajamento com o governo e doadores. Esta pesquisa enfatiza a necessidade de um processo transparente, regularizado e democrático para a inclusão de organizações da sociedade civil nas negociações políticas.

Sociedad civil, educación primaria y ayuda sectorial: experiencias del África subsahariana
Las tendencias actuales de las reformas en el sector educativo muestran un cambio tanto en la distribución de la ayuda internacional como en el nuevo rol de los actores de la sociedad civil como formadores e impulsores de políticas. Este ensayo analiza la transformación en los roles de la sociedad civil en Burkina Faso, Kenia, Malí y Tanzania. Si bien las nuevas propuestas en el sector educativo han generado oportunidades para que la sociedad civil participe a nivel nacional, la investigación indica que también han surgido importantes retos para el diálogo con el gobierno y los donantes. La investigación resalta la necesidad de crear un proceso transparente, ordenado y democrático para que la sociedad civil participe en la formulación de políticas públicas.

Introduction

Since the late 1990s, efforts to revitalise and expand basic education systems in Sub-Saharan Africa have changed in two important new directions: they increasingly highlight a role for civil society, and they also encourage the use of sector-wide approaches in which foreign aid is pooled to support a single national plan (Buchert 2002; Kruse 2003; Lexow 2003). This contribution looks at the experience of civil-society actors in this new policy context, focusing in particular on the policy and watchdog (as opposed to service-delivery) roles of civil-society organisations (CSOs). It synthesises research conducted in four countries in 2006 – Burkina Faso, Kenya, Mali, and Tanzania.[1]

This contribution explores both how education-sector plans frame a new role for civil-society actors; and how civil-society actors themselves are taking up these new policy and watchdog roles. It addresses two key questions: in new sector plans and sector-wide efforts to reform basic education, have civil-society actors gained a seat at the education policy table? What factors limit or encourage their effective engagement in policy and advocacy roles?

Our studies show that CSOs are increasingly expected to be partners in the formulation, implementation, and monitoring of national education-sector plans – and in this sense have a growing policy voice. However, capacity and coordination among these actors vary substantially by country, as do the formal opportunities available for their participation. Thus, our study suggests that initiatives that hope to build national civil-society policy capacity in the education sector (of the type currently being promoted through the Fast-Track Initiative funding for 'Civil Society Education Funds', which we discuss in our conclusion) will need to be carefully targeted to address such variations in capacity and policy context.[2]

Research design

For the purpose of this research, the term 'civil society' is used to refer to organised groups or associations that *'are separate from the state, enjoy some autonomy in relations from the state, and are formed voluntarily by members of society to protect or extend their interests, values or identities'* (Manor *et al.* 1999). A wide range of CSOs is often active in the education sector, including national and international NGOs, parents' associations, teachers' unions, student organisations, faith-based organisations, private provider groups, community-based organisations, research organisations, and networks or coalitions. Research on the evolving advocacy and policy roles being played by civil-society actors often highlights tensions between these roles and service provision, as well as limitations in CSO capacity (CEF 2005, 2007a, b; Cornwall and Gaventa 2001).

Our research began with a desk study of the history of national educational development in each country, a review of current education-sector policies, and a review of the history of civil society in the country. Desk studies were followed by field research undertaken in teams for three or more weeks in each country. Interviews with 30–50 CSOs were carried out in each country, across all the main types of CSO mentioned above. These CSOs were identified through policy documents and by using a snowball sampling technique, in which CSOs and other officials were asked for key CSOs in the sector. Sixty interviews with major donors to the education sector and a small number of government officials were also conducted, in order to better understand their relationships with and approaches to civil-society participation.

We used our interviews with CSOs, donors, and governments to explore the history, capacities, interests, values, resource base, degrees of influence, and levels of coordination among CSOs active in the national education-sector policy arena. We compared the CSO experience at the design and implementation phase of new education-sector programmes in each country, and analysed inter-CSO relations, CSO–government, and CSO–donor relationships. Drawing on Lister and Nyamugasira (2003) and others, we also explored whether CSOs have been 'invited' to the policy table or have themselves 'created' new policy spaces (Manor *et al.* 1999; McGee *et al.* 2002; Tomlinson and Foster 2004).

Four countries were selected for our study: Burkina Faso, Kenya, Mali, and Tanzania. All four have moved towards greater political freedom since the late 1990s and all four have developed Poverty Reduction Strategy Papers (PRSPs) that emphasise the importance of basic education. All four of the countries considered in our study have national education-sector plans in place, each strongly focused on improvements at the primary level. In each country, sector funding is provided by a significant number of international donors, many of which participate in an annual joint review of the sector. Three of our case countries have also been approved for the Fast Track Initiative, which creates another mechanism for sector-wide coordination (Tanzania has not yet applied). National sector plans and donor sector funding for the four countries are described in Table 1.

Despite many similarities, the four case countries are quite different in terms of their size, political histories, levels of poverty, and dependency on foreign aid (see Table 1). There are also significant differences in the way their governments approach the provision of basic education. Both Kenya and Tanzania made a commitment to universal free primary education, in the context of newly invigorated systems of parliamentary democracy in 2000. In contrast, Burkina Faso and Mali began their sector programmes with much lower rates of access to schooling. Their governments have not promised universal free access – in part, perhaps, because of their tighter presidential systems of democracy, and the long history of disarray among opposition parties, which creates less voting pressure on governments.

Education-sector plans and the political opportunity structures for CSO engagement

A fundamentally new direction in the national education-sector plans for each country in our study is the emphasis on partnership with non-government actors and engagement with civil society. A review of sector-programme documents found the terms 'partnership' and

Table 1: Basic statistics from the four case countries

	Burkina Faso	**Mali**	**Tanzania**	**Kenya**
Government	Multi-party democracy (Leadership by former military dictator from 1987)	Multi-party democracy 1992 (Leadership changed in 2002, but no organised opposition)	Multi-party democracy 1995 (*De facto* rule by single party)	Multi-party democracy 1992 (*De facto* single-party rule until 2002)
Population (million)	12.8	13.1	37.6	33.5
GDP/capita (PPP, 2004)[3]	1169	998	674	1140
Overseas Development Assistance as percentage of GDP	12.6	11.7	16.1	3.9
Population on less than $2/day (%)	71.8	90.6	89.9	58.3
Free primary-education policies	Constitutional right – but fees in place	Constitutional right – but fees in place	Abolition of fees announced 2001	Abolition of fees announced 2003
Education sector* plan	PDDEB (1999) *Plan décannal du développement de l'éducation de base*	PRODEC (1999) *Programme décennal de développement de l'éducation*	PEDP (2001)[4] Primary Education Development Plan	KESSP (2005–10) Kenya Education Sector Support Program
Aid to basic education/child†	$18.20	$19.00	$8.40	$12.80
Gross primary enrolment ratio‡	58	66	106	112
Primary completion rate‡	31	38	54	95
Adult literacy rate (%)‡	22	19	69	74

Source: UNDP (2006); Except for: † UNESCO (2007) data for 2003–2004; and ‡ World Bank (2005) data for 2005.

'participation' used extensively. But the overall imagery of 'partnership' in these documents is focused on financing and service provision: community-level and private-sector inputs into achievement of basic education goals is viewed as essential in all four countries. In the Burkina Faso and Mali sector plans, a large share of the improvement in access to basic education is expected to come from private, community, or NGO-funded schools. While this is less the case in Kenya and Tanzania, their national sector plans also recognise the value of the contributions made by private partners.

In contrast, national sector programme documents for the four countries in the period 2000–2005 mention policy engagement, advocacy, or watchdog roles for civil society much more rarely. Only in Tanzania is direct reference made to 'advocacy' as a legitimate role for civil-society actors. Each sector plan highlights NGOs over teachers' unions as key civil-society interlocutors.

When sector programmes *do* mention concrete accountability, policy, or oversight roles for civil-society actors, these are primarily related to the local or decentralised level of the system. Thus, most sector plans introduce new mechanisms for the engagement of community-level actors in the oversight of schools, and many also include earmarked funding for schools under the management of school-level committees. Our research did not study the quality of this local-level CSO engagement, but it did suggest some limitations. Across our case studies, most school committees have highly prescribed functions (purchase of materials, fundraising) and little connection to larger organised CSOs. In some cases (Mali in particular), there is confusion about which local-level authorities are responsible for schools. Local management committees thus do not appear empowered to voice concerns at the local level, nor are they able to feed the collective voice of parents and communities to the national level. None of the sector plans suggest how decentralised accountability roles for CSOs can be scaled up to provide coherent oversight or representation at the national level.

Concrete structures or processes for engaging CSOs in national policy-setting processes are also rare. For example, while all four sector plans mention the value of stakeholder consultation, none provides a clear framework or benchmarks for civil-society consultation and engagement in national planning process; neither do they propose a transparent, regularised process for choosing civil-society representatives in key policy discussions. As we shall see later, this absence of a transparent procedural framework allows governments to control who sits at the policy table, and often leads to the exclusion of CSOs that have potentially critical or destabilising viewpoints.

Furthermore, the kind of partnerships encouraged in sector programmes tend to be in the form of consultation between ministries of education and CSOs, neglecting the wider opportunities for enhancing legislative oversight. No formal opportunities for CSOs or the public to engage elected officials in the review of education policies (as, for example, might occur in parliamentary democracies through education-specific standing committees) are suggested. This is a problematic emphasis in contexts where centralisation of power in the executive and a history of patrimonial politics tends to limit the development of citizen engagement in formal democratic processes.

Finally, it is worth noting that while the engagement of civil-society participation in education policy processes is crucially dependent on the wider policies for CSO registration and sanction, none of the sector plans mentions this wider context. In all four of the case countries, a decade of political liberalisation, combined with new levels of international funding, has yielded a rapid growth in the number of NGOs and other CSOs. However, in each country, national governments still limit CSO advocacy and watchdog activities, through threats of deregistration, choosing of favourites, and state domination of the media.

Changing dynamics of CSO engagement in the education sector

Both sides of the CSO–government equation shape the degree to which CSOs participate in the national education-policy arena. National education-sector plans in all the case countries seem to have created a context within which civil-society actors are 'invited to the table' for consultation more frequently by governments than had historically been the case. However, roles and expectations for CSO–government and CSO–donor engagement vary considerably across the countries, as do levels of CSO autonomy, coordination, and mobilisation. In the terms suggested by Lister and Nyamugasira (2003), it matters both whether CSOs are '*invited*' to the policy table by government, and whether CSOs have the autonomy and resources to '*create*' and define their own policy roles and spaces.

Below, we first explore CSO experiences in the policy processes that have unfolded around each country's new education-sector plan. We then we look at the responses from different types or categories of civil-society actors.

Tanzania

In Tanzania, CSO engagement is relatively well coordinated and includes impressive use of evidence-based policy advocacy. The CSO coalition, the Tanzania Education Network (TEN/MET), is effective in mobilising a wide range of members around a common policy platform. TEN/MET includes international NGOs (INGOs) in its membership, and has benefited substantially from their funding and international leverage (in particular through the Commonwealth Education Fund). However, its leadership is primarily drawn from national NGOs, and significant attention is paid to building links to sub-national groups, though links to rural community-based organisations and citizens are still weak.

CSO efforts to play effective monitoring and watchdog roles in Tanzania have not been well received by government. Tensions heightened in 2005–2006 when the government placed an interdiction on a national watchdog (Haki-Elimu) and tried to prevent its participation at the policy table. There is also a perceived weakness in the capacity of the CSO coalition to reach rural and more marginalised CSOs and citizen groups. Civil-society capacity, in terms of popular mobilisation, and development of local authorities (including school management committees) is just emerging.

The Tanzanian experience is characterised by:

- Expansion of policy space for CSOs in the new sector programme, in part 'created' by CSOs themselves, through advocacy and research, use of media, and leveraging of international networks and actors. However, government has tried to contain criticism and contention, and favours complementary service providers. Rules for CSO engagement in sector-programme design and oversight are neither transparent nor formalised.
- Considerable coordination among CSOs, though led in large part by national NGOs. In contrast to Burkina Faso, Kenya, and Mali, the national parents' association is weak.
- Common platform for CSO coordination emphasises equity and quality improvements – holding government accountable for the delivery of services.
- CSO engagement is coordinated, focused on accountability, and independent. However, this is the most contentious CSO–government relationship among our case countries.

Burkina Faso

CSOs in Burkina Faso were initially marginalised in the policy discussions that led to the formulation of the education-sector plan in 2002, particularly teacher unions. However, the development of a national education CSO coalition, the Cadre de Concertation en Education de Base (CCEB), has led to new civil-society voice on issues of gender, curricular reform, and regional planning. By 2006, CSO consultation at the national and regional levels in Burkina Faso had become routine. Furthermore, the establishment of a CSO–government governed pooled fund for non-formal education projects (a unique feature of the Burkina sector programme) seems to have created a dynamic space for new CSO initiatives and stronger CSO voice in education policy processes.

However, in contrast to many other civil-society coalitions, CCEB has not made universal free access to primary education a central part of its mobilisation efforts. The coalition still has limited capacity for monitoring national educational quality and equity issues, and limited ability to engage a wider public on education issues. In contrast to Tanzania, relations between CSOs and government are not conflictual: CSOs rarely criticise the government in the media or other public forums.

The Burkina Faso experience is characterised by:

- Expansion of government-controlled ('invited') policy space for all CSOs, especially at decentralised levels (with some innovative mechanisms to support CSO management of parts of the sector programme).
- NGOs increasingly coordinated around efforts to directly provide for expansion of access and creation of curricular alternatives.
- Broad endorsement of gradualist, *faire-faire* (partnership) approach to expanding and improving basic education.
- CSO engagement that is complementary and collaborative – especially at decentralised levels. However, there are limited signs of CSO capacity for popular contention or engagement in watchdog or accountability roles.

Kenya

In Kenya, CSOs came together at the time of the country's first fully free multi-party elections, and formed the ElimuYetu Coalition (EYC). This coalition played a very important role in lobbying citizens and political leadership – its campaign and research on school fees and declining enrolments helped influence the winning political party to declare abolition of elementary-school fees upon its election. However, since 2002, EYC has lost much of its capacity and voice. Since 2007, civil-society actors have tended to focus their energies on gaining individual leverage inside the Ministry of Education, through complementary service and contracting roles, instead of through active advocacy and monitoring. While some CSOs have emerged as trusted policy partners in the recent education sector-wide approach (SWAp) (around issues such as gender and early-childhood education), there is little evidence of coordinated capacity for monitoring government and donor commitments to universalising good-quality education.

Competition for funding, and various views about the right direction for future education-sector expansion within the education civil-society sector may partially explain this deterioration in collective CSO action in Kenya. However, the lack of CSO coordination also reflects larger tensions in Kenya's political system. In Kenya, CSOs continue to feel the threat of government reprisals for their critical advocacy and monitoring work, and the NGO umbrella body has become heavily politicised. Furthermore, CSOs have little traction with parliamentarians; the main focus of their engagement is with the Ministry of Education and donors.

The Kenyan experience is characterised by:

- Expansion of policy space for CSO engagement, in part 'created' by CSO advocacy in the lead up to the 2002 elections. However, government continues to view CSOs primarily as implementers, not as policy interlocutors.
- Some coordination among CSOs in the education sector – especially strong around thematic issues (gender, early-childhood education). But competition, even among networks, is common.
- The loss of a common platform for CSO coordination after the government's abolition of school fees. There has been a distinct decline in overall capacity and effectiveness of the

national EYC. While key CSOs still belong to the EYC, many also advocate for policies that enhance their own interests.
- CSO engagement that is routine and frequent, but relatively uncoordinated. There are limited signs of CSO capacity for popular contention or engagement in watchdog or accountability roles.

Mali

CSO engagement in education policy in Mali has a distinctive history. On the one hand, the 1990s witnessed an impressive level of coordination among NGOs involved in the community-school movement, in part funded from INGOs and donor organisations. However, the 1990s also saw strong efforts to limit the power of Mali's teachers' unions and national post-secondary student associations in educational decision making. Perhaps not so surprisingly, there are contradictory views from these different CSOs on the degree of voice they had in the design of the education-sector plan. Many local CSOs view the sector plan as being largely donor led, and modelled from a pre-established policy-reform model. Teachers' and parents' associations and some national NGOs feel they were not adequately consulted, and continue to object to key aspects of the sector programme. This is in contrast to the view of INGOs and NGOs with strong international links and traditionally large roles in direct service provision, which feel that the sector plan was the result of wide consultation, and are pleased that the government has adopted several of the lessons learned from the NGO-sponsored community-school movement, including building proactive school-level management structures for civil-society participation.

Although a number of CSO coordinating groups have emerged in Mali since the late 1990s, CSOs in Mali (as in Kenya) tend to bargain with government and donors individually rather than collectively. At the time of our research in 2006, CSO engagement in Mali's education-sector programme appeared fragmented and disorganised. In addition, our research found that many Malian CSOs lacked understanding of the decision-making spaces for civil-society actors within the sector programme. Few participated in the consultative structures, joint evaluation missions, or joint thematic groups. The fragmentation and lack of coordination among CSOs may help explain why donors and civil-society actors alike noted an overall diminishment of CSO participation in the education-policy arena since the design of the sector programme in 1999, a perception in sharp contrast to opinions expressed in our interviews in the other case countries.

The Mali experience is characterised by:

- Expansion of government-controlled ('invited') policy space for CSOs, but with differential treatment by type of CSO, and limited information sharing between government and NGOs. Decentralisation of governance seems to confuse rather than enhance CSO policy leverage, although government wants the main CSO contributions at this level.
- Limited coordination among NGOs and between NGOs and other CSO actors.
- No effective, shared CSO platform for operating in the sector – deep disagreement about the main decentralisation reforms.
- CSO engagement is fragmented and offers a limited counterweight at the national level. Actors contend for specific interests, and bargain with government as individual organisations.

Capacities and tensions among different types of CSO

Using our case-study data, we also explored how the various interests and relationships among different types of CSOs engaged in the education sector were affecting CSO capacities and voice in national policy settings. While considerable variation appeared within each actor category when looked at across national context, some broad generalisations about their capacities, motivations, and interests are possible. Here we summarise our findings by type of CSO.

INGOs and NGOs emerged as the most prominent and visible CSO actors in new national education-sector programmes. While INGOs and NGOs continue to work in project mode, there was wide recognition of the need to work at a system level, and within emerging sector plans. There was a clear perception among INGOs and NGOs that a small subset of actors, namely those that have repositioned themselves as complementary service providers and who have international connections, are more frequently invited to the policy table in the context of the new sector programmes. Tensions between INGOs and national NGOs varied by country – but appeared to be less problematic in the countries with the stronger national coalitions (Tanzania and Burkina Faso). Functioning civil-society coalitions with substantial leadership from national organisations appeared to support a sense of local ownership and control among domestic NGOs in two of our cases, helping to ward off the claims of domination by Northern NGOs that are found in many other studies of civil society in Africa.

Teachers' unions remain perhaps the most powerful, well-organised, and representative of civil-society actors – especially so in Mali and Kenya (though not in Tanzania). In addition, these organisations have played a powerful historical role in advocating for democratic transitions. However, our research suggested that unions remained somewhat marginalised players within sector programmes, primarily because of their focus on employment issues. Government efforts in most countries appear to focus more on containing the disruptive capacity of unions than on engaging with them to improve the quality of teaching. Many unions remain sceptical of core reforms in new sector plans – including decentralisation reforms and plans to hire para-professionals. However, even in countries like Mali, where teachers' unions have opposed major aspects of the sector programme, unions are now committed to working with government towards the expansion of basic education. Our research suggests that the time has come to reconsider the role of teachers' unions in sector programmes – focusing both on their capacities for professional socialisation and mobilisation, and their broader contribution to the fabric of democracy.

Faith-based organisations bring considerable resources and capacities to the education policy table. They represent large constituencies in each of our case countries, and often have experience in running their own schools. However, the engagement of faith-based organisations in national sector planning is quite diverse. In Tanzania and Kenya, Christian and Muslim organisations are routinely consulted by government, and work effectively with national CSO education coalitions. In Mali and Burkina Faso, faith-based organisations are more marginalised in the policy process. We also noted, drawing on the Kenya case, that inherent tensions can arise between secular national education systems and faith-based bodies around the control of schools and school curriculum. In Kenya, for example, the churches are still interested in regaining ownership of previously nationalised secondary schools, and sometimes align with the private-sector provider group. Like teachers' unions, faith-based groups represent both general citizen interest and the particular interests and values of their members.

National parents' associations differ considerably in terms of their representativeness, autonomy from the government, and organisational capacity. National parents' associations in Kenya and Mali collect membership fees and have some degree of organisational effectiveness – for example, membership lists, newsletters, an executive, and regular meetings. Burkinabe parents' associations are linked in a confederated structure at the national level, which has provincial and regional representation, while Tanzania's national parents' association, WAZAZI, originated as an arm of the ruling socialist party, primarily to facilitate the interaction between government and a growing number of community-initiated secondary schools. These are important, constituency-based bodies, but only in the Kenyan case did the national parents' association appear to have a sustained voice on national education-sector policies.

Private providers and the business community: There has been a rising number of private educational providers in all four of our case countries since the late 1990s, supported in part by the new openness to private provision in new education-sector plans. Kenya, Mali, and Tanzania each have an active CSO that represents the interests of private providers within the educational policy arena. In addition, Kenya has a coalition of private providers from informal urban settlements. While governments tend to consult with these new provider groups, tensions sometimes emerge over their demands for increased government subsidies for private schools. Perhaps more importantly, national business associations (including chambers of commerce) seem to be relatively disengaged from national policy processes related to basic education, except in the case of Kenya.[5]

Comparison across our case studies suggested that *coordination among civil-society* actors makes an important contribution to CSO ability to effectively engage in the national policy arena in education. Yet, across the four countries studied, historical divisions and tensions among different CSO groups, especially between teachers' unions and NGO service providers, and between international and national NGOs, appeared to limit CSO coordination, undermining their ability to make significant policy gains. Perhaps it is for this reason that, regardless of CSO type, the organisations we interviewed viewed their own capacity to act as policy watchdogs and to mobilise citizens' voice as both limited and weak, and uniformly recognised the need for more effective inter-CSO coordination. Many CSOs noted the valuable role played by international initiatives, such as the Global Campaign for Education and the Commonwealth Education Fund, in supporting their efforts to establish a new policy presence. However, such externally led efforts were felt at times to displace the need for the development of national capacities (as in Kenya). Most nationally based CSOs argued for the need for a strong locally led effort whose features emerged from the distinct features of civil society in each national context.

CSO–government and CSO–donor relationships

Changes in CSO–government and CSO–donor relationships are an important outcome of new sector programmes in education. Across all our case countries, there has been a drop in direct funding from bilateral donors to NGOs, a heightened level of policy dialogue between donors and government, and a new (but relatively untested) framework calling for the engagement of CSOs. We were thus not surprised to find many similar trends in CSO–government relationships across our case countries, differing more in degree than in kind. Here we summarise some of the key features of changing relationships between CSOs, governments, and donors engendered by education-sector programmes in our four case studies.

CSO–government relationships

Our case interviews with government officials and donor organisations suggested that CSOs are now accepted participants in education-sector programmes and in such regular mechanisms as the joint annual donor review of education-sector programmes. However, governments still have the ultimate say over who gets invited to the policy table, and for which purposes – regularised, transparent processes for selecting civil-society participants were rare. In the absence of clear rules, governments tend to select the organisations they perceive to be least contentious and most helpful. CSO winners and losers are apparent: while most governments consult with a variety of CSO actors, they tend to marginalise teachers' unions in the design and implementation of sector programmes, favouring those INGOs and national-level organisations that provide services in the sector and have the capacity for technical training. The significant potential that organisations with independent constituency bases – such as teachers' unions and parents' associations – have in terms of leveraging public engagement in educational issues is often neglected by governments.

Across all four countries, government–CSO relations are fraught with tension and confusion about appropriate CSO roles and mandates, including questions about how to ensure that CSOs are working in a complementary fashion within new sector programmes. Government officials sometimes raise the idea that CSOs should report on their activities to government and (in a few interviews) noted that CSOs should contribute their resources directly to a pooled sector fund. For their part, CSO actors found it very difficult to work with government as subcontractors, preferring to seek funding from external sources. They distrust government management and disbursement of resources. However, many CSOs (particularly well-established NGOs and INGOs) view the opportunity to work collaboratively with the government to meet sector goals with enthusiasm.

Relations between CSOs and donors

CSO–donor relationships are changing rapidly in the context of new sector programmes. Our findings suggest that CSOs are unsatisfied with the level and scope of donor support for their policy and advocacy efforts, and wary of donor initiatives that place CSOs in subcontracting roles *vis-à-vis* government. In Kenya, Mali, and Tanzania, many CSOs described a drop in international funding for their activities – sometimes a precipitous one. In Mali in particular, several organisations expressed frustration with the fact that donors still tend to channel funds through their own national NGOs rather than directly to Southern groups. In Burkina Faso, CSOs also cautioned that when donors delay disbursements of sector funds, due to government failure to meet conditions, CSOs' activities suffer. CSOs in all countries noted a decline in opportunities to meet with international technical and financial partners in the period following the introduction of sector programmes. However, in some contexts (particularly Tanzania), several CSOs praised donors for helping them to leverage a greater degree of CSO engagement in national policy processes.

A significant finding across our case studies was the degree to which donor organisations lack a well-informed and coordinated strategy for supporting CSO involvement in the education sector. We were surprised at how little bilateral donor organisations seemed to know about local CSOs and their capacities – or even about the funding given by various branches of their own organisations to education-sector CSOs. As an example, we found local DFID staff unaware of the funding provided by the UK government to the Commonwealth Education Fund, a programme that funds national civil-society activities in both Kenya and Tanzania. At the time of our field research in 2006, several donors were considering ways of supporting CSO advocacy efforts in education. But donors preferred to fund small research or information-sharing exercises among CSOs. With the exception of Tanzania, donors had generally shown limited interest in providing the kind of core funding that might enable national CSOs to engage in sustained programmes of research or advocacy. Many donors continued to prefer to channel funds through their own national NGOs, for reasons of familiarity and trust, and had only begun to experiment with direct funding of Southern organisations. In addition, donors did not have clear rules or transparent processes for selecting which CSOs they interact with and support.

Perhaps not surprisingly, given their reliance on donor funding, most CSOs we interviewed did not express sustained interest in monitoring and playing a watchdog role *vis-à-vis* the commitments and activities of donor organisations themselves.

Conclusion

The civil-society experiences drawn from our four country case studies suggest that important changes have occurred for CSOs in the context of new sector programmes in education. These changes include at a minimum government recognition of the need for more regular consultation with civil-society groups, greater interest among donors in funding the advocacy and policy watchdog roles played by civil-society groups, and in some cases, evidence of mounting civil-society capacity for effective engagement in debates about national education policy.

However, our study also points to key challenges in this new era of civil-society engagement, confirming some of the findings of others who have questioned the degree to which the policy and advocacy roles played by civil-society actors are enhanced by new sector programmes in education (Doftori and Takala 2005; Kruse 2003; Lexow 2003; Miller-Grandvaux *et al.* 2002; Samoff 2004). In all four countries, governments had not established transparent and regularised processes for civil-society engagement in the policy process – CSO participation was even more muddied in systems undergoing rapid administrative decentralisation. There is clearly a need for transparent procedural frameworks at the national level, including rules around the selection of CSO representation, a regular timetable for consultation, and more active encouragement of engagement with parliamentary bodies.

For civil-society actors, our case studies suggest that considerable gains in civil-society voice come with more effective coordination and coalition building, particularly as illustrated in Burkina Faso and Tanzania. In these two contexts, coalitions helped to dampen traditional tensions between Northern and Southern NGOs, and between NGOs and unions, and created opportunities for civil-society actors to hedge against government efforts to choose favourites. However, the CSO coalitions studied in this research appeared to be quite weak in reaching out beyond ministries of education, to mobilise communities and citizens, or even engage with parliamentarians. Coalitions seemed to miss out on the crucial opportunities for expanding public engagement offered by constituency-based organisations like parents' associations and teachers' unions. CSO capacity for monitoring government commitments to free access, better quality, and more equitable provision of basic education over the longer term also appeared quite fragile in all our case studies – though Burkina Faso and Tanzania suggest more positive trends. As illustrated by the Kenya case, initial policy gains by a coalition do not guarantee sustained action.

Our study offers several key insights for external groups wishing to fund or support more effective civil-society engagement, including the recently launched Civil Society Education Fund initiative developed by the Global Campaign for Education, which received funding from the donor-led Fast Track Initiative in December 2008. Initiatives that hope to build national civil-society capacity in the education sector will need to be carefully targeted to existing capacities and relationships among CSOs, and the political opportunity structures that limit CSO policy engagement in each national context. While sustained support for the development of broad-based and nationally led coalitions is clearly needed, a 'one size fits all' model seems unlikely to take hold given such diverse policy starting points. Further, external support is likely to be most effective when it targets the glaring gaps in current civil-society engagement in the sector. Thus, efforts that build direct links to communities through constituency-based organisations – that try to leverage national policy makers in locations outside the ministry of education (for example, parliamentarians, the judiciary, and the executive), and that encourage regular efforts to monitor and publicise the performance of both governments and donors in meeting their commitments to universal, quality basic education – should receive special attention.

Acknowledgements

This research was sponsored by the Canadian International Development Agency (CIDA), the International Development Research Centre (IDRC), the Comparative, International and Development Education Research Centre at the University of Toronto, Canada, and the University of Ottawa, Canada.

Notes

1. The country case studies, and a number of background desk studies (including Bangladesh, Mozambique, Senegal, and Zambia), are available on the project website: http://cide.oise.utoronto.ca/civil_society (retrieved 16 November 2009).
2. For a history of the Civil Society Education Fund Initiative, see CEF (2007b) and Save the Children UK *et al.* (n.d.).
3. Purchasing power parity (PPP) is 'an exchange rate that accounts for price differences among countries, allowing international comparison of real output and incomes' (UNESCO 2007). PPP is often used to compare the standards of living across countries, giving a better picture than GDP per capita alone.
4. PEDP is focused on the primary sector; a costed plan for the whole education sector was under development during the period of our field research in 2006. The Education Sector Development Plan (ESDP) of 2001, although covering the whole sector, was not costed and therefore not frequently referred to by participants.
5. The Commonwealth Education Fund (which is financed by DFID and managed by a group that includes ActionAid, Oxfam, and Save the Children) has long advocated for the engagement of the business community in basic education issues (CEF 2007b).

References

Buchert, L. (2002) 'Towards new partnerships in sector-wide approaches: comparative experience from Burkina Faso, Ghana and Mozambique', *International Journal of Educational Development* 22: 69–84.
CEF (2005) 'Global Mid-Term Review', London: Commonwealth Education Fund.
CEF (2007a) 'Driving the Bus: The Journey of National Education Coalitions', London: Commonwealth Education Fund.
CEF (2007b) 'Funding Change: Sustaining Civil Society Advocacy in Education', London: Commonwealth Education Fund.
Cornwall, A. and J. Gaventa (2001) 'From Users and Choosers to Makers and Shapers: Repositioning Participation in Social Policy', *IDS Working Paper 127*, Brighton, UK: Institute of Development Studies.
Doftori, M. and T. Takala (2005) 'Role of NGOs in the Context of Education Sector Development Programs in Developing Countries', paper presented at the 11th EADI General Conference: Insecurity and Development, Regional Issues and Policies for an Interdependent World, Bonn, 21–24 September.
Kruse, S. (2003) 'SWAps and Civil Society: The Roles of Civil Society Organizations in Sector Programs – Synthesis Report', *NORAD Report 1/2004*, Oslo: Norwegian Agency for Development Cooperation.
Lexow, J. (2003) 'SWAps and Civil Society: The Role of CSOs in Zambia's Basic Education Sub-Sector Investment Programme (BESSIP)', Oslo: Norwegian Agency for Development Cooperation.
Lister, S. and W. Nyamugasira (2003) 'Design contradictions in the new architecture of aid? Reflections from Uganda on the roles of civil society organizations', *Development Policy Review* 21 (1): 93–106.
Manor, J., M. Robinson, and G. White (1999) 'Civil Society and Governance: A Concept Paper', Brighton, UK: Institute for Development Studies.
McGee, R., J. Levene, and A. Hughes (2002) 'Assessing Participation in Poverty Reduction Strategy Papers: A Desk-based Synthesis of Experience in Sub-Saharan Africa', *Research Report 52*, Brighton, UK: Institute of Development Studies.

Miller-Grandvaux, Y., M. Welmond, and J. Wolf (2002) 'Evolving Partnerships: The Role of NGOs in Basic Education in Africa', USAID, available at http://www.glp.net/c/document_library/get_file?p_l_id=473710&folderId=12858&name=DLFE-1712.pdf (retrieved 8 November 2004).

Nelson, J. (2006) 'Democratic Politics and Pro-poor Services: Unpacking the Concept of Reform', paper prepared for the Workshop on The Politics of Service Delivery in Democracies, Stockholm, 27–28 April.

Samoff, J. (2004) 'From funding projects to supporting sectors? Observations on the aid relationship in Burkina Faso', *International Journal of Educational Development* 24: 397–427.

Save the Children UK, Oxfam GB, and ActionAid (n.d.) 'National Civil Society Education Funds: A Briefing Paper', available at http://www.commonwealtheducationfund.org/downloads/documents/briefingpaper.pdf (retrieved 16 November 2009), London: Save the Children UK; Oxford: Oxfam GB; London: ActionAid; London: Commonwealth Education Fund.

Tomlinson, B. and P. Foster (2004) 'At the Table or in the Kitchen? CIDA's New Aid Strategies, Developing Country Ownership and Donor Conditionality', Briefing Paper, Halifax, Canada: Canadian Council for International Co-operation.

UNDP (2006) *Human Development Report*, New York, NY: UNDP.

UNESCO (2007) *EFA Global Monitoring Report*, Paris: United Nations Educational, Scientific and Cultural Organization.

World Bank (2005) 'Education Statistics Version 5.3', available at http://web.worldbank.org/WBSITE/EXTERNAL/TOPICS/EXTEDUCATION/EXTDATASTATISTICS/EXTEDSTATS/0,,menuPK:3232818~pagePK:64168427~piPK:64168435~theSitePK:3232764,00.html (retrieved 5 January 2010).

Marching to different rhythms: international NGO collaboration with the state in Tanzania

Sheila Aikman

This contribution examines relationships between international NGOs and state education institutions in their efforts to achieve Education for All. It does this through an investigation of Oxfam GB's multi-level and multi-strategy approach to education in Tanzania. Looking at three components of this programme, it explores what a 'one-programme approach' means for Oxfam GB's education work and investigates its partnerships and advocacy relationships at the local and national levels with different state education institutions and agents. The boundaries of partnership and collaboration are discussed and it concludes that advocacy practices need to be viewed as multiple, part of a process, and emergent.

À des rythmes différents : collaboration des ONG avec l'État en Tanzanie
Cette contribution traite des relations entre les ONG internationales et les institutions d'enseignement publiques dans leurs efforts en vue de garantir l'Éducation pour tous. Pour ce faire, elle examine l'approche à niveaux et stratégies multiples d'OXFAM GB concernant l'éducation en Tanzanie. Elle étudie, en se penchant sur trois éléments de ce programme, ce que signifie une « approche à un seul programme » pour les travaux menés par Oxfam GB dans le secteur de l'éducation et examine ses partenariats et relations de plaidoyer aux niveaux local et national avec différents agents et institutions publics du secteur de l'éducation. Les frontières qui définissent un partenariat et une collaboration sont traitées et ce document conclut que les pratiques de plaidoyer doivent être considérées comme multiples, s'inscrivant dans des processus et en cours d'émergence.

Marchando em ritmos diferentes: colaboração de ONGs internacionais com o estado na Tanzânia
Esta contribuição artigo examina as relações entre ONGs internacionais e instituições educacionais estatais em seus esforços para alcançar a Educação para Todos. Ele faz isto através de uma investigação da abordagem da Oxfam GB de vários níveis e estratégias para educação na Tanzânia. Examinando três componentes deste programa, ele explora o que significa uma "abordagem de programa único" para o trabalho sobre educação da Oxfam GB e investiga suas parcerias e relações de advocacy em nível local e nacional com diferentes instituições educacionais estatais e agentes. As fronteiras da parceria e colaboração são discutidas e o artigo conclui que as práticas de advocacy precisam ser vistas como múltiplas, parte de um processo e emergentes.

ACHIEVING EDUCATION FOR ALL THROUGH PUBLIC-PRIVATE PARTNERSHIPS?

Marchando al son de varios tambores: la cooperación entre ONG internacionales y el Estado en Tanzania

Este ensayo analiza la relación entre ONG internacionales e instituciones de educación estatales que trabajan en el marco de la iniciativa "Educación para Todos". Se investigó la metodología multiestrategia y multinivel que impulsa Oxfam GB en Tanzania. Tras examinar tres componentes del programa, el ensayo esclarece lo que significa para Oxfam GB el "método de programa unitario" para la educación, y examina sus alianzas y relaciones de incidencia a nivel local y nacional con distintas instituciones y actores de la educación estatal. Se exploran también las fronteras que delimitan las alianzas y colaboraciones. El ensayo concluye que la incidencia siempre es de carácter múltiple, está sujeta a emergencias y es el producto de procesos.

Introduction

This contribution examines relationships between international NGOs and state education organisations and institutions in their efforts to achieve Education for All. It does this through an investigation of Oxfam GB's[1] multi-level and multi-strategy approach to education – its 'one-programme approach'. Informed by a human-rights framework, international NGOs (INGOs) such as Oxfam engage diverse state actors and institutions through multiple strategies aimed at leveraging change towards commonly agreed goals of Education for All (EFA). The contribution explores what a one-programme approach means for Oxfam GB's education work and the nature and diversity of relationships it embraces with state entities at different levels of INGO action: sub-national (local, community, 'grassroots'), national, regional, and global.

Using examples of education work being undertaken by Oxfam GB in Tanzania, it investigates concepts and practices of its partnerships and advocacy relationships at the local and national levels with different state education institutions (district councils, school management associations, education ministry departments) and agents (ministers, planners, inspectors, teacher trainers, and others). Through these examples, it looks at how partnerships are developed, roles established, and legitimacy maintained. It begins by exploring how the one-programme approach modelled by Oxfam GB's education team has been shaped by developments in both the global education-policy arena and the move towards rights-based programming and working in alliances by UK INGOs.

INGOs as transnational advocates in the EFA arena

At a meeting in June 2008, Oxfam GB's education team committed itself to 'moving beyond creating pockets of ephemeral change in disparate countries towards playing a part in creating long term sustainable change on education and other basic social services' (Oxfam GB 2008). This team – comprising national, regional, and global education coordinators, advocacy and lobby officers, media, funding, and campaign managers – discussed how the concept of a one-programme approach could help explain and strengthen their work on education and basic social services through articulating their common goals and mapping out their interconnections and potential synergies.

Oxfam GB's work has encompassed education projects, and livelihoods and humanitarian programmes that have had educational components for many decades; however, formal education was not considered part of its core work until the late 1990s. It has a long history of training, adult literacy, and some school construction and materials supply, but it was only with a restructuring and refocusing of Oxfam's work through a human-rights lens and human-development framework in 1998 that education emerged as one of its main 'strategic change objectives' (Oxfam GB 1998). Linked with health under a 'basic services' banner, achieving the right to basic education became one of five rights around which the INGO's work is structured. Education is viewed as being of critical importance for human development, through its promise of developing capabilities with which individuals can strive towards overcoming poverty in its multiple expressions (Watkins 2000).

Education, conceived as an enabling right, is at the heart of the general INGO shift towards a rights-based approach to development aimed at leveraging change through working in alliances and networks. This shift is well illustrated through the role of UK INGOs, and Oxfam was a key player in the formation of the Global Campaign for Education, itself a 'paradigmatic instance' of a new wave of transnational advocacy (Mundy and Murphy 2001: 125). Mundy (2006) argues, furthermore, that education is now embedded in a widening consensus on the core features of 'good' global development and a new development compact. Education's particular expression of this compact is apparent in the Dakar Framework and the Education for All movement, which 'has become part of a broad-based consensus about "what works" among bilateral and multilateral development agencies, a rallying call for heads of state and focus for transnational advocacy' (Mundy 2006: 24). As transnational actors, Oxfam and other INGOs such as ActionAid have shed lingering remnants of education service-delivery practices to engage in advocacy and campaigning 'mobilized around a well-developed action frame that links the problem of educational access to the wider issues of debt relief, human rights and global equity and targets erosion of national commitments to free, publicly provided educational services' (Mundy and Murphy 2001: 125). The EFA consensus has become a strong focus for international NGO advocacy concerned with not only leveraging change for education goals – and these often narrowly defined in terms of universal primary and, more recently, secondary schooling – but using these as an entry point for influencing wider issues of distribution of resources and recognition of rights.

In his book *From Poverty to Power*, Green (2008) sets out what he describes as his contribution to an evolving debate within and outside of Oxfam about the importance of efforts to overcome inequalities of power, assets, and opportunities. He articulates the concept of a new development compact in terms of a complex process, a 'subtle interplay between citizens and states in terms of a combination of citizens actively demanding their rights for justice within their societies and states which are accountable to citizens and able to guarantee their rights' (Green 2008: 14). This brings the nexus between citizen and states sharply into focus as the centre of concern for INGO efforts. Working with both citizens and states, he argues, is both compatible and desirable, even though they 'march to different rhythms' (Green 2008: 14).

This kind of development compact and the processes it implies brings new significance to the role of state agents and institutions in the work of INGOs. Where formerly relationships may have been framed in terms of complementarity, with INGOs providing educational services where the state could not reach, the reformation of INGOs into transnational advocacy organisations concerned with rights suggests a new way of working. Moreover, this change requires INGOs (as complex multi-level organisations with projects and programmes operating at local, national, regional, and global levels) to have a keen understanding and awareness of how 'marching rhythms' may differ between international, national, and local organisations in different socio-historical spaces around the globe.

A multi-layered, multi-faceted strategy for EFA

It was noted at the turn of the last millennium, that the move to a rights framework poses tough challenges for INGOs in terms of their structure, their fundraising and 'brand', their spending decisions and priorities, and their relations with others, not least government (Edwards *et al.* 2000). In an article first published in 1993 and reprinted in 2002, Edwards outlines what he saw then as a need for 'a proper, multi-layered, and multi-faceted strategy for NGO advocacy which relates themes, targets, objectives, activities, roles, and responsibilities together in a coherent way' (Edwards 2002: 104). He produced a model framework for international advocacy that illustrated how such a strategy might look in theory, 'which integrates detailed policy work with public campaigning; which is rooted in real experience; and which embraces the whole organization in pursuit of a common cause' (Edwards 2002: 104).

In 2008, a similar model framework was discussed by Oxfam GB's education staff in local offices, national offices, and international headquarters as a tool for understanding and improving the articulation of different dimensions of its education work in different sections within the organisation and in diverse countries (see Table 1). The purpose was to use the framework to help build cohesion and coherence around a common goal of access to quality education for all. Members of the team – from country education coordinators, through regional advocacy advisers, global lobbyists, and global campaign managers, to media officers – used the

Table 1: A one-programme approach to education programming in Tanzania

Advocacy focus	'Level'	Types of advocacy
Global commitments and resources (UN agencies, international finance institutions, Fast Track Initiative, bilateral donors) developing a global campaigning force	Global	Analysis, research, and documentation Lobby on models of financing Work with key partner Gobal Campaign for Education (GCE) Link citizen movements to global decision making Lobby for UN reforms Global Week of Action; Oxfam 'For All Campaign'
Commitments and resources, regional governance structures (for example, Southern African Development Community, African Union)	Regional	Analysis, research, and documentation with key partners Facilitate regional alliance building Policy advocacy to influence regional bodies
Legislation, education policies, and review processes, budgets of national governments	National	Support civil society and government dialogue on budgets, policy, planning, and accountability Engage parliamentarians and legislators Popular mobilisation (for example, Global Week of Action)
Organisation of the delivery of education (decentralised government)	District	Facilitate effective functioning of district education networks Build capacity of partners and district authorities for analysis, research, and documentation
School management (decentralised government, NGOs, private sector)	Local	Carry out programme research Foster linkages between sectors Support of people's organisations Facilitate critical information Document experience and learning

Source: Oxfam GB after Abani (2007); Oxfam GB (2008).

framework to map their distinctive activities and contributions at different levels to help visualise inter-relationships and complementarities in strategies.

Working closely with the Global Campaign for Education since its start in 1999, Oxfam GB's Oxford-based global advocacy and campaigns team has become highly professional and efficient, expanding its home-based UK campaigning force to new levels in 2005 during the Make Poverty History campaign and the G8 meeting in Gleneagles. Since then it has also been working intensively with the Global Campaign for Education to broaden and strengthen the alliance with new European Global Campaign for Education members and with Southern organisations, particularly national civil-society education coalitions, through the tripartite management of the Commonwealth Education Fund by Oxfam GB, ActionAid, and Save the Children UK (CEF 2008). Oxfam GB also operates through eight regional offices as well as national offices, many of which have led the way in advocacy and campaigning, such as the advocacy-based programme developed in the Philippines in the late 1990s, supported through the East Asian regional office. Others, however, found the shift to an advocacy and rights-based approach challenging. For some, it was an unfamiliar and threatening way of working, imposed from above with inadequate support and limited appreciation of what this change implied for them. With little experience on which to model their work, or cultural patterns and practices that were inimical to confrontational advocacy practices, some national and local teams struggled to incorporate advocacy and campaigning in a way meaningful to their education work. For some years, the INGO's education work as a whole struggled to bridge a separation between 'advocacy and campaigning' and 'programme'.

Slowly over the 2000s, this situation changed: campaigning was decentralised from a specialist unit in the UK to the regional and national offices and programmes. As these offices have gained confidence in their new role, they have been challenging Northern models of advocacy and engagement in a slow process of 'domestication' of the concept and practices of advocacy and lobbying, tailoring them to their diverse cultural and linguistic contexts. Local and national programmes now not only identify their own advocacy and campaigning targets and messages, but are also developing their own practices geared towards their own understandings of how to influence change for good-quality EFA. In this way, advocacy has slowly lost its sense of being 'something bolted on to mainstream activities as an optional extra' (Edwards *et al.* 2000).

Oxfam GB's education programme today is, therefore, concerned with developing relationships with state institutions and agents, in order to exert leverage and advocacy for change and through a variety of action and activities.

INGO–state relations in Tanzania

As noted above, a focus on the nexus between citizen and state implies new kinds of relationships with state institutions and government bodies. This section looks at three examples of INGO work with state education institutions, drawing from the education work of Oxfam GB in Tanzania. They will be briefly examined in terms of the nature of the relationship between Oxfam GB and the state, the roles of different actors and organisations, and what they indicate about INGO legitimacy and accountability. They are drawn from INGO programme publications (both printed and web based) and my personal field notes.[2] They are examples of qualitatively different kinds of relationships with different state education institutions and their representatives. The first is an example of the transition from a welfare-based approach to a rights-based approach, the second an example of a 'partnership' with district councils for the development of a pedagogical innovation, and the third an example of an advocacy programme by an INGO–national education coalition alliance.

ACHIEVING EDUCATION FOR ALL THROUGH PUBLIC-PRIVATE PARTNERSHIPS?

Oxfam GB's work in Tanzania is organised in a 10-year framework for action and sustainability for the period to 2017, focusing on work in the areas of livelihoods and vulnerability, governance, and education. The work is designed for maximum impact at every level from the five-year-old child to the Prime Minister's office (Oxfam GB 2007). Nested within Oxfam GB's global education aim of achieving access to quality basic education for all, the Tanzania programme has its own specific national aim of 'enhancing the quality and relevance of, and equitable access to, education to further strengthen Tanzania's skill base, foster active citizen participation, and reduce both income and non-income poverty' (Oxfam GB 2007: 9). It aims to do this through three strategies. The first two examples – empowering pastoralist peoples through education and improvement of formal basic education through pedagogical innovation – are designed to feed into and provide a direct source of evidence for the third – education policy advocacy (including research, lobbying, and campaigning).

Research and advocacy for pastoralist education

Oxfam's pastoralist education programme in Ngorongoro District has a small budget, but ambitious aims. The INGO has been working in Ngorongoro District since 2000, and since 2005 has been working on an integrated pastoralist programme with livelihood security and diversification, food security, and education components. Its broader goal is one of enhancing a strong and vibrant pastoral civil society, and effective and accountable governance with policy advocacy at district and national levels in six countries in the Horn of Africa and East Africa (part of a 15-year Regional Pastoral Programme). In this way, the project's aims are an example of Green's (2008) 'subtle interplay between citizens and state'.

The education component of this programme, with a focus on preschools and youth and adult literacy, has evolved out of support to preschools. Maasai parents recognised a value in the literacy and numeracy skills (if not other skills) that primary schooling offered, and so were concerned that their children dropped out during the early grades, if they attended at all. They perceived this problem as stemming from a lack of familiarity with the institutionalised nature of schooling where all teaching and interaction was through a language the children did not speak (Kiswahili). Consequently, parents in some villages (*bomas*) set up preschools with volunteer Maasai women teachers to prepare their young children for the sharp shock of leaving home and attending primary school. For some years, Oxfam GB provided very basic learning materials to the preschools and supported the construction of dormitories for primary schools to improve conditions for young Maasai pupils and, though this, established a collaborative relationship with the Local Government Authority (LGA).

In 2007, Oxfam GB embarked on a new strategy based on the outcomes of research commissioned in 2006. The research investigated options and opportunities for ensuring equitable access to schooling for pastoralist boys and girls from a diversity of mobile, semi-mobile, and settled households. The research (Kariuki and Puja 2006) indicated that LGA officials, inspectors, and teachers displayed a high level of cooperation and willingness to collaborate on improving teacher training, school facilities and transport, and support for a proposed Oxfam-supported pilot project for diverse means of delivering primary education suitable for the needs of different groups of children (for example, through satellite schools for young people in their communities, mobile schools to accompany mobile herders, especially boys, and boarding facilities adjacent to primary schools in the larger villages and towns). Oxfam GB staff participated in community and LGA meetings to discuss the research findings, and the LGA was supportive in terms of developing ideas into a pilot. However, the limits of LGA collaboration and of their ability to collaborate became apparent over issues of the relevance of the curriculum.

While teachers were faced with challenges of teaching monolingual Ma-speaking students – either because they were not Ma-speaking themselves or because the syllabus and materials were in Kiswahili (the language of primary schooling throughout the country) – the response from the LGA officers was to frown upon any use of Ma in the schools and label it 'unconstitutional' (Kariuki and Puja 2006: 24). This rigidity at the local level was a direct response to national centralised control over curriculum development, prescriptive content, and the rigid national examination system. The legislative limitations were compounded by prejudice about pastoralists' intellectual abilities and 'backward culture and tradition', and a belief in the importance and superiority of the national culture and language policy for the cohesion of the nation (Kariuki and Puja 2006: 25).

The education component of the INGO's pastoralist programme in Ngorongoro District was, therefore, the outcome of support to initiatives to provide Maasai parents with access to formal schooling and through direct material support for the delivery of primary schooling by the LGA. By working with the LGA over several years through this 'welfare' type approach and direct support, the INGO set the foundations for a relationship of trust and goodwill. This paved the way for a potential new collaboration and partnership through an innovative pilot programme aimed at ensuring the right of all children to access education. However, the collaboration is bounded by LGA considerations of what is suitable for a partnership and what they understand as appropriate within the confines of a nationally prescribed and nationally sanctioned monolingual and monocultural model of schooling. Challenging spheres of control and curriculum-policy decision making are not acceptable professionally or personally, and touches on contested and contentious questions of values. Leveraging change in this situation requires the INGO to implement a long-term integrated strategy engaging multiple levels – personal, local, and national.

Partnering for sustainability – education quality improvement through pedagogy

In 2004, Oxfam GB Tanzania together with the District and Municipal Councils in the Shinyanga Region developed a project for school-based teacher professional development aimed at improving learning outcomes and educational quality through an active pedagogy and teacher mentoring process, known as 'Education Quality Improvement through Pedagogy – Equip'. The relationship between the two implementing agencies was conceived as a partnership, with a Memorandum of Understanding outlining respective roles and responsibilities. As a project, it brought together a wide range of state actors and departments, such as the Schools Inspectorate, the Teachers' Service Unit, and different education officers and officials within the LGA. The INGO and LGA shared the objective of improving the quality of teaching and learning. The INGO had overall responsibility *vis-à-vis* the donor (EU) for the management and technical implementation, and directly employed six project officers and an overall manager who coordinated the project activities on a daily basis. Data for a mid-term review of the programme were collected through interviews (Mmbando and Mukyanuzi 2007), which took place one year before the end of EU funding, and produced findings and recommendations that throw light on the functioning of the partnership and how it was perceived by different 'stakeholders' from the within LGA.

The review revealed limitations in the LGA's participation in planning and financial management and oversight, which may have contributed to a lack of sense of ownership of the project. This is manifest in terms of irregular and poor functioning of the Project Coordination Committee, the overall decision-making body for the project, which was chaired by the District Commissioner – who, because of other prioritised commitments, failed to call and attend regular meetings (Mmbando and Mukyanuzi 2007: 11). This was considered to have affected project efficiency and delayed implementation schedules. At that time, too, the project was viewed as 'Oxfam's Equip project', and there were bottlenecks in implementation attributable to, among other things, a situation whereby those with executive responsibility for the project within the LGA were not in the positions of influence or authority necessary to overcome a state of inertia at the executive level. This indicates shortcomings in the nature of Oxfam's understanding of the political structure and decision-making lines, both formal and informal, within the LGA in the early stages of the project, which had subsequent implications for the partnership. It also indicates a lack of shared purpose of the project, neglect of potentially useful documents such as the Memorandum of Understanding, and potential weaknesses in respect or understanding of the values, beliefs, and culture of the other partners' institutions. Nevertheless, at the school and classroom levels the project was slowly but successfully transforming teacher–student relations, and new cadres of teacher peer mentors were changing relationships and motivation among staff.

In the final year of the project (2008), however, a change took place.[3] Taking into account comments from the mid-term review, Oxfam GB turned its attention to developing an exit strategy and to planning a handover process with the LGA. A series of meetings took place with senior education officers in the LGA who were committed to the new pedagogical training model (having seen its impact on teachers and students in the classroom). They understood that, with their involvement, the training model could be consolidated and expanded, and so embarked on their own internal advocacy process to ensure participation and commitment from LGA budget holders. Meetings between the INGO and LGA openly discussed remaining budgets and future needs in a new ethos of collaboration and equality. LGA decision makers were involved in discussion of priority spending on the remaining budget and in planning a strategy for handover of control of the project. A gradual process of transfer of power took place, which was evident in the way different LGA stakeholders prioritised and participated in these meetings.

This new phase of the project – though now less of a 'project' and more of an ongoing process of pedagogical renewal through teacher support within the LGA – has involved new roles, as Oxfam GB has scaled back its involvement, completed its outstanding scheduled training activities, and pared down its training team. It continues with only one trainer working in the LGA in a new mentoring role, drawing on professional skills, trust, and respect that he built up over the earlier phase of the project. The LGA team, with some 'backstopping' training and mentoring support from Oxfam GB, has been actively working out ways to consolidate the pedagogical training model, document its components, and begin a concerted process of advocacy (together with the INGO) to integrate the model into the national teacher-training strategy.

This partnership developed over several years and has undergone a shift in power and control from the INGO to the LGA. Underpinning the relationship has been a set of shared goals and the development of trust and compatible ways of working. Over time, the nature of the activities and relationship have changed such that senior LGA officials have become partners in advocacy for the sustainability of the pedagogical training model, as well as active agents for policy change at national level.

Education policy advocacy

At the national level, Oxfam GB's education work is focused on policy advocacy carried out through the national civil-society education coalition – the Tanzanian Education Network (TENMET). TENMET was established in 1999 and was a founding member of the Global Campaign for Education. TENMET has an advocacy mandate to provide an 'informed collective voice' for its member organisations, so as to influence policies for basic quality education for all in Tanzania (www.tenmet.org). During its first decade, its work has been oriented to help it become a strong advocacy organisation, with a clear plan of action and an ability to respond to its diverse membership. It has worked steadily over the decade to gain access to national and donor policy-making forums and get 'around the table' so that it can influence policy and, ultimately, practice. Its small secretariat has had financial support from its member organisations, INGOs and, since 2004, through the Commonwealth Education Fund. A study looking at the capacities and challenges of civil-society organisations as partners in the formulation, implementation, and monitoring of national education plans and policies (Mundy 2008) notes that TENMET seems to be relatively strong in terms of its ability to represent its constituencies, in its organisational capacities, in terms of its autonomy from government in the national arena, and the degree to which it is led by members of national civil society (Mundy 2008: 21).

The coalition has a seat on national education policy-making forums, such as the Primary and Secondary Education Development Plans (PEDP and SEDP), and plays an active role in the annual Education Sector Reviews, for which TENMET publishes its analysis and sets out its policy positions. At times, though, it is viewed with a degree of wariness by members of the government – for example, when it boycotted a national education-policy review in 2006 because the government had banned one of its strident campaigning members, Haki Elimu (Tomlinson and Macpherson 2007a: 41). To participate effectively in the policy spaces to which it now has regular access, TENMET's contribution, like those of national education coalitions in neighbouring countries, has to be based on its ability to engage in policy debate with others around the policy table. Oxfam's policy-advocacy work with TENMET is, consequently, about supporting it to achieve a relationship of respect through, 'not just strengthening the voice of civil society to be audible, it's about having a more informed and intelligent voice ... through evidence-based research so that education matters can be presented in an informed manner which is most likely to have impact' (Tomlinson and Macpherson 2007b: 16).

This relationship is built through demonstrable skills that contribute to good advocacy, such as the ability to critique policy documents, write policy briefs, use evidence (for example, documentation of improved learning outcomes through the implementation of the Equip pedagogical model in Shinyanga), good organisational and financial management, and the management of research. It involves using knowledge derived from good linkages that its member organisations maintain with grassroots realities and which give the coalition legitimacy in the eyes of government policy makers. Important, too, is the ability to be independent and 'establish good relations at all levels of both Government and donors, while maintaining our own point of view and taking a stand on matters of disagreement or misunderstanding' (www.tenmet.org).

Studies carried out by TENMET members into government budget allocations and expenditures on education at national and local levels have provided evidence for advocacy. Nevertheless, this evidence has had to be used judiciously, as advocacy on financial matters and budgets is not welcomed by government officials. A review of TENMET's budget work for the Commonwealth Education Fund notes that access to budgetary information requires a sensitive but persistent approach, and any attempts to raise issues of budgets and allocations requires very solid evidence in order to be taken seriously (Perry 2008). TENMET has learned through experience that, despite promises from the government to move towards increased transparency and accountability, the culture of state institutions and government offices remains 'secretive and suspicious of any efforts to seek information on financial matters. Stiff bureaucracy and suspicions hampered access to information at different levels of the government, meaning that findings were rarely a true reflection of allocation and expenditure across the board' (Perry 2008: 42).

Policy-advocacy work, then, is about setting up conditions so that education-policy decision makers are receptive to what the INGO and the coalition have to say about what matters in education and what will improve the implementation of policies. Carrying out effective advocacy involves the nurturing and development of a range of relationships with individuals, and gaining recognition and respect for contributions and insights based on credible and reliable evidence.

The nature of INGO–state relationships for EFA in Tanzania

These brief examples illustrate something of the diversity and multiplicity of INGO–state relationships, and provide insights into state institutions themselves as heterogeneous and multi-layered. They also demonstrate how the term 'partnership' can be used for a wide range of different kinds of relationship, some of which may not necessarily be reciprocal or equitable. The Shinyanga context is an example of partnership for a common purpose within the education system, which served to enhance the professionalism and status of teachers, as well as the status of education in the region measured through children's higher test scores and learning outcomes. In this context, the partnership involved education officials working alongside the INGO in advocacy activities and bringing an 'insider' authority and credibility to their lobbying of education officials and colleagues at the national level for expansion of the pedagogical model.

The partnership in Shinyanga District between INGO and LGA is illustrative of a collaborative relationship built on common goals and shared understandings, where the different organisations bring complementary skills and resources and where they have negotiated mutually acceptable ways of working together. There are parallels here with some of the hard-earned achievements of the national education coalition and recognition it has gained as a stakeholder at the policy-negotiating table (where it has valuable contributions to make to the process). This kind of relationship between the INGO and the LGA has not materialised in Ngorongoro District. Where the terrain for engagement has been uncontroversial – supply of educational materials, supporting access to flexible modes of educational delivery – collaboration has developed, but in politically sensitive areas, such as control over curriculum content and language policy, the divergent goals indicate a lack of shared understandings.

TENMET is, however, pushing the boundaries and shaping the terrain for engagement through its budget analysis and advocacy. The Tanzanian government still hesitates to recognise the validity of civil-society monitoring in this area, and education bureaucracies are slow to emerge from an institutional culture of opacity. Where agendas are not compatible and agreed ways of working together cannot be negotiated, such as over issues of language and curriculum relevance or discriminatory attitudes and prejudices, other strategies need to be sought that involve relationships with broader social networks and/or individuals within education institutions able to perceive alternative educational scenarios and prepared to take a moral stance.

Towards a one-programme approach for leveraging change

To what extent do these three different types of education action in Tanzania come together in a coherent multi-level, multi-strategy, one-programme approach? How do they contribute to the INGO's national aim of enhancing the quality and relevance of equitable education through the active engagement of Tanzanian citizens and the actions of an accountable, responsive state? What are the threads that could knit this work together?

One thread is people: how the teams are structured and how they develop their overall aim and shape and understand the contribution of each component. In the Tanzania case, the role of the national education coordinator is key to developing and maintaining an oversight of the three components, providing management and professional education support as well as leading the national advocacy component. The Ngorongoro District service-delivery support approach has paved the way for a more collaborative relationship between INGO and LGA for a diversified model of primary-education provision. This component of the overall INGO programme is providing evidence about the nature of changes in practices, relationships, and processes in order to enhance the quality, relevance, and equity of schooling for young Maasai children, but its ability to do this is limited locally. There needs to be leverage applied at national policy level too. With good evidence, high-quality research, and well-documented practice, the coordinator, in partnership with TENMET, can advocate for change at the national policy level.

Curriculum development and language in education policy, however, are highly charged political arenas. Yet there are opportunities that can be seized, and allies to work with for a more equitable educational experience for the Maasai, especially through the attention being given in EFA and donor forums to the challenges of reaching the 'hard to reach', 'marginalised' groups and adopting a more nuanced approach to quality education. With well-researched, well-documented evidence, the Ngorongoro can be used to understand and eventually remove blockages at the local level through informed policy making at the national level and, moreover, to bring a contextualised and more complex understanding of how to achieve EFA at the international level. Spinning strong threads between all levels of the 'one programme' is important.

In Shinyanga, documenting the process and the outcomes of the Equip project has been a top priority since 2008. The future scaling up and sustainability of the pedagogic model relies on being able to demonstrate and convince district, regional, and national government of its ability to promote qualitative change in learning environments, classroom relationships, and increasingly, learning outcomes. This documentation is now, slowly, being used for advocacy, by the INGO together with TENMET, to raise awareness of what Equip has done, to influence not only policy but also practice through influencing, for example, the Teacher Education Development and Management Strategy and the Education and Training Sector Development Programme (2008–2017). Holding national education conferences on education quality together with TENMET, as well as research-dissemination seminars, are other actions being taken to increase the discussion and debate on the evidence being produced from both of the local-level projects. The local-level work, then, feeds directly into advocacy at national level and, through Oxfam GB, the Global Campaign for Education, and other alliances such as the Africa Network for Education for All (ANCEFA), into global campaigning and policy.

The threads that link the INGO with state education representatives need to be kept strong through various actions. Invitations are extended to directors of primary education and teacher-training directorates as important ways of informing and building productive relationships with government officials, ministers, and advisers who may otherwise work in relative isolation from each other and from exposure to NGO work. These are also important forums for sharing between NGOs and INGOs in Tanzania. These activities build the legitimacy of the INGO and its education team of Tanzanian nationals in the policy arena through demonstrating its direct and practical experience of classroom pedagogies and locally contextualised meanings of quality.

Advocacy is an integral part of this Tanzania programme and not 'something bolted on'. Advocacy, moreover, needs to be understood as a diverse set of activities and, as the Ngorongoro component illustrates, this process may need to be gently nourished through actions which at times may have more of a 'service delivery' flavour to them. This is a challenging way to work, as it demands good communication and nimble structures for collaborative programme development so that individuals with diverse aims, perspectives, skills, and expertise can understand not only their own but also each others' contributions to the whole. Where experiences, priorities, timeframes, and values differ widely from level to level and place to place, this is not an easy way of working. In Tanzania it is emergent and gaining confidence.

Conclusion

Edwards' (2002) multi-layered and multi-faceted model framework is a useful analytical tool for reflecting on the coherency, cohesion, and effectiveness of a 'one-programme approach'. It encourages reflection on relationships within and across the programme in terms of objectives, activities, roles, and responsibilities. It allows for an analysis of ways in which roles differ but can complement each other within one country and how they link vertically. And it allows for an evaluation of the extent to which different actors at different levels have made the change to an advocacy approach, asking how different contributions work in their own ways towards the achievement of the right to an education.

This framework has facilitated the unpacking of 'advocacy', revealing its practices to be multiple and part of a process. Advocacy, moreover, is built upon a diversity of relationships: formal and informal, short and long term, comfortable and uneasy. In the education arena, the INGO–state relationship is being defined in the context of a global development compact and global EFA consensus, where schooling is a public good and state responsibility. Education advocacy, in all its dimensions, is about relationships with state institutions and actors.

And the framework can also be used to ask questions about how evidence for advocacy is developed, how it is used, and by whom. As Mundy (2006: 45) notes, universal public access to free basic education has achieved status and legitimacy as a global public good on a scale not realised during the 20th century. But what does the evidence from the grassroots, from the learners and parents in Ngorongoro for example, say about what free basic education as a public good should look and feel like? Advocacy and lobby for the right to education has become lobby for the right to schooling and quality, addressed instrumentally through new buildings and changes in teacher–pupil ratios, and measured through exam scores. INGO action inside state schools tells a complex, nuanced, and contextualised story about what quality is, whose rights are respected, and whose freedoms valued.

The boundaries of partnership and collaboration were found between INGO and LGA in Ngorongoro over questions of rights to language and whose knowledge is valued in the curriculum, and between the national coalition and the ministry of education over financial transparency, control, and accountability. In each case, the NGO and state institution were 'marching to different rhythms', but in the cacophony lie opportunities for new kinds of understanding and new relationships forged through action that is joined coherently to local, national, and global advocacies.

Acknowledgements

I would like to thank Ellen Binagi, Mary Soko, and Fred Kwame for all their collegiality and support over the years. Their insights and work have influenced this contribution, though the points made are my own perspectives.

Notes

1. The article refers specifically to the work of Oxfam GB except in instances of advocacy and campaigning done jointly through Oxfam International, where 'Oxfam' is used.
2. See www.oxfam.org.uk and www.commonwealtheducationfund.org. My field notes are from programme advisory visits in 2007 and 2008.
3. I participated in this process in the role of education adviser.

References

Abani, C. (2007) 'AIM2', presentation for Southern Africa Regional Education Meeting. Oxfam GB, Pretoria, South Africa, July.

CEF (2008) *Empowering Civil Society on Education: Commonwealth Education Fund Achievements*, London: Commonwealth Education Fund.

Edwards, Michael 1993 (2002) '"Does the doormat influence the boot?" Critical thoughts on UK NGOs and international advocacy', *Development in Practice* 3 (3): 163–175, reprinted in Deborah Eade (ed.) *Development and Advocacy*, Oxford: Oxfam, 2002, pp. 95–112.

Edwards, M., D. Hulme, and T. Wallace (2000) 'NGOs in a Global Future: Marrying Local Delivery to Worldwide Leverage', New York, NY: Ford Foundation.

Green, D. (2008) *From Poverty to Power: How Active Citizens and Effective States can Change the World*, Oxford: Oxfam International.

Kariuki, W. and G. Puja (2006) 'Education Options for Pastoral Communities in Ngorongoro District, Tanzania', unpublished report, Dar es Salaam, Tanzania: Oxfam GB.

Mmbando, J. and F. Mukyanuzi (2007) 'Mid-Term Review of Education Quality Improvement through Pedagogy – Equip', unpublished report, Dar es Salaam, Tanzania: Oxfam GB.

Mundy, K. (2006) 'Education for All and the new development compact', *Review of Education* 52: 23–48.

Mundy, K. (2008) 'Basic Education, Civil Society Participation and the New Aid Architecture: Lessons from Burkina Faso, Kenya, Mali and Tanzania', Toronto, Ottawa, and Gatineau: Ontario Institute for Studies in Education (University of Toronto), University of Ottawa, Canadian International Development Agency, and International Development Research Centre.

Mundy, K. and L. Murphy (2001) 'Transnational advocacy, global civil society? Emerging evidence from the field of education', *Comparative Education Review* 45 (1): 85–126.

Oxfam GB (1998) 'Fundamental Review of its Strategic Intent', Oxford: Oxfam GB.

Oxfam GB (2007) *National Change Strategy for Tanzania 2007–2017: Our Scaled-up Plan of Action to Reduce Extreme Poverty*, Dar-es-Salaam, Tanzania: Oxfam GB.

Oxfam GB (2008) 'Reinvigorating the Basic Social Services Programme: Updating Our Programme and Policy Positioning', unpublished Aim 2 Global Meeting Report, 1–13 June, Oxford: Oxfam GB.

Perry, V. (2008) *Civil Society Engagement in Education Budgets: A Report Documenting Commonwealth Education Fund Experience*, London: Commonwealth Education Fund.

Tomlinson, K. and I. Macpherson (2007a) 'Driving the Bus: The Journey of National Education Coalitions', London: Commonwealth Education Fund.

Tomlinson, K. and I. Macpherson (2007b) 'Funding Change: Sustaining Civil Society Advocacy in Education', London: Commonwealth Education Fund.

Watkins, Kevin (2000) *The Oxfam Education Report*, Oxford: Oxfam GB.

The roles of non-state providers in ten complementary education programmes

Joseph DeStefano and Audrey-marie Schuh Moore

This contribution reviews ten case studies of complementary education programmes conducted by the USAID-funded Educational Quality Improvement Program 2. The state–non-state relationship in each case is explored to reveal the arrangements that permit non-state providers to extend the reach and improve the effectiveness of education, particularly for populations that are underserved by the state system. Non-state providers improve on the standard models of state schooling by changing the mix of inputs at the school level, altering the institutional incentives that govern how schools operate, and setting up political accountability relationships closer to the points of service delivery.

Les rôles des prestataires de services non publics dans dix programmes d'éducation complémentaire
Cette contribution examine dix études de cas de programmes d'éducation complémentaire menés par le Programme d'amélioration de la qualité de l'éducation 2, financé par USAID. La relation État-entités non publiques dans chaque cas est examinée afin de mettre en évidence les arrangements qui permettent aux prestataires non publics d'étendre la portée et d'améliorer l'efficacité de l'éducation, en particulier pour les populations mal desservies par le système public. Les prestataires non publics améliorent les modèles standard de la scolarisation publique en changeant la sélection d'intrants au niveau des écoles, en modifiant les moyens d'incitation institutionnels qui régissent le fonctionnement des écoles et en mettant en place des relations de reddition de comptes (de « redevabilité ») politique plus près des niveaux de prestation des services.

As funções de provedores não-estatais em dez programas educacionais complementares
Esta contribuição revê dez estudos de caso de programas educacionais complementares conduzidos pelo Programa 2 de Melhoria de Qualidade Educacional financiado pela USAID. A relação entre estado–não-estado em cada caso é explorada para revelar os arranjos que permitem que provedores não-estatais estendam o alcance e melhorem a efetividade da educação, particularmente para populações que são mal-servidas pelo sistema estatal. Provedores não-estatais melhoram os modelos-padrões do ensino estatal ao mudar o conjunto de inserções em nível de escola, alterando os incentivos institucionais que governam o modo como as escolas operam e estabelecendo relações de accountability política mais próximas dos pontos de implementação de serviço.

ACHIEVING EDUCATION FOR ALL THROUGH PUBLIC-PRIVATE PARTNERSHIPS?

El papel de los proveedores no estatales en 10 programas educativos complementarios

Este ensayo examina 10 casos de estudio de los programas educativos complementarios que el Programa 2 de Mejoramiento de la Calidad Educativa realizó con fondos de USAID. Analiza en cada caso la relación entre actores estatales y no estatales a fin de entender cómo se celebraron acuerdos para que los proveedores no estatales ampliaran el alcance y la eficacia de la educación, en particular para poblaciones con poca cobertura del sistema estatal. Los proveedores no estatales mejoran el modelo tradicional de la educación estatal adjudicando en diferente forma las aportaciones que reciben las escuelas, variando los incentivos institucionales que rigen su operatividad y estableciendo mecanismos de transparencia locales y por tanto más cercanos a las escuelas.

Introduction

Education is a key component to improving economic competitiveness, raising incomes, improving health, and achieving sustained growth. The provision of basic education has long been regarded as the government's responsibility (Rose 2007), justified on the grounds that if left solely to the free market, the public would underinvest in education, reducing the positive contributions to society (Colclough 1996, cited in Rose 2007). However, despite government efforts to reach universal education, 75 million children of primary-school age remain out of school (UNESCO 2008) and countless others are poorly served by the public sector and drop out.

State and non-state partnerships are often created to reach the most underserved. These partnerships play a significant role in the development agenda, in which organisations from one sector (government, private, or non-government) work in partnership with those from other sectors to achieve educational goals (Edwards and Hulme 1995; Teamey 2007). UNESCO Institute of Statistics data compiled by the Aga Khan Foundation reveal that non-state schooling is a growing trend. One-third of the increase in access to primary education from 1991 to 2004 in 136 developing countries was in non-state schools (Aga Khan Foundation 2007).

The case for non-state providers derives mainly from their ability to address the state's failure to effectively and efficiently deliver services (Teamey 2007). The perceived comparative advantage of non-state providers is grounded in their ability to better understand organisational forms, agendas, and practices (Teamey 2007: 5). Non-state providers tend to be less hierarchical, more democratic and flexible, committed to working and serving the poor, and have fewer profit-seeking motives, making the delivery of services more cost-effective (Teamey 2007). Their more flexible organisational structure and dedicated agendas allow them to be perceived as more innovative, accountable, and effective in terms of cost and delivery, while having greater knowledge of community needs than state providers (Teamey 2007).

This contribution reviews the experience of non-state providers in managing complementary education programmes in ten countries.[1] The objective is to examine the nature of the state–non-state relationships across the ten cases and how they successfully serve populations that would otherwise not have access to education.

Overview of the ten cases[2]

In 2006 and 2007, the USAID-funded Education Quality Improvement Program 2 (EQUIP2)[3] completed ten case studies of complementary education programmes in Afghanistan,

Bangladesh, Egypt, Ghana, Guatemala, Haiti, Honduras, Mali, and Zambia. In the cases studied, non-governmental networks of support are able to help communities organise and operate effective schools. In some of the cases, locally recruited, less-educated and often minimally compensated teachers produce educational outcomes that match or exceed what regular public schools obtain. The community-based schools use management approaches that ensure smaller classes, support instruction in local language, promote regular attendance by both teachers and students, and provide continuous support and training for teachers and families.

Not only are these complementary programmes more effective at providing access to otherwise underserved populations, some of them were shown to be more educationally cost-effective than government schools. For example,

- Village-based schools serving remote hamlets in Upper Egypt have higher rates of completion and better pass rates in the national examination. These schools are in fact twice as cost-effective as government schools at producing a fifth grader who can pass the national exam.
- Bangladesh Rural Advancement Committee (BRAC) primary schools have completion rates 30 per cent higher than public schools, and their students are almost three times as likely to meet basic competencies as public school students. BRAC schools are more than seven times as cost-effective as public schools.
- In Guatemala, Programa Nacional de Autogestión para el Desarrollo Educativo (PRONADE) primary schools are twice as cost-effective at producing completers.

Table 1 provides a summary of the cost and cost-effectiveness results for the ten case studies.

Critical aspects of state and non-state provision of education

State–non-state relationships are evolving rapidly. Non-state providers are collaborating in the provision of basic education to fill a void in the public sector (Rose 2007; Teamey 2007); to respond to demand that the public sector is not satisfying (DeStefano *et al.* 2007; Rose 2007; Teamey 2007); to relieve pressure on the public sector, and to try to maximise the educational return for each dollar invested (Patrinos and Sosale 2007). The question is how can state–non-state collaboration best increase the reach and improve the quality of basic education?

Table 2 provides a summary of the roles played by non-state and state actors in each of the ten cases.

Institutional and legal frameworks

The institutional and legal framework includes the legal statutes and charters that guide the rules of the game, as well as the implementing regulations and arrangements according to which the education system functions (DeStefano and Crouch 2006; Rose 2007). These rules, regulations, and charters define the space in which non-state actors function, manoeuvre, and collaborate with state entities in service-delivery and/or policy dialogue (Rose 2007; Teamey 2007). The provision of a supportive legal framework is central to the emergence of viable state–non-state partnerships (Brinkerhoff 2002, cited in Teamey 2007) and is the basis for facilitating a positive environment for non-state provision of services.

An aspect of the institutional framework that stands out in all ten cases as critical to the success of non-state provision is official state recognition of the education obtained by students in non-state schools. Whether the schools are counted in official statistics appears less important than whether the achievements of students enrolled in non-state schools are acknowledged and transferrable to the public sector. In the cases studied, the achievements

ACHIEVING EDUCATION FOR ALL THROUGH PUBLIC-PRIVATE PARTNERSHIPS?

Table 1: Cost-effectiveness of complementary education (Comp Ed) programmes compared to public schools in each country

	Afghanistan COPE		Afghanistan IRC		Bangladesh BRAC		Egypt Community Schools		Ghana School for Life[4]	
	Comp Ed	Public	Comp Ed	Public	Comp Ed	Public	Comp Ed	Public	Comp Ed	Public
Annual cost per pupil	$38	$31	$18	$31	$20	$29	$114	$164	$39	$27
Completion rate	50%	32%	68%	32%	94%	67%	92%	90%	91%	59%
Cost per completer	$453	$485	$132	$485	$84	$246	$620	$911	$43	$135
Students meeting learning outcome	94%	–	99%	–	70%	27%	94%	73%	81%	9%
Cost per learning outcome	$482	–	$134	–	$120	$911	$659	$1248	$53	$1500
	Guatemala PRONADE		Haiti Community Schools		Honduras Educatodos		Mali Community Schools		Zambia Community Schools	
	Comp Ed	Public	Comp Ed	Public	Comp Ed	Public	Comp Ed	Public	Comp Ed	Public
Annual cost per pupil	$119	$155	$54	$77	$40	$102	$47	$30	$39	$67
Completion rate	98%	62%	37%	32%	61%	68%	67%	56%	72%	72%
Cost per completer	$729	$1500	$437	$725	$197	$803	$421	$322	$376	$655
Students meeting learning outcome	–	–	33%	50%	–	–	51%	43%	40%	35%
Cost per learning outcome	–	–	$1317	$1450	–	–	$825	$729	$939	$1873

BRAC – Bangladesh Rural Advancement Committee; COPE – Community Organized Primary Education; IRC – International Rescue Committee; PRONADE – Programa Nacional de Autogestión para el Desarrollo Educativo.

of students in non-state schools are officially recognised. Students who meet criteria for entry into a particular grade are able to transfer into government schools at the appropriate level. Students who complete primary school in complementary settings are allowed to take the end-of-cycle exam; if they pass and obtain the appropriate educational certification, they then have the option to continue their post-primary schooling in the government system. For example, 65 per cent of students enrolled in the School for Life programme in northern Ghana were subsequently integrated into the formal system (Casely-Hayford and Ghartey 2007). This is true even in the four cases, including Ghana, in which non-state schools

Table 2: The various roles played by state and non-state actors in the EQUIP2 case studies

	Official recognition	Curriculum	Teachers Selection/ Mgmt	Training/ Support	Pay	Governance & accountability	Financing
Afghanistan: Community Schools	Yes, able to transfer/ continue	Official	Community	NGO	Community	Community/ NGO	NGO Community
Afghanistan: Home-Based Schools	Yes, able to transfer/ continue	Official	Community	NGO	Community (volunteer)	Community/ NGO	NGO Community
Bangladesh: BPS	Yes, able to transfer/ continue	Official	Community/ NGO	NGO	NGO	Community/ NGO	NGO Community
Egypt: Community Schools	Yes, able to transfer/ continue	Modified, developed with MOE	Community	NGO/ MOE	MOE	Community/ NGO/MOE	MOE NGO Community
Ghana: School for Life	Yes, able to transfer/ continue	Independent	Community	MOE/ NGO	Community (volunteer)	Community/ NGO	NGO Community
Guatemala: PRONADE	Yes, able to transfer/ continue	Official	Community	NGO/ MOE	MOE through community	Community/ MOE	MOE
Haiti: Community Schools	Yes, able to transfer/ continue	Official	Community	NGO	Community	Community/ NGO	NGO Community
Honduras: Educatodos	Yes, able to transfer/ continue	Modified	NGO	NGO	NGO (volunteer)	NGO	NGO MOE
Mali: Community Schools	Yes, able to transfer/ continue	Modified	Community	NGO	Community	Community/ NGO	NGO Community
Zambia: Community Schools	Yes, able to transfer/ continue	Official	Community	Community	Community	Community	Community

BPS – BRAC Primary Schools; Mgt – Management; MOE – Ministry of Education.

make use of curricula that are significantly different from the official national curriculum. In all the cases, communities support non-state schools in part because they are assured that their children's education will be recognised, and the possibility of continuing to further levels of education will not be closed off to them (DeStefano et al. 2007). One of the early lessons of the community schools in Mali was that parents wanted the community schools to provide a full primary cycle (DeStefano 1996).

Institutional conditioning factors

The political, legal, social, and cultural institutions define the conditions in which non-state actors operate. The interests, values, ideologies, goals, resources, decision-making processes, and organisational structures embedded in these institutions determine the outcomes of state–non-state partnerships (Teamey 2007).

In all the cases reviewed, non-state providers contributed to improved schooling most significantly through the institutional factors governing the selection, management, training, support, and payment of teachers. Pre- and in-service training are among governments' most widely used strategies to raise instructional quality. However, conventional teacher training is expensive and teachers, once trained, command higher salaries, raising the overall recurrent cost of education. Furthermore, once employed, state teachers often fail to report to rural regions and usually lack the appropriate ongoing instructional support needed to facilitate learning in the classroom (Villegas-Reimers 2003). The non-state examples studied all use alternative approaches to conventional teacher training.

Selection and hiring: All the non-state school programmes studied promote community selection and management of teachers. In Bangladesh, BRAC develops and enforces criteria for community selection of teachers (DeStefano *et al.* 2007). In Honduras, the NGO implementing the Educatodos project organises the learning centres and recruits volunteers to staff them (DeStefano *et al.* 2007). In all ten cases, there is no state involvement in the selection and hiring of teachers. Analysis of the cases indicates that the relationships between teachers and communities are a critical feature in effective non-state schools (DeStefano *et al.* 2007). Centralised, professional systems for training, certifying, hiring, and deploying teachers grew up in part as a response to the wide disparities across communities and to correct for local influences on hiring decisions (for example, nepotism or explicit *quid pro quo* arrangements) (Tyack 1974). The approaches used by the complementary models studied are purpose-built responses to the shortcomings of the centralised system – namely, the distance such systems create between teachers and the community in which they serve, and the increased costs associated with a professionalised teaching corps. Over time, safeguards will need to be developed to ensure that local management of teachers does not recreate the problems centralised systems evolved to correct. Likewise, relying on non-professional teachers with quasi-voluntary status cannot constitute a long-term strategy for provision of schooling.

Training and support: In nine of the ten cases, NGO intermediaries ensure the training and, more importantly, ongoing support for teachers once they have been recruited. In Egypt, Ghana, and Guatemala, a combination of ministry and NGO resources is used to reinforce teacher capacity. In Egypt and Ghana, government teacher-training and curriculum institutions develop and implement the initial training programmes for teachers, as well as periodic refresher courses. The NGO partners that implement the programmes provide the ongoing supervision and on-site support for teachers (DeStefano *et al.* 2007). In Guatemala, the ministry initially contracted with NGO intermediaries to provide training and ongoing support to teachers in PRONADE schools (DeStefano *et al.* 2007).

In all the cases, NGOs are able to ensure regular supervision and on-site support for teachers at levels not usually attained by government. Teachers in the non-state schools are usually visited monthly by a support person, and also participate in facilitated meetings with other teachers on a regular basis (DeStefano *et al.* 2007). This approach emphasises the strategic choices and capacities critical to improvements in service delivery – and which NGOs bring into state – non-state partnerships (Ramanath 2005).

Pay: In six of the ten cases, communities rely on their own resources to pay their teachers. In two of those six cases – Home-Based School in Afghanistan and School for Life in Ghana – teachers are in fact considered volunteers, and may only receive occasional in-kind support (DeStefano *et al.* 2007). BRAC pays the teachers recruited by the communities (DeStefano *et al.* 2007). Educatodos provides small stipends to the people who volunteer in their learning centres (DeStefano *et al.* 2007). In only two of the cases does the government pay the teachers in the non-state schools. In Egypt, the government created a special category in the civil service so that community-school teachers can be put onto the ministry payroll

(DeStefano et al. 2007). In Guatemala, the ministry allocates funds for PRONADE schools and then distributes those resources directly to the communities who then pay the teachers (DeStefano et al. 2007).

Governance and accountability

Governance structures establish the decision-making apparatuses regarding programme direction, accountability, and external relationships (Rose 2007; Stone 1996, cited in Teamey 2007). Parent governance committees and school management committees ensure that non-state schools operate effectively and meet their goals (DeStefano et al. 2007). The external support of NGOs improves monitoring and evaluation systems, contributes to the development of an improved information base, and often strengthens the capacity of both state and community actors to take part in improved service delivery (Freeman and Faure 2003).

All of the non-state models studied rely on community-based mechanisms for school governance and day-to-day accountability. School management committees select and hire teachers, set the school schedule, manage school finances, and make all the decisions necessary to keep the school running (DeStefano et al. 2007). In Guatemala, local school management committees have official status and must meet government-defined criteria to be recognised and receive government support (DeStefano et al. 2007).

In all the cases, except the unsupported community schools in Zambia, NGOs support the operation of school management committees. This includes setting criteria for membership, providing training for committee members, and offering ongoing supervision and support.

Accountability in all the cases is limited to the management aspects of the non-state schools. Communities supervise their schools to make sure they are open and teachers and students attend regularly. Communities are usually accountable to the NGOs that perform oversight visits to schools. In Bangladesh, BRAC supervises the implementation of its policies on school organisation, curriculum, and instruction, and has a highly structured system of monitoring and quality assurance.

School management committees are fiscally accountable to the community and the NGO partners who manage the programmes. In the case of Guatemala, local committees are accountable to the ministry for managing public funds (DeStefano et al. 2007). In Egypt, the ministry includes the community schools in its regular supervision and support, and has conducted evaluations of these schools (DeStefano et al. 2007).

None of the cases have accountability for academic performance. In Ghana, students who finish the School for Life programme are tested by the government to determine if they are eligible to continue in a state school,[4] but those results are not used to hold communities or the implementing NGO accountable for school performance (DeStefano et al. 2007). In Bangladesh, Egypt, Mali, and Zambia, students from the non-state schools all take the same primary-cycle exams as students in state schools, but (as is the case in government schools) there is no system of accountability linked to those results (DeStefano et al. 2007). Accountability in state-managed education is limited to operational or fiscal accountability. The approach in the non-state cases appears to be the same, but – through reliance on local governance and management, especially regarding the selection and hiring of teachers – non-state schools obtain a higher degree of operational accountability.

Financing non-state provision of education

One of the critical factors in improved service delivery is better use of resources (Besley and Ghatak 2007). The EQUIP2 research demonstrates that allocating resources to non-state providers can offer a more cost-effective means to reach underserved populations (DeStefano *et al.* 2007). Non-state schools in many countries receive government funds, through a variety of mechanisms, such as payment of teacher salaries, provision of inputs, grants-in-aid, scholarships, loans, and vouchers. Public subsidies to non-state providers allow states to expand access at lower cost, provide schooling choices to families, or improve access for otherwise underserved populations (Aga Khan Foundation 2007).

In Zambia, unsupported community schools almost exclusively rely on their own resources.[5] In Afghanistan, Bangladesh, Ghana, Haiti, and Mali, NGOs provide substantial financial support to the operation of the non-state school programmes. Communities still contribute in each of those cases – often mobilising in-kind contributions of labour or support for teachers, as well as paying the fees that contribute to the operating budgets of the schools. In all those cases, the NGOs obtain resources from development agencies or foundations (DeStefano *et al.* 2007).

Only in Egypt, Guatemala, and Honduras are government resources allocated to non-state schools. In Egypt, as stated earlier, the government pays the teachers in the community schools. In Honduras, government and USAID resources are used to cover the costs of setting up and supervising the learning centres (DeStefano *et al.* 2007). In Guatemala, government resources are allocated directly to communities to operate schools (DeStefano *et al.* 2007).

One could argue that only in the three cases where government invests a significant portion of the cost of the complementary programmes is there a true state–non-state partnership. In the other cases, the government is merely allowing non-state providers to fill some of the empty space in the public education system.

In all of the cases, the financial sustainability of the state–non-state arrangements is uncertain. The provision of education, whether directly by the state, by non-state actors, or through state–non-state collaboration, requires a continued allocation of resources to cover operating costs and make needed investments. The non-state-supported programmes in this study are all subject to the same financial challenges faced by the public sector – namely, will enough resources be allocated each year to ensure continued operations? Fiscal constraints that make it hard for the state to meet its financial obligations would both impinge on government willingness to allocate resources to non-state providers and constrain the abilities of communities and non-state actors themselves to contribute to funding their operations. Non-state-supported programmes, however, face an additional financial challenge in that they often rely on some external source of funding that by design is temporary. Six of the ten programmes studied are funded by time-constrained projects. In all those cases, the continuation of the programmes will require another funding source to take on the operating costs at the end of the project. Poor communities without formal tax bases cannot be expected to shoulder the full financial burden. This issue is illustrated by the two cases where communities are essentially funding their own schools (Haiti and Zambia), where the schools are chronically under-resourced and suffer for it (DeStefano and Miksic 2007; DeStefano *et al.* 2007). Governments themselves may either replace the external funding with public-sector allocations to the non-state actors (something that is being promoted as a possibility in Haiti), or could absorb the non-state schools into the public sector (as has been the case in Afghanistan). Guatemala perhaps best illustrates how state commitment to non-state provision, outside the context of a specific project, can establish a more viable long-term financial arrangement, albeit one that is still dependent on continued government willingness and ability to allocate sufficient resources (DeStefano *et al.* 2007).

The nature of state–non-state collaboration in the ten cases

Preconditions for successful state–non-state collaborations include (Brinkerhoff 2002; Mayhew 2005, cited in Teamey 2007):

- the willingness and capacity of the government to work with non-state providers;
- government capacity to move from basic levels of engagement to dialogue, and short- and long-term contracts with non-state providers;
- accountability structures that can regulate and manage the partnerships;
- political will to engage in open and constructive discussions;
- a representative civil society.

In the ten cases, two patterns of state–non-state interaction emerge. In seven of them, the interaction started at the basic levels and was limited – government simply allowed the non-state actors to provide education. However, in most of these cases, government interaction with non-state providers evolved or is continuing to evolve to include more government promotion of non-state provision, but not direct funding. In one case (Zambia), it has evolved to include funding, albeit of such a limited amount that it continues to constrain non-state provision.

Bangladesh is an example where the government only grudgingly allows BRAC to operate schools and collaboration has not even reached the basic level of engagement. BRAC operates wholly independently of the government and is seen by the government as competition for external funding. The lack of government will and capacity to transparently manage partnerships is the principle factor constraining the development of a more purposeful state–non-state relationship in Bangladesh (DeStefano et al. 2007).

The community and home-based schools in Afghanistan and the community schools in Mali began operating in an environment of benign neglect on the part of the government. Institutionally weak governments and severely underdeveloped education systems left lots of room for non-state actors to operate (DeStefano et al. 2007).

In Afghanistan, NGOs began providing education in defiance of government restrictions on who could attend school during periods when government capacity to deliver services was essentially non-existent. As the political situation in Afghanistan evolved, the NGOs built more formal relationships with a government that was increasingly concerned with absorbing schools previously run by non-state providers. The Afghan government promotes NGO support of community-based schooling in regions it still has trouble serving, but again sees that as a temporary measure (DeStefano et al. 2007).

In Mali, community schools have long filled the voids in an education system that for many years barely served students outside of main population centres. As NGOs increasingly supported community-based schooling, official policy evolved from merely allowing community schools to operate, to actively promoting their development and official recognition. A 1994 law authorised any community to open a school, and conferred official status on those schools that could meet a simple set of criteria. A ministry office was created to develop guidelines for community schools, increasing the government's capacity to handle relationships with non-state providers (DeStefano et al. 2007).

Haiti is perhaps the starkest example of non-state providers filling in for a weak public sector. Government recognises various forms of non-state education, including private, church-affiliated, and community schools, but provides virtually no support to them. Government views community schools in particular as inferior quality. The state tolerates non-state providers because it has to. More than 80 per cent of students in Haiti attend non-state schools. In 2007, the state developed criteria and procedures for the licensing and accreditation of non-state schools and, with external support, has built capacity to catalogue and monitor their operation. Given that growing capacity, and with World Bank prodding and funding, Haiti is considering how to pilot the allocation of state funds in the form of scholarships for students to attend non-state schools that are becoming licensed and accredited (DeStefano and Miksic 2007).

ACHIEVING EDUCATION FOR ALL THROUGH PUBLIC-PRIVATE PARTNERSHIPS?

In Ghana, government policy evolved from merely permitting programmes like School for Life to operate, to explicitly addressing the role of non-state actors in sector plans. In 2003, the government formulated an education plan that includes strategies to encourage non-state actors to provide schooling, to support complementary programmes designed to serve hard-to-reach children, and to integrate non-state and formal schools (DeStefano et al. 2007). However, the government has, thus far, been unable to translate that policy support into operational or financial support.

In Zambia, communities formed their own schools when no public school was nearby or when families could no longer afford the costs associated with government schooling. By the late 1990s, Zambia was witnessing tremendous growth in non-government schools. Zambia, like Ghana, recognised that non-state initiative was in fact a key component in helping it meet the objectives of Education for All. Official policy in 1996 stated that 'The Ministry will assist communities and voluntary organizations that wish to develop their own schools', and promised technical assistance, educational materials, and state-funded teachers. At one point, 30 per cent of education funds allocated to districts was set aside for community schools, and places in teacher-training institutions were reserved for community-school teachers (DeStefano et al. 2007).

Egypt, Guatemala, and Honduras present a contrast to those discussed above, because the state played and plays a significant role in each country in setting up and funding non-state schools. Egypt is distinct from Honduras and Guatemala, because the government's role is limited to supporting a pilot, not partnering with non-state providers to extend the reach of the public sector.

The Egyptian government launched the community-school initiative in partnership with UNICEF. From the beginning, the ministry paid teachers' salaries, invested in developing curriculum and teacher-training programmes, and provided materials. NGOs delivered the ongoing support and training. The ministry's objective was to maintain and evaluate the quality of 200–300 community schools and draw lessons from them for state-operated schools. The state–non-state relationship in Egypt could be characterised as joint experimentation (DeStefano et al. 2007).

In contrast, in Guatemala and Honduras, the government, acting as the principal, sees the benefit in allocating funds so that non-state actors, serving as the agents, can provide educational opportunities which the state cannot.

USAID initiated the Educatodos programme in Honduras in the early 1990s. At that time, the Secretariat of Education was committed to experimenting with alternative delivery models, particularly for youth and young adults who had never completed primary education. In 1995, the government embraced the Educatodos programme and began recognising its graduates as having finished primary school and those who could pass the equivalent of ninth grade were allowed to enter upper-secondary school. In addition, the government provided texts and audio learning materials for the programme, and contributed significantly to its funding. Government provided on average 32 per cent of the costs from 1995 to 2003, and has been increasing that share each year towards the target of 100 per cent by 2010 (DeStefano et al. 2007).

The Guatemalan government launched PRONADE to enlist local effort in the provision of education in remote areas. The programme exists as an arm of the ministry and is over 90 per cent financed with government funds. Resources are allocated directly to community-based committees that hire teachers and manage the schools. In addition, the ministry contracts with education service providers for technical assistance to schools, oversight, and data collection. A government office manages the allocation of school resources to the communities (for materials and teachers' salaries) and provides technical assistance and teacher-development services (DeStefano et al. 2007).

ACHIEVING EDUCATION FOR ALL THROUGH PUBLIC-PRIVATE PARTNERSHIPS?

Figure 1 summarises the range of relationships between the state and non-state actors in each of the ten programmes studied. The two axes capture the variations in these relationships. The horizontal axis concerns the degree to which public resources flow to non-state providers. The vertical axis shows the different nature of the interaction between state and non-state entities.

Five of the cases cluster towards the 'no state resources/benign neglect' corner of this two-dimensional space. Moving up from Bangladesh, to Afghanistan, to Mali, and to Ghana along the state–non-state interaction axis reflects the degree to which those governments actively promote non-state provision. Haiti is slightly to the right of these four, indicating that the government intends to pilot some funding for non-state schools.

Egypt, Zambia, Honduras, and Guatemala are distinctly different from this first group of countries. Egypt is only midway up the vertical axis, because the state does not contract with non-state operators of schools as a separate education-supply strategy. Zambia does try to do that, and is therefore slightly higher, but it provides only minimal amounts of resources for community schools, so is to the left of Egypt. Honduras and Guatemala are distinctly more advanced towards a true principal–agent set of relationships, with government funding providing almost all of the resources to non-state actors to run schools.

What difference do these relationships make? The countries in the lower left section of the chart face serious challenges concerning the sustainability of non-state provision. In all these cases, the programmes rely on external sources of funding, and make no provisions for what will happen when that funding ends. In Afghanistan, the programme schools are simply absorbed into the government system, a reasonable way for education provision to continue in those communities, but, by design, eliminates the non-state component of those supply

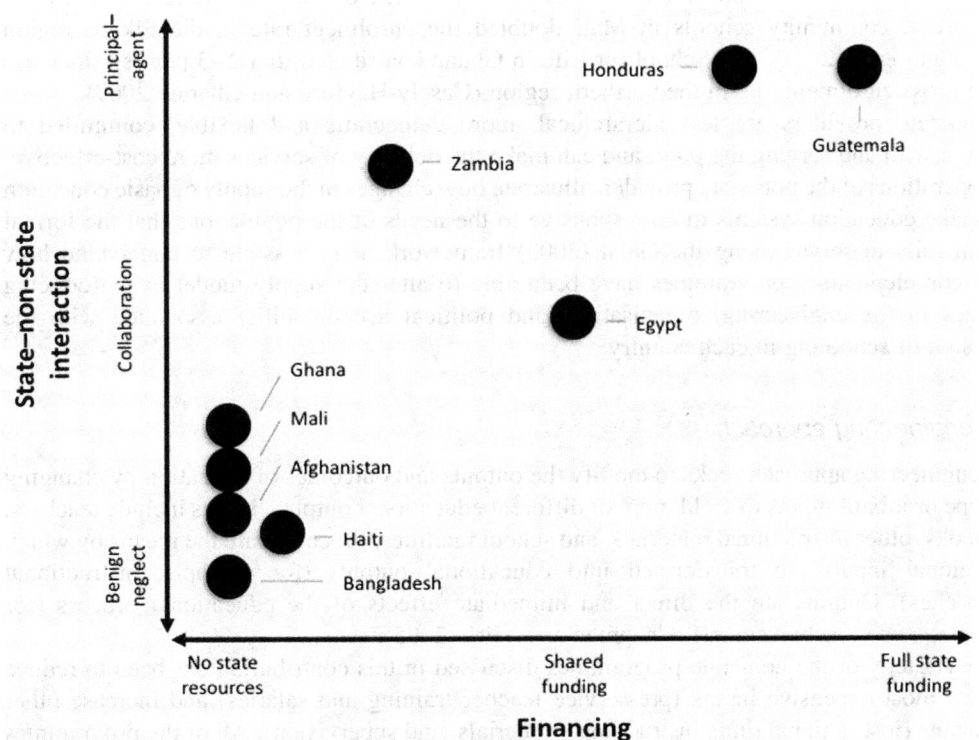

Figure 1: The range of state–non-state relationships

models (which was what enabled those schools to operate successfully in the first place). An alternative approach would have the government take the place of the external funder and continue to support NGOs and communities in the organisation and operation of schools.

BRAC (Bangladesh) is distinct because it relies on private, foundation, and development-agency funding to operate its network of 33,500 schools. It acts as the agent for those institutions which take the place of the government as the principals interested in the public benefits of education. In a country where public-sector corruption is recognised as a severe constraint (DeStefano et al. 2007), channelling external resources to BRAC for non-state organisation of schooling may be a prudent investment strategy.

Government neglect of non-state schools in Ghana, Haiti, Mali, and Zambia means that they operate as chronically under-resourced institutions (especially in Haiti). While the government in Zambia intends to use non-state providers to augment the public sector, the limited resources made available to community schools means that most of them are also underfunded. In Haiti, Mali, and Zambia, non-state provision of schooling remains constrained because it relies on the capacity of the poorest segments of society to mobilise resources.

How non-state provision improves education

Non-state providers in the cases reviewed in this study extend the reach of the education systems in the countries in which they work, and contribute to improved education effectiveness, in terms of enabling students who would otherwise not have access to education to complete primary education and achieve measurable learning outcomes. Of the cases studied, community schools in Zambia account for 25 per cent of the enrolment in primary schools, BRAC schools meet the educational needs of 50 per cent of the school-age population in rural areas, community schools in Mali doubled the enrolment rate in the Sikaso region (DeStefano et al. 2007), and School for Life in Ghana contributed to a 2–3 per cent increase in the gross enrolment rate in the northern region (Casely-Hayford and Ghartey 2007).

Non-state providers are less hierarchical, more democratic and flexible, committed to working with and serving the poor, and can make the delivery of services more cost-effective. The operations of the non-state providers illustrate how changes in the supply of basic education can make education systems more responsive to the needs of the populations that the formal system fails to serve. Using the Galal (2002) framework, it is possible to understand how these complementary programmes have been able to alter the supply model by introducing changes in the engineering, organisation, and political accountability associated with the provision of schooling in each country.

The engineering approach

The engineering approach seeks to modify the outputs and outcomes of education by changing the type or mix of inputs to yield more or different educational outputs. Inputs include teachers, textbooks, other instructional materials, and school facilities. Processes are the means by which educational inputs are transformed into educational outputs (for example, instructional approaches). Outputs are the direct and immediate effects of the educational process (for example, student achievement) (Chapman and Miric 2005).

The strategy of the non-state programmes discussed in this contribution has been to reduce the two most expensive inputs (pre-service teacher training and salaries) and increase other key inputs (instructional time, instructional materials, and supervision). All of the programmes studied spend less on teacher salaries as a share of total programme costs than do government schools. All provide pre-service training that is short and targeted. The savings thus garnered are used to cover the expenses of additional, more frequent classroom support, direct instructional supervision, and materials. The inputs being maximised – school-based teacher support, teacher and student attendance, and presence of instructional materials – offset the lower levels of initial teacher training and compensation in ways that yield higher levels of cost-effectiveness in some cases (as shown in Table 1).

Does the nature of the relationship between the state and the non-state providers in these cases impact the ways in which the supply models are re-engineered? NGOs operating in the margins left available by inadequate state supply are free to introduce innovations to help their community schools become more successful. For example, the School for Life was launched in northern Ghana as a supply model that could provide the equivalent of three years of primary schooling in nine months, until all the out-of-school children in a village have participated. By not having to broker a relationship with the government, non-state providers like School for Life are better able to innovate and 'break the mould' of the prevailing state model of schooling.

In Egypt, the non-state actor and the ministry worked together to launch an alternative supply model. The state was interested in addressing the inadequacy of the public system in serving the educational needs of rural hamlets in Upper Egypt. Educational authorities were involved in designing the re-engineered model and the ministry was willing to contribute resources to a model that represented a deliberate, dramatic departure from the public-sector norm.

Like Egypt, the Guatemalan government realised that a different supply model would be needed to better reach populations in rural areas. The Ministry of Education, working with NGOs and funding agencies, devised the means to partner with local communities in the provision of schooling. Decision making is granted to communities to design the mix of inputs needed to meet the educational needs of their children.

In all the cases, except Haiti, non-state providers introduced or helped introduce re-engineered approaches to the supply of schooling. Haiti's exceptionality is mostly due to the fact that non-state providers attract students not by offering innovatively engineered approaches to education, but rather by appearing as official as possible. The tendency therefore is to adhere to official curriculum, calendar, and hours of operation to the point where, even when communities manage their own schools, they enforce a model that is emulative of the official government system.

Organisational approach

In the organisational approach, the ministry is interested in a particular outcome (quality education), but has to rely on teachers and other actors to obtain it (Welmond 2004). Welmond (2004) argues that it is not enough just to manipulate or influence inputs to ensure change in classroom or partnership behaviour. For behaviour to change, there needs to be incentives and a clear system of accountability to ensure that those incentives only go to those who deserve them.

In the ten cases, the incentives for behaviour change are embedded in the non-state management of service provision. NGOs deploy field staff to monitor and support schools and communities, offering the incentives of (a) participating in an NGO-supported programme, (b) receiving outside resources, and (c) having a school. For a teacher, a community-based school provides interesting work, community recognition, and some level of compensation for women (or men) who often have few other alternatives (Kemmerer 1990, cited in Terway *et al.* in press). These incentives encourage teachers to be present in the classroom – one factor identified as contributing to the effectiveness of the complementary models (DeStefano *et al.* 2007). A second type of incentive is found in the instructional process itself. Research indicates that availability of instructional materials, effective supervision, and a structured work environment that allows teachers to do their work have incentive value (Hanushek *et al.* 2001, cited in Terway *et al.* in press).

Accountability is ensured by the on-the-ground presence of the non-state provider. Teachers, families, and communities know that the school is being monitored and the management committee must report to the NGO's representatives on the use of resources and the operation of the school.

Where government plays a more direct role, an additional set of incentives is introduced. In Egypt, community members who are recruited as teachers obtain a civil-service post. The system encourages them to gain further qualifications and aspire to the official teacher category and its higher status and pay. In Guatemala and Honduras, communities self-organise in response to the incentive of government funding for running a school or learning centre. Government in these cases relies on non-state intermediaries to monitor and interact with the communities, while also acting as the final authority to which accounts must be rendered.

The political-accountability approach

The political-accountability approach argues that if community members can influence education leaders in their formulation of education policies and practices, they can improve educational outcomes (Welmond 2004). If the distance between the policy decision and the client is reduced, and the relationship between service provider and client is more direct, then service provision can be both more responsive and accountable to the intended beneficiary.

The programmes in this study alter the political accountability arrangements of the formal sector in ways that allow schooling to be more responsive and accountable at the point of service delivery.

First, the management structures within the non-state programme ensure monitoring and reporting for operational and financial accountability. Second, every non-state school has a management committee with decision-making and monitoring authority. Increased NGO and community oversight of these programmes provides accountability mechanisms that are frequently not available in state schools. Through local governance structures, communities are more engaged in teacher selection and management, and teachers are therefore answerable to them. In this way, the accountability connection is as short as possible: service providers (teachers) are directly answerable to the clients (the families). NGOs provide an additional layer of accountability to back up the community.

These cases offer no evidence that the nature of the state–non-state relationship impacts these kinds of accountability mechanisms. In Egypt, where the government pays the teachers, the local accountability connection is still maintained because teachers are hired by the communities and monitored by the implementing NGOs. Likewise, in Guatemala and Honduras, the intermediaries and the communities themselves maintain the tighter management and oversight relationships that ensure greater degrees of responsiveness and accountability.

Conclusion

The concept of state and non-state partnerships is increasingly being discussed in the literature as a way of effectively addressing the provision of education to underserved populations. While there is variation across countries in how effectively the partnerships have worked and how long they are sustainable, the Galal (2002) framework highlights the ways in which state–non-state partnerships work to effectively provide access to quality education to large numbers of otherwise underserved children.

The ten programmes studied by EQUIP2 have assisted state systems in reaching large numbers of students that had limited or no access to education. BRAC has reached over one million children. PRONADE has educated more than 455,000 students. Zambian community schools serve more than 500,000 children, many of whom are orphaned or vulnerable.

While the long-term sustainability of these programmes is often uncertain and highly dependant on continued external funding, they provide a more flexible environment that allows providers to creatively mix inputs and processes so that schools can better cater to the needs of underserved communities. The partnerships can often lead to more cost-effective attainment of educational outputs such as completion and learning.

Notes

1. Complementary models of education are defined as programmes designed specifically to complement the government education system in each country and are *not* meant as non-formal alternative programmes. In each case, the programmes provide a different approach to helping children obtain the same educational objectives as students in state schools. Also, in each case, the programmes serve populations that have limited or no access to government-provided schooling.
2. The data presented in this section are based on the series of EQUIP2 studies conducted between 2004 and 2007 compiled in DeStefano *et al.* (2008) and DeStefano and Miksic (2007).
3. EQUIP2 – the Education Quality Improvement Program 2 – is a USAID-funded project that operates education projects in 20 to 30 countries and generously provided the funding for this research.
4. The learning outcomes for public-school students in Ghana are based on Criterion Referenced Test (CRT), given to a national sample of 10 per cent of students in grade 6 each year, and measuring learning performance in language and mathematics. On that test, only 8.7 per cent of the sixth grade students achieved the minimum competency level in English. See DeStefano *et al.* (2007).
5. While the government in Zambia has experimented with grants-in-aid to community schools, the amounts and extent of those grants have been very limited. Most community schools survive on their own means. See DeStefano *et al.* (2007).

References

Aga Khan Foundation (2007) 'Non-state Providers and Public–Private–Community Partnerships in Education – Contributions Towards Achieving EFA: Opportunities and Challenges', paper presented at the UKFIET Conference 'Going for Growth? School, Community, Economy, Nation', Oxford University, Oxford, 11–13 September.

Besley, Timothy and Maitreesh Ghatak (2007) 'Provision of Public Services by Non-state Actors', paper presented at the Annual Bank Conference on Development Economics (ABCDE), Slovenia, 17–18 May.

Brinkerhoff, J. (2002) 'Government–nonprofit partnership: a defining framework', *Public Administration and Development* 22 (1): 19–30.

Casey-Hayford, Leslie and Adom Baisie Ghartey (2007) 'The Leap to Literacy and Life Change in Northern Ghana: An Impact Assessment of School for Life', Accra: School for Life.

Chapman, D. W. and S. Miric (2005) 'Teacher Policy in the MENA Region: Issues and Options', background paper prepared for the Middle East and North Africa Division, Washington, DC: The World Bank.

DeStefano, Joseph (1996) 'Community-based Primary Education: Lessons Learned from the Basic Education Expansion Project (BEEP) in Mali', Washington, DC: USAID, Bureau for Africa, Office of Sustainable Development.

DeStefano, Joseph and Luis Crouch (2006) 'Education Reform Support Today', Educational Quality Improvement Program 2, Washington, DC: Academy for Educational Development.

DeStefano, Joseph and Emily Miksic (2007) 'School Effectiveness in Maissade, Haiti', Educational Quality Improvement Program 2 Case Study, Washington, DC: Academy for Educational Development.

DeStefano, Joseph, Audrey-marie Schuh Moore, David Balwanz, and Ash Hartwell (2007) 'Reaching the Underserved: Complementary Models of Effective Schooling', EQUIP2, Washington, DC: Academy for Educational Development.

Edwards, M. and D. Hulm (eds.) (1995) *Non-Governmental Organizations: Performance and Accountability: Beyond the Magic Bullet*, London: Earthscan.

Freeman, Ted and Sheila Dohoo Faure (2003) *Local Solutions to Global Challenges: Towards Effective Partnerships in Basic Education, Final Report, Joint Evaluation of External Support to Basic Education in Developing Countries*, The Hague, the Netherlands: Ministry of Foreign Affairs.

Hanushek, E. A., J. F. Kain, and S. G. Rivkin (2001) 'Why Public Schools Lose Teachers', *Working Paper No. W8599*, Washington, DC: National Bureau of Economic Research.

Galal, A. (2002) 'The Paradox of Education and Unemployment in Egypt', *Working Paper No. 67*, Cairo: Egyptian Center for Economic Studies.

Patrinos, Harry Anthony and Shobhana Sosale (2007) 'Public–private partnerships in education', in Harry Anthony Patrinos and Shobhana Sosale (eds.), *Mobilizing the Private Sector for Public Education: A View from the Trenches*, Washington, DC: The World Bank.

Ramanath, R. (2005) 'From Conflict to Collaboration: Nongovernmental Organizations and their Negotiations for Local Control of Slum and Squatter Housing in Mumbai, India', unpublished PhD dissertation, Virginia Polytechnic Institute and State University, Blacksburg, VA.

Rose, Pauline (2007) 'NGO Provision of Basic Education: Alternative or Complementary Service Delivery to Support Access to the Excluded?', *CREATE Discussion Paper No. 3*, Brighton, UK: University of Sussex.

Teamey, Kelly (2007) 'Whose Public Action? Analyzing Inter-sectoral Collaboration for Service Delivery: A Literature Review on Relationships between Government and Non-state Providers of Services', Birmingham, UK: Economic and Social Research Council, University of Birmingham.

Terway, Arushi, Carolyn Pugliese, and Audrey Moore (in press) 'Doing more for less: an analysis of why complementary education schools out do government schools?', *International Review of Education*.

Tyack, David B. (1974) *The One Best System: A History of American Urban Education*, Cambridge, MA: Harvard University Press.

UNESCO (2008) 'Education for All by 2015, Will We Make it?', EFA Global Monitoring Report, Paris: UNESCO.

Villegas-Reimers, Eleonora (2003) *Teacher Professional Development: An International Review of the Literature*, Paris: UNESCO – International Institute for Educational Planning.

Welmond, M. (2004) 'Concept Paper: Education Policy in the Middle East and North Africa', Washington, DC: The World Bank.

Reaching the underserved with complementary education: lessons from Ghana's state and non-state sectors

Leslie Casely-Hayford and Ash Hartwell

Between 1995–06 and 2005–06, more than 85,000 children between the ages of 8 and 14 years participated in a complementary education programme in rural areas of northern Ghana. School for Life, a non-profit organisation, provides nine months of instruction in the children's spoken language. An impact assessment of the programme demonstrates that complementary education programmes are able to help children attain basic literacy in their mother tongue within a shorter timeframe and more cost-effectively than formal state primary-school systems can.

Faire parvenir l'éducation complémentaire aux personnes mal desservies : leçons tirées des secteurs public et non public du Ghana
Durant la période de 1995/96 à 2005/06, plus de 85.000 enfants d'entre 8 et 14 ans ont participé à un programme d'éducation complémentaire dans des zones rurales du nord du Ghana. School for Life, une organisation à but non lucratif, propose neuf mois d'instruction dans la langue parlée par les enfants. Une évaluation de l'impact du programme a démontré que les programmes d'éducation complémentaire sont en mesure d'aider les enfants à atteindre un niveau d'alphabétisme de base dans leur langue maternelle dans un délai plus bref et de manière plus économique que ne le peuvent les systèmes de scolarité primaire de l'État.

Alcançando os sub-atendidos com educação complementar: lições de setores estatais e não-estatais de Gana
Entre 1995–06 e 2005–06, mais de 85.000 crianças com idade entre 8 e 14 anos participaram de um programa educacional complementar em áreas rurais do norte de Gana. A organização School for Life, que não possui fins lucrativos, oferece nove meses de instrução no idioma falado das crianças. Uma avaliação do impacto do programa demonstra que os programas educacionais complementares são capazes de ajudar as crianças a obter alfabetização básica em sua língua materna dentro de um prazo mais curto e de forma mais efetiva em termos de custos do que os sistemas formais escolares primários do estado.

ACHIEVING EDUCATION FOR ALL THROUGH PUBLIC-PRIVATE PARTNERSHIPS?

Llegar hasta poblaciones aisladas con educación complementaria: experiencias de actores estatales y no estatales en Ghana

Durante los últimos 12 años, más de 5 mil niños de entre 8 y 14 años de edad del ámbito rural del norte de Ghana han participado en algún programa escolar complementario. Escuelas para la Vida, una organización sin ánimo de lucro, ejecuta un programa escolar de nueve meses en los idiomas maternos de los niños. Un reciente estudio de impacto indica que los programas escolares complementarios logran la alfabetización de los niños en su idioma materno en menos tiempo y con costos menores que las escuelas primarias del Estado.

Introduction

As the target date for achieving the Millennium Development Goals (MDGs) and Education for All (EFA) goals draws closer, governments in Sub-Saharan Africa are beginning to realise that non-state actors are helping close the access, quality, and achievement gaps, particularly in deprived and hard-to-reach areas of the continent. The debates for closing the final 10–15 per cent access gap through alternative routes to basic education in Sub-Saharan Africa began in the early 1990s, but it was not until the mid-2000s that visible signs of state interest in non-state activities began to materialise. Ghana is no exception. While the civil-society sector was making significant strides and learning to achieve access among the poorest, isolated, and most remote populations, government was moving ahead on provision to the majority of children in the hard-to-reach areas. Towards the end of the Ghanaian government's Education Strategic Plan (ESP 2000–2009), the last 10 per cent of children outside the state system appeared to be more difficult to reach, and this required a look at alternative approaches.

Despite the positive access trends, education in Sub-Saharan Africa is still failing to meet the basic literacy and learning needs of children, particularly in deprived rural areas of the continent (Casely-Hayford 2003; DeStefano *et al.* 2007; UNESCO 2005). Research by Filmer and Pritchett (1999) shows that poor children are much more likely to be out of school than their wealthier counterparts. Work by Filmer *et al.* (2006) broadened the EFA debate to include the question of achieving an acceptable level of learning, and not merely access and completion.

As governments continue to fail to provide *quality* education in poor, hard-to-reach rural areas, non-state actors have been experimenting with alternative approaches to the conventional schooling system in these same areas (Casely-Hayford *et al.* 2007; Farrell and Hartwell 2008; Hartwell 2008). These approaches have often been termed 'complementary education', and share some of the following characteristics: serving underserved areas; school schedules taking account of the work demands on children; locally relevant and simplified curriculum; the medium of instruction in the mother tongue; teachers with no formal pre-service training but provided with ongoing mentoring and supervision, along with management and implementation structures that involve collaboration between non-state actors and government agencies (Casely-Hayford 2003; Hartwell 2008). These models increasingly demonstrate their ability to reach deprived and endemically poor areas, and provide education that promotes a quality learning environment to the populations they serve.

This contribution focuses on the impact of the School for Life (SfL) model, which has influenced the state sector's notions of quality provision within Ghana's predominantly remote rural northern districts. It primarily draws on the results of an external impact assessment undertaken in 2007, in which one of the authors was the external evaluator. The contribution begins by considering the emergence of complementary education systems in Ghana before moving to an analysis of the outcomes and impact of the SfL programme. The final sections review the challenges that non-state actors face in financing and providing complementary education within the context of meeting EFA objectives.

The emergence of complementary education and non-state actors in Ghana's education sector

Northern Ghana (comprising Northern, Upper East, and Upper West administrative regions) accounts for almost a third of Ghana's land area and is inhabited by about 10 per cent of its population, with a population density of less than 25 people per square kilometre. Poverty is endemic in northern Ghana, with the people facing formidable challenges with regards to water, food security, and employment opportunities. A significant percentage of girl children – between the ages of 12 and 18 years – migrate from the north to urban areas to find employment and earn money in order to prepare for marriage. There are also significant challenges related to child fostering and the poor perception of girls' education in the region, which encourages parental preference for boys' education due to the traditional roles of the girl child, inheritance patterns, and security of parents in their latter years (Casely-Hayford 2000).

Approximately 40 per cent of school-age children are out of school across the north, the majority of whom are girls (Hartwell *et al.* 2006). The great majority of children in northern Ghana do not complete the compulsory nine years of primary schooling. The National Education Assessment (NEA) indicated that, 'In Ghana, 75% of sixth graders are not able to read and write in any language, and 90% do not achieve basic numeracy skills' (MOE 2008).

As the 1990s drew to a close, the question of quality provision for many of Ghana's rural poor remained unanswered. Ghana, at a policy level, is committed to achieving universal primary education. The 1992 Constitution mandated that government would make provision for universal primary education (Republic of Ghana 1992), and in 1996, the Ghana government launched 'Free and Compulsory Universal Basic Education' (FCUBE), a programme intended to ultimately reach all children (MOE 2002). Preliminary work by ActionAid Ghana and the Danish Friendship Groups Association pointed to the fact that formal education systems were not flexible in providing education in harsh rural contexts where large family size and dependence on farm labour among children were priorities (Casely-Hayford 2000, 2003).

In the early 1990s, Danish researchers supported by the Ghana Danish Friendship Association embarked on an ethnographic study of the farming patterns and educational needs of northern Ghanaian families and found that the timing of the school day was pivotal to accommodate children who needed to work on the family farm in the morning. The studies also found that education needed to be more relevant to local needs and curriculum should be better integrated with the social and economic realities of the area (Casely-Hayford 2000). In 1995, the School for Life programme was started by two Danish Ghanaian organisations and funded by the Danish International Development Agency (DANIDA), on the premise that flexible school hours were a key to reaching children who were out of school and not traditionally earmarked for education within the farming family (Casely-Hayford 2000; Casely-Hayford *et al.* 2007).

In response to the unique educational problems in northern Ghana, the SfL Programme developed a functional literacy programme for out-of-school children. The programme was designed as a complementary education programme for children between the ages of 8 and 14 years. In this context, 'complementary' meant that the schools provide an educational programme for underserved groups that is recognised by the government, organised often by a non-state organisation, involves the community, and typically has a number of innovative features to enhance and accelerate access and learning. The programme offered a nine-month cycle of afternoon classes in the mother tongue,[1] aimed at assisting children attain basic literacy, numeracy, and life skills – preparing pupils to join the formal primary-education system. SfL classes are operated within villages, while formal primary schools are typically 5–8 km distant from the SfL villages, and can only be reached by older children and youths.

The SfL programme started in 1995 as a pilot project in two districts of the north with 50 classes in each district. The two partners to the programme – the Ghana Development Communities Association and the Ghana Friendship Groups in Denmark – succeeded in developing an effective model to provide functional literacy[2] for out-of-school children in these rural areas. Following this success, the scale of delivery was increased during the second and third phases of the programme. In Phase 2 (1998–2003), SfL was operated in eight districts and benefited 40,000 children. In Phase 3 (2003–2008), the programme area expanded to cover ten districts and 48,000 children, with mainstreaming, advocacy, and replication becoming an integral part of the programme strategy.

By the late 1990s, SfL had grown in scale, reaching close to 50,000 children, and was showing signs of success in helping children break through to literacy within a nine-month cycle. The majority (65 per cent) of these children were then being mainstreamed into the primary 3 and primary 4 levels of government schools after graduating from SfL. This level of integration saved the parents' direct and indirect costs of sending children to 2–3 years of formal schooling. The SfL approach was introduced to the Ministry in 1996 at a conference hosted by USAID Ghana, but was not widely recognised as a viable system until 2006, when the Education Quality for All (EQUALL) project began operations.

By mid-2003, SfL was gaining recognition through the commissioned study by USAID on 'Reaching Underserved Populations with Basic Education'. This study helped USAID design its new five-year education strategy for Ghana. In 2005–06, USAID included the SfL approach within its education programme strategy for Ghana. The USAID-supported EQUALL project emerged from the design work of a consortium of non-state actors in 2005–06,[3] and brought the SfL programme into the forefront of delivering complementary education to Ghana's rural poor.

As USAID began to finance the EQUALL project, including the complementary education component of the project implemented by SfL, the Ministry of Education (MOE) began to recognise the impact of the SfL approach as a potentially viable approach for reaching underserved areas of northern Ghana. These geographic areas had previously shown the greatest resistance in closing the enrolment gap. SfL made presentations in 2006–07 to the MOE's Access and Participation thematic working group in charge of guiding the education-sector work for attaining goals within the MOE's Education Strategic Plan.

Another major thrust which provided public visibility for the complementary education programmes in northern Ghana was the government's approach to poverty and education targeting embedded in the 1st and 2nd Ghana Poverty Reduction Strategy documents. These documents recognised that over 500,000 children were out of school in Ghana and that alternative/complementary education approaches would be needed in order to reach out-of-school children. This work led to the government's own Education Strategic Plan, which suggested that, in order to ensure equal access for the final 10 per cent of Ghana's school-aged children who were out of school, non-state actors would be required to assist government; the report included complementary education systems as one approach to close the net/gross enrolment gap (MOESS 2007).

As the SfL programme was emerging from obscurity, the main donor (DANIDA) also required that SFL make a stronger case to government, so that its approaches would be mainstreamed. Phase 1 resourcing and programme strategies for the SfL programme were mainly focused on full-scale implementation of the approach. Phases 2 and 3 began to support advocacy and mainstreaming components of SfL, in order to gradually hand over more of its implementation work to government. In Phase 2, increased government ownership and support to the programme were pilot tested in two districts. The results were abysmal, with the District Education Office taking possession of the motorbikes funded through the programme, but not following through with their agreement to supervise and ensure the programme was monitored (School for Life 2001).

Phase 3 tested out the engagement of smaller NGOs to implement the SfL approach, with SfL sharing its methods and training potential with SfL partners. The SfL impact study found that this had limited effectiveness due to the small size and lack of funding for NGOs implementing literacy work, particularly among school-aged children (Casely-Hayford *et al.* 2007). Beginning in October 2008, Phase 4 went even further in supporting more NGOs to receive training and help scale up the SfL approach across the north of the country.

Despite the emphasis on scaling up as the programme entered its 4th phase, elements of the donor's desire to 'mainstream' the SfL approach were reflected in DANIDA's decision to scale down the service-delivery side of SfL and increase advocacy for government to take on SfL in partnership with local NGOs. The movement away from service delivery and the idea that the programme could be scaled up by other NGOs in northern Ghana was not supported by evidence from the impact assessment (Casely-Hayford *et al.* 2007). There were few NGOs in northern Ghana capable of scaling up the approach and in a financial position to do so. This means that, although there were large numbers of out-of-school children in some areas, the complementary education programme might not continue unless government or other donors are willing to finance and support this approach.

The impact of School for Life's programme in northern Ghana

The impact assessment of SfL was designed to provide evidence to government and other donors on the effectiveness of the SfL programme. The impact study was based on a one-year participatory study. It was designed largely as a carefully sampled qualitative tracer study, based on perspectives of former pupils, and perspectives of comparative peers who were in school, and family perspectives. Over 77 in-depth interviews were conducted with ex-SfL youths and their families along with over 50 non-SfL peers and their families in communities which had participated in the programme three, six, and nine years previously. The impact study traced over 77 children in nine target schools across three study districts who were currently enrolled in the primary to Senior Secondary School (SSS) levels of education, in order to elicit their experiences of the SfL programme. The information collected focused on what they had learned, and how these experiences had shaped and changed their own life, their family and communities' lives. In addition to the qualitative analysis from interviews and focus groups, the study examined records and reports of SfL and the Ministry of Education for the period 1995–2007. The study also analysed the factors contributing to programme success, and the impacts the programme made on the ex-SfL students and ex-SfL facilitators across northern Ghana (Casely-Hayford *et al.* 2007).

The SfL impact study reveals that over 85,000 children and over 4000 rural communities had been reached by the SFL programme across 12 districts in Ghana's Northern Region over a period of 12 years. Close to 90 per cent of the 85,000 children had completed the SfL programme and become functionally literate, with almost 70 per cent transitioning to the formal education system at upper primary levels. There was on average a 6.6 per cent drop out in the programme over the 12-year period.

Access

Overall, the impact assessment reveals that SfL has had a positive impact on improving access and retention of children over the 12-year period of its programme interventions.

ACHIEVING EDUCATION FOR ALL THROUGH PUBLIC-PRIVATE PARTNERSHIPS?

The integration of former SfL students into the formal system was having a positive impact on the gross enrolment rate[4] for public primary schools in the north, helping the government to move towards Universal Basic Education, gender parity, and improving the quality of education. It is estimated that the SfL programme increased access to primary education by 14 per cent, from a gross enrolment rate of 69 per cent in the north to 83 per cent. Further, the SfL rate of completion and transition into grade 3 was 70 per cent, in comparison to the survival rate of pupils in public schools from P1 to P3 of 48 per cent (BED 2006; Hartwell 2008).

A total of 55,606 SfL graduates (32,520 males and 23,086 females) were integrated into the formal school system between 1995–96 and 2005–06. This represents 69.9 per cent of the total that graduated from the SfL programme – a tremendous achievement given the fact that the first phase of SfL was not particularly focused on ensuring integration. Levels of integration consistently increased over the 12 years despite endemic barriers to access, including the high poverty incidence and negative socio-cultural barriers that often prevent girls from attainment in the public primary system (early marriage, child fosterage to 'aunties', and betrothal practices). This was a result of increasing parental and community support for the female SfL students, as parents saw the literacy outcomes of their children in the programme (Casely-Hayford *et al.* 2007). Figure 1 shows enrolment, drop-out, and graduation trends in SfL from 1995–96 to 2005–06.

According to the impact assessment, SfL had also made remarkable progress in addressing gender inequality by helping parents change their attitude about the value of girls' education. This resulted in improving girls' retention rates and lowering drop-out rates in the primary schools across the north, where former SfL students were integrated. At least 40 per cent of those enrolled in the SfL programme were females, of whom 54.2 per cent entered the formal system over the 10-year period.[5] In terms of gender parity, retention, and completion rates among girls, SfL has had a positive impact on the number of girls remaining in school and transitioning to higher levels of education. According to district education officers, head teachers, and school records, ex-SfL girls constituted a large proportion in the classes at the junior- and secondary-school levels, particularly when considering the rural characteristics of

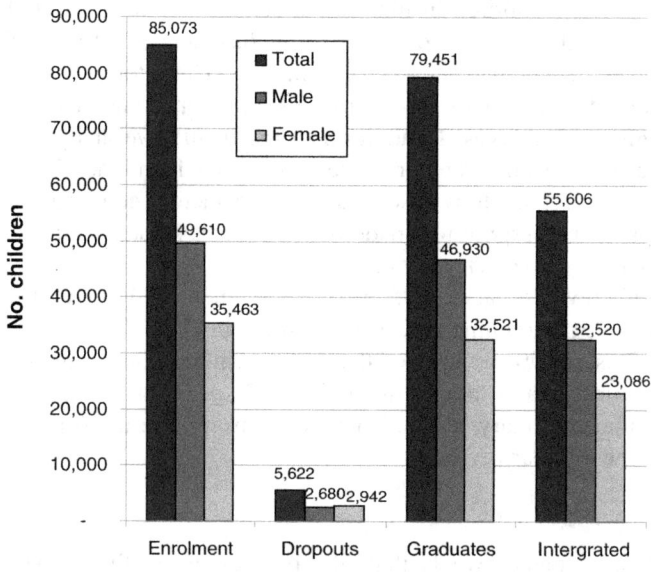

Figure 1: Total enrolment, drop outs, graduation, and integration of SfL learners, 1995–96 to 2005–06

school intake. Female former SfL students made up, on average, 18 per cent of the junior-secondary school population studied, and 16.3 per cent of the senior-secondary school population.

SfL also demonstrates strong retention and completion rates in public schools, in comparison to students who have not gone through SfL (Casely-Hayford et al. 2007). The SfL impact assessment reveals that 70 per cent of graduates were admitted to P3 or higher after a government placement assessment was conducted at community and district level. In all the sampled study districts for the impact assessment, promotion rates[6] of the *former SfL students in public schools* was very high, ranging between 97.7 per cent (2003) and 92.9 per cent (2005).

Learning outcomes

The impact assessment found that the nine-month SfL literacy cycle provides a solid foundation for students to move from mother-tongue literacy to second-language acquisition in English. In 2003, SfL requested that the Government Education Service conduct a survey to test SfL pupils towards the end of the nine-month cycle. The results showed that 81.2 per cent of the children tested were able to meet the minimum standards for literacy and numeracy at grade 3 levels (Hartwell 2008). The values embedded in the SfL curriculum contribute to the former SfL students being disciplined, confident, and self-motivated. This, coupled with high academic performance, earned former SfL students leadership roles in their classes and schools (including in governance), and they were seen by their peers as role models (Casely-Hayford et al. 2007). The SfL participatory teaching approaches have direct impact on helping children feel confident, become self-assertive, and enjoy learning. The in-depth interviews revealed that former SfL students learn to analyse, ask questions, and become critical thinkers through the participatory methods used by the SfL facilitator, and the curriculum.

Teachers noted, and literacy testing demonstrated, that that SfL makes a significant contribution to the literacy and numeracy performance among the ex-SfL learners once they join formal school. Interviews with head teachers and teachers revealed that ex-SfL learners were outperforming non-SfL students in the same class in the Ghanaian language, English, and mathematics. Literacy tests revealed that SfL students were performing at the same level as non-SfL students in the English-fluency tests in primary grade 6 and junior-secondary grade 3. Several other instruments used to track performance of SfL students, along with in-depth interview of their teachers, district education officers, and non-SfL colleagues, revealed that they were outperforming non-SfL students in other core subject areas. According to teachers, district education officers, and in-depth interviews with peers in the same class, SfL students are able to learn independently, particularly once integrated into formal primary schools where teachers are often not punctual nor reliably regular in attending school. Former SfL students also often help their peers pursue reading and writing activities in English and Ghanaian language classes, when teachers are late or absent; they help their peers learn to read using the phonetic approach to literacy which they learn in the SfL programme.

The ripple effect within the family and community

Interviews with parents and family members of former SfL students revealed that SfL makes a positive impact at the family and community levels. At the family level, former SfL students are able to assist their family with basic reading and writing tasks in the home. They are also able to transfer the knowledge of how to read to help their siblings and, in some cases, their parents learn to read. Most importantly, former SfL students were found sharing the developmental messages of social change with their families and communities. Lessons on malaria prevention, environmental health and sanitation, family planning, and sustainable agriculture were all being talked about with families of former SfL students. Many of the families interviewed during the impact assessment revealed that they were still practising better hygiene, beginning to plan their family size, critically thinking about gender equality, and improving their agricultural practices through reduced bush burning. Interviews from the impact assessment, particularly among community members who had not had SfL classes running for over five years, revealed that changes in behaviour were sustained long after the SfL programme had stopped in the community.

The greatest impact of the SfL programme at the family and community levels was in relation to people's new-found awareness concerning the importance of 'good-quality education'. The life histories collected among former SfL students and parents in the impact assessment revealed that children who would not have had a chance to enter the formal system were working hard to demonstrate to their parents that they could succeed and were worth the investment, particularly girls.

The government's own appraisal of SfL

In addition to the external impact evaluation, the Ghanaian government carried out its own assessment of the SfL programme in 2006 (BED 2006). This was probably even more influential in demonstrating the results of SfL in a way that would have an impact on public policy, concluding that: 'The study led to a firm discovery that non state actors were indeed mainly involved in running the innovative complementary education programmes' (BED 2006: 4).

The MOE/BED study confirmed the success of SfL in achieving high rates of access, completion within their own programme, and transition to primary schooling in general, pointing to the following reasons for the 'comparative advantage':

- Flexible school environment;
- High levels of community involvement and more child-centred pedagogical approaches adopted by complementary schools – 'factors which are normally absent in mainstream schools' (BED 2006).

The most interesting results were in relation to:

> the high academic successes of pupils within the nine month SfL cycle could be attributed to the level of teacher/community commitment to succeed as well as the availability of teaching learning materials. The text book ratio in the SfL system was 1:1 and the pupil teacher ratio was also pegged at 25:1. These ratios indicated the comparatively high levels of attention that the SfL pupils received. Comparatively the pupil/teacher ratio (PTR) for the mainstream primary schools in northern region was 40:1. (BED 2006: 15)

The cost of operating the complementary system was also found to be substantially lower than that of the public system. The annual recurrent costs of educating a public-school child in northern Ghana was approximately $70.8 compared to $38 per child for one year of SfL (2008 figures). The majority of costs for the public system were in salaries, while a greater proportion is spent on non-salary inputs, including learning materials, in the SfL programme. The government study found that 97.8 per cent of education recurrent costs were used for salaries, while only 2.2 per cent remained for quality delivery of education in state primary schools, compared to 4 per cent for salaries or facilitator stipends in SfL, leaving 96 per cent for inputs into the education delivery of the SfL programme (BED 2006: 17). Both the SfL impact assessment and the government assessment of complementary education found that the SfL programme was saving the government a significant amount of funding and was effective in helping children attain basic literacy in deprived rural contexts where trained teachers were often unwilling to live. According to the impact assessment, the SfL programme had saved the Government of Ghana over $6,023,168 by educating over 85,073 children to grade 3 equivalent (Casely-Hayford et al. 2007).

The final recommendations from the government's 2006 'Study of Complementary Education' suggest that 'complementary schools should be part of the public system of education. Absorption of the schools should be done in phases. Existing complementary schools in the three northern regions should be absorbed first. Those in the southern sector should be absorbed based on experience gained in the northern sector' (BED 2006: 17). The report also acknowledges the value of complementary schools as an effective alternative to provision of three grade levels of primary schooling in deprived areas, and that complementary schools should be used as preparatory school for admission to upper primary grades. This was a major step forward in a context where the government had previously not fully recognised the contributions of non-state providers in delivering education services to rural areas.

Further evidence of closer collaboration between SfL and government was apparent through the report's role in highlighting the unique character of complementary education systems, and stating some of the good practices that government schools should adopt. These include: community awareness creation/animation before schools are established; phonic/syllabic teaching method; small class sizes; the use of vernacular or local dialect as the medium for instruction; the use of textbooks written in the vernacular; and community involvement and ownership. Finally, the government report suggests that the operation of complementary schools should be funded through the government's capitation (per-student) grant scheme (BED 2006). The report ends by stating that the:

> *initiative of non state actors to send children in hard to reach areas ... including drop outs should be supported. These children constitute a critical mass whose exclusion from the educational system will make the realisation of UPE [universal primary education] an impossible task. A Government policy in this direction is worth pursuing to complement capitation and school feeding policies to enhance primary school enrolment.* (BED 2006: 19)

The MOE findings had far-reaching effects on accelerating the government's next steps to developing a policy on complementary education. The study helped the MOE develop the framework, which later became the 'Complementary Basic Education Policy Document' (finalised in October 2007) – the drafting of which involved defining the regulatory and policy context, the goals and strategies, the institutional framework, and financial implications of complementary education.

Influence of SfL on state provision of basic education

Not only has SfL had positive outcomes for those learning through its programme, but it has also had a multiplier effect through its influence on state provision. Through demonstration of what can be achieved, along with building a constructive relationship with government officials, the success of the programme has been recognised by district and national governments. This has resulted in the programme becoming integrated into government policy, as well as government learning lessons for its own provision (as noted above). However, this is not without its challenges.

The MOESS Draft Document on Complementary Basic Education (2007) advocates that government take the lead in supporting complementary education to reach underserved rural children and youth. However, it initially downplayed the vital role of non-state actors as the primary force and organising agency for complementary education in deprived rural areas. Although the draft makes clear the need to reach the out-of-school child, and notes the success of SfL and other initiatives in meeting this need, there are significant policy challenges. MOE does not have the capacity, or the bureaucratic means, to undertake the kind of radical shift in standard policies and procedures that characterise the management and support of a complementary education programme (Farrell and Hartwell 2008).

At the district level – which is charged with the responsibility for primary education[7] – there is evidence of support for complementary education, and the influence of SfL is strong. This is demonstrated by a number of significant decisions and processes:

- Several District Education Offices (DEOs) have signed Memoranda of Understanding with SfL, recognising the legitimacy of the schools, and agreeing to regular consultations and support.
- DEOs participate in the identification and selection of new sites for SfL classes, taking into account the location of existing schools, and population densities and distribution.
- DEOs conduct end-of-programme student assessments, using a test for literacy and numeracy appropriate for grade 3.
- Schools, with the support of DEOs, accept SfL graduates into their classes at grade 3 and grade 4 (depending on the pupil's performance in the assessment test).

In addition to these direct indicators of district support for SfL, the influence of SfL on the state at the district and regional levels is visible in the demand generated among teachers in the formal system that have requested training in the SfL methodology. Over 600 teachers (P1 to P3 level) across 431 schools have been trained in the north of Ghana (Casely-Hayford *et al.* 2007). Another major influence is that SfL facilitators/teachers are becoming part of the teaching service. Some become contract teachers paid by the District Assemblies to support teaching and learning in remote-area schools after their service with SfL. The SfL programme has, through EQUALL, been able to support over 80 complementary teachers to enter the government's Untrained Teacher Diploma in Basic Education (UTDBE) and obtain formal teacher qualifications.

At the national level, in addition to the assessment and draft policy paper commissioned by MOE, donors are recognising the strength and opportunities provided by a complementary education system for the deprived hard-to-reach rural areas of Ghana. The growing interest among new donors, such as DFID and UNICEF, for complementary education programmes in Ghana has helped to ensure that government takes more interest and monitors non-state actors' provision of education services.

Despite the increasing support by the donor community for non-state actors to deliver basic education, the Ghanaian government's current aid strategy further centralises aid financing in the public sector, with little guidance as to how non-state actors will collaborate in service delivery. The government's Aid Policy Document suggests that the preferred support mechanism for the government is multi-donor budgetary support (MDBS), which will provide fungible financing to the education sector (Government of Ghana 2008).

The future and sustainability of complementary education programming will depend to a large degree on the relationship forged between non-state and state actors with respect to the complementary policy implementation, and possibilities for government funding. One option would be to allocate school capitation grants to districts for those pupils enrolled in complementary education classes. At the district level, DEOs would then be authorised to provide these funds to SfL, or other providers that meet specified criteria to support operations at the SfL sites. This approach would, in some ways, be similar to the traditional grant-in-aid system used many years ago to provide public funds to non-profit, non-state education providers.

Another approach is to follow the path of Burkina Faso, which has set up a social investment fund for non-state actors to provide complementary education in remote areas.

As the SfL model highlights, successful implementation of complementary education programmes by non-state actors depends on development partners and governments recognising promising models of educational development and ensuring that these are 'mainstreamed' into the wider education system. This requires recognition of the particular circumstances, management capacities, and characteristics of programmes that demonstrate a different set of skills and demand more responsive government support for successful implementation.

Conclusions

Northern Ghana's three regions still contain well over 500,000 children out of school. Given the fact that it is highly unlikely that *all* children in northern Ghana will enter the formal education system – due to the timing and scheduling of classes, coping strategies of rural families, labour patterns, and lack of funds for parents to support all children in school – complementary education programmes will remain a viable alternative and more cost-effective policy option for government.

The speed and efficiency with which Ghana meets its education goals will require closer state and non-state interaction in relation to the provision of educational services in hard-to-reach rural areas of Ghana. The realisation of these goals will also depend on whether the state accepts an overall policy framework that welcomes non-state interaction to attain mutually beneficial goals. This relationship will require an increased understanding of the comparative advantages of diverse education service providers implementing programmes across diverse geographic and content lines. The evidence presented in this contribution suggests that moves are being made in this direction, but more work is needed to compare countries where states have accepted the comparative advantage of non-state actors and supported them to deliver basic education to their children (for example, Bangladesh, Burkina Faso, Egypt, Ethiopia, and Mali).

There are also moves within the Government of Ghana and Parliament to ensure more accountability among non-state actors, particularly NGOs operating in Ghana. With the increased thrust towards multi-donor budgetary support, the climate for private–public partnerships among state and non-state actors appears to be opening, particularly if Universal Primary Education is to be attained in Ghana's remote rural areas.

The non-state sector will require full approval and support by the state in order to assist in the realisation of these goals, which will likely involve state financial support or co-financing arrangements. This state–non-state partnership may also result in shared learning in how to deliver quality education in remote rural areas on a sustainable basis, and help improve teachers' accountability within public schools and ultimately improve quality provision particularly at lower-primary level in remote rural areas.

When considering the way forward for state and non-state provision of complementary education in Ghana, there are three major policy questions:

- Who should pay?
- Who should deliver the programme?
- Should there be more choice and competition at the local level to increase the accountability of public teachers in deprived rural areas?

The policy issues arising from the School for Life case also raise the question: how can government work in partnership with non-state actors and communities to achieve Learning for All through improved management, community engagement, more frequent and systematic support for teachers and schools, and greater instructional time devoted to early literacy?

ACHIEVING EDUCATION FOR ALL THROUGH PUBLIC-PRIVATE PARTNERSHIPS?

The evidence presented in this contribution shows that this is possible. However, for it to happen on a larger scale, will require sector policies by government which are more inclusive of non-state partnerships, and long-term core financing for non-state providers extending provision to hard-to-reach populations.

Notes

1. As of 2008, SfL was working in eight local languages. The selected language must have a written form.
2. 'Functional literacy' means the pupil is able to read a lower-grade primary text with fluency and comprehension. Fluency means reading at the rate of approximately 60 words per minute (see Abadzi 2006).
3. The consortium was led by the Education Development Corporation (EDC), a private non-profit organisation based in the USA.
4. The primary gross enrolment rate is calculated by dividing the total number of children in primary school by the primary school-aged population.
5. A higher proportion of girls than boys was being integrated into the formal education system from SfL when comparing the proportion of girls and boys who graduated from SfL with those who were integrated over the 10-year period.
6. Promotion in the public primary-school system is mainly based on attendance and achievement rates.
7. About 80 per cent of funding, including all recurrent funding, for basic education comes from the Ministry of Education to the District Education Offices (DEOs), and all DEO staff are employees, not of the district, but of the Ghana Education Service.

References

Abadzi, H. (2006) 'Efficient Learning for the Poor: Insights from the Frontier of Cognitive Neuroscience', Washington, DC: The World Bank.

BED (Basic Education Division) (2006) 'A Study of Complementary Education Systems in the Three Northern Regions of Ghana', Accra: Ministry of Education, Science and Sport.

Casely-Hayford, Leslie (2000) 'Education, Culture and Development in Northern Ghana: Micro Realities and Macro Context: Implications for Policy and Practice', unpublished DPhil thesis, University of Sussex, Brighton, UK.

Casely-Hayford, Leslie (2003) 'Reaching Underserved Populations with Basic Education in Deprived Areas of Ghana: Emerging Good Practices, Section 1 and Section 2', Accra: CARE.

Casely-Hayford, Leslie, Adom Basie Ghartey, and the SfL Internal Impact Evaluation Team (2007) 'The Leap to Literacy and Life Change in Northern Ghana: An Impact Assessment of School for Life (SfL), Final Report', Accra: UNICEF Ghana.

DeStefano, Joseph, Audrey-marie Schuh Moore, David Balwanz, and Ash Hartwell (2007) 'Reaching the Underserved: Complementary Model of Effective Schooling', Washington, DC: EQUIP2 and USAID.

Farrell, Joseph and Ash Hartwell (2008) 'Planning for Successful Alternative Education: A Possible Route to Education for All', Paris: International Institute for Educational Planning/UNESCO.

Filmer, Deon and Lant Pritchett (1999) 'The effect of household wealth on educational attainment evidence from 35 countries', *Population and Development Review* 25 (1): 85–120.

Filmer, D., A. Hasan, and L. Pritchett (2006) 'A Millennium Learning Goal: Measuring Real Progress in Education', *Working Paper No. 97*, Washington, DC: Center for Global Development.

Government of Ghana (2008) 'Ghana's Aid Policy', Accra: Ministry of Finance and Economic Planning.

Hartwell, Ash (2008) 'Learning for all: alternative models and policy options', in William K. Cummings and James H. Williams (eds.) *Policy-Making for Education Reform in Developing Countries: Policy Options and Strategies*, Lanham, MD: Rowman & Littlefield.

Hartwell, Ash, Annababette Wils, and Yijie Zhao (2006) 'Reaching out-of-school children: sub-regional disparities', *Journal of Education for International Development*, 2: 2, available at http://www.equip123.net/jeid/articles/3/volume2-issue2comp.pdf (retrieved 2 December 2008).

MOE (2002) 'Education Sector Review (ESR)', Accra: Ministry of Education.

MOE (2008) 'Education Sector Performance Report', Accra: Ministry of Education.
MOESS (2007) 'Complementary Basic Education Policy Document', unpublished document, Accra: Ministry of Education, Science and Sport.
Republic of Ghana (1992) 'Constitution of the Republic of Ghana', Accra: The Republic of Ghana.
School for Life (2001) 'Final Report of the Mid Term Review Team: Functional Literacy Program for Children', Tamale, Ghana: Ministry of Foreign Affairs and DANIDA.
School for Life (2004) 'Project Document Phase 3: School for Life Programme; Functional Literacy and Development', School for Life.
UNESCO (2005) 'Children Out of School: Measuring Exclusion from Primary Education', Montreal: UNESCO Institute for Statistics.

Public–private partnerships or privatisation? Questioning the state's role in education in India

Prachi Srivastava

This contribution examines the Government of India's proposed public–private partnership (PPP) strategies in education in its Tenth and Eleventh Five Year Plans. The analysis aims to ascertain the state's role as financier, manager, and regulator of education in view of the proposed PPP strategies. The analysis shows that strategies strongly link PPPs in education with privatisation, and further, that despite assertions of 'a greatly expanded role for the state', the proposed strategies result in a diminished role for the state in education financing, management, and regulation.

Partenariats publics-privés ou privatisation ? Mise en cause du rôle de l'État dans le secteur de l'éducation en Inde
Cette contribution traite des stratégies de partenariats public-privé (PPP) proposées par le gouvernement indien dans le secteur de l'éducation dans ses Dixième et Onzième plans quinquennaux. Cette analyse cherche à déterminer le rôle joué par l'État en tant que financier, responsable et organisme de contrôle de l'éducation par rapport aux stratégies PPP proposées. L'analyse montre que ces stratégies établissent des liens solides entre les PPP du secteur de l'éducation et la privatisation et, de plus, que malgré les affirmations concernant un « rôle très élargi pour l'État », les stratégies proposées aboutissent en fait à un rôle réduit pour l'État dans le financement, la gestion et la réglementation de l'éducation.

Parcerias públido-privadas ou privatização? Questionando o papel do estado na educação na Índia
Esta contribuição examina as estratégias propostas de parceria público-privada (PPP) do governo da Índia em educação em seu décimo e décimo primeiro plano de cinco anos. A análise visa verificar o papel do estado como financiador, gerente e regulador da educação em vista das estratégias propostas de PPP. A análise mostra que as estratégias conectam fortemente as PPPs em educação com privatização, e além disto, que apesar das afirmações de "um papel significativamente maior do estado", as estratégias propostas resultam em um papel reduzido do estado no financiamento, gerência e regulação da educação.

¿Alianzas público-privadas o privatización? Interrogantes sobre la participación del Estado en la educación en India
Este ensayo analiza las estrategias del gobierno de India para impulsar las alianzas público-privadas (APP) en los Planes Quinquenales X y XI del sector educativo. La investigación

examina el papel del Estado como financiador, administrador y regulador de la educación, en el marco de las estrategias APP propuestas. A pesar de afirmar que "habrá una mayor participación del Estado", los resultados demuestran que las estrategias APP impulsan la privatización de la educación y terminan reduciendo la intervención del Estado en el financiamiento, la administración y la regulación del sector.

Introduction

The aim of this contribution is to analyse the Government of India's proposed strategies for public–private partnerships (PPPs) in education in its two most recent plans – the Tenth and Eleventh Five Year Plans – as an indication of the wider policy landscape influencing education provision in India. A 'strategy of inclusive growth', of which education is one of seven components, and delivering education in 'PPP mode' are the guiding mantras in India's eleventh development plan. The Planning Commission of India states that: 'Achieving the 11th Plan targets for health and education requires a greatly expanded role for the state in these areas. This is because access to essential public services such as ... education ... is not an automatic outcome of rising incomes. It calls for deliberate public intervention to ensure delivery of these services' (Planning Commission 2006b: 101). Therefore, public intervention was analysed in view of proposed PPP strategies in education. This was done by applying a revision of Greenaway's (1991) framework used to examine the role of the state in the delivery of services considered merit goods, namely the state's role as financier, manager, and regulator.

This contribution analyses key documents from the Tenth Five Year Plan (2002–2007) leading up to and including the Eleventh Five Year Plan (2007–2012).[1] The Eleventh Plan Planning Commission established a number of sector-wise working groups, steering committees, and task forces to make policy recommendations. In education, there were nine working groups and three steering committees.[2] Given the focus on inclusive growth and in the interest of space, recommendations from two of these, the Basic Education and Literacy Working Group and the Development of Education of Scheduled Caste/Scheduled Tribe/Minorities/Girls and other Disadvantaged Groups Working Group, are included here.

The analysis shows that beyond repeated instances of education delivery 'in PPP mode', an articulation of specific PPP models in the proposed strategies is missing. Furthermore, the strategies strongly link PPPs in education with privatisation rather than mechanisms of genuine partnership between public and private or other non-state actors, indicative of a dramatic 'paradigm shift' (Sengupta 2008) associated with India's macro-economic liberalisation policy. In line with this paradigm shift, the analysis shows that despite repeated assertions of 'a greatly expanded role for the state' in social sectors, namely education, proposed PPP strategies result in a diminished role for the state in the areas of education financing, management, and regulation in favour of privatised strategies of delivery.

Privatisation strategy and PPPs: situating the Tenth and Eleventh Five Year Plans

It is generally recognised that 1991 was the landmark year for privatisation policy prescriptions in India (Naib 2004; Sengupta 2008). The wave of privatisation began with an economic crisis and a worsening of the fiscal deficit in 1985–86 and culminated in the macro-economic crisis of

1991 (Naib 2004). In response, the New Economic Policy of 1991 was introduced promulgating market liberalisation and privatisation of many state-owned enterprises, influenced largely by the World Bank's standard structural adjustment package. Sengupta (2008) asserts that these policy prescriptions constituted a dramatic and controversial 'paradigm shift' for India. She sees their persistence and expansion with successive government changes as puzzling, since they are contrary to the ideals that favoured a large role for the state in the development of post-independent India.

There is evidence to suggest that while the New Economic Policy may have been politically expedient, its consequences were not fully considered (Gouri 1997), and further, that it had negative effects on the poor and disadvantaged (Sengupta 2008). The mid-term appraisal of the Tenth Plan acknowledges 'a problem of rural distress' (Planning Commission 2005: 2) for small-scale farmers and landless labourers linked to the deceleration of growth in agriculture despite wider economic growth. Still, liberalisation, disinvestment in state-owned enterprises, and harnessing private-sector investment in 'hard' development sector initiatives are generally accepted as the main catalysts for India's recent economic success. There is little attention in the wider policy discourse on the role that the concerted promotion of a home-grown industrial base in a protectionist environment over the four decades following independence may have played in fostering certain preconditions allowing liberalisation and privatisation policy prescriptions 'to take' more favourably compared with the experience of most African and Latin American countries that followed similar policy packages.

Nonetheless, and in line with the paradigm shift, PPPs have been promoted by the Department of Economic Affairs of the Ministry of Finance as the preferred strategy to build and expand India's infrastructure, specifically in the highways, railways, ports, airports, telecommunications, and power sectors, with the World Bank and the Asian Development Bank taking the lead in technical assistance on project and institutional development (see Department of Economic Affairs 2007). Not surprisingly, suggestions involve 'creating an enabling framework' for private-sector investment by simplifying taxation; a preference for mega-projects managed by larger private owners as opposed to small-scale private investment; and expediting the approval process. The speed with which the Department of Economic Affairs seems to have agreed in principle to these prescriptions is noteworthy, as is the presentation of large-scale PPPs as a monolith – the only feasible way for India to meet growing infrastructure needs in the Eleventh Plan (Department of Economic Affairs 2007).

Establishing a strategy for PPPs is not limited to infrastructure projects. In 2002, the Working Group on Public–Private Partnership was established under the Prime Minister's Office, through which the PPP Sub-Group on Social Sector was established in 2003. This sub-group was tasked with exploring the feasibility of PPPs in social-sector development, including elementary education, despite hesitation in the wider literature on the suitability of such strategies in delivering services intertwined with basic human rights (Burgos 2004).

Consistent with its neo-liberal tone, the report of the PPP Sub-Group on Social Sector posits PPPs not only as more effective and efficient than the classically characterised lumbered bureaucracy, but as empowering mechanisms against an essentially oppressive state with 'its origin[s] in the general distrust of bureaucracy and the oppressiveness of state. Involvement of community, family neighborhoods and voluntary organizations under PPP is observed to have led to empowerment of citizens' (Planning Commission 2004: 3). Yet, rather than a focus on citizens, the report's rhetoric addresses the concerns of 'customers' in accessing basic social services. Instead of using PPPs as a way to hold the state accountable to oppressive or exclusionary mechanisms in accessing essential services, the benefits are expressed as a 'clear customer focus for enhanced social services' (Planning Commission 2004: 5) shrouded in classic neo-liberal terminology of greater cost-effectiveness, higher productivity, accelerated delivery, and recovery of user charges.

Furthermore, the report uncritically accepts that budgetary allocations 'will fall short of the requirements' (Planning Commission 2004: 15) to meet the Millennium Development Goals (MDGs) and other development targets to justify the expansion of PPPs rather than questioning the underfunding of social sectors by the state. In education, the PPP Sub-Group proposes using PPPs to resolve the well-known problem of teacher absenteeism and credible inspections as 'an alternative to the traditional approach of providing services through in-house facilities. Community participation through supervision of schools and involvement of non-profit service agencies in providing social services is being increasingly favoured and encouraged by the governments' (Planning Commission 2004: 15). This suggestion is taken forward in the Eleventh Plan Approach Paper: 'For locally delivered services, such as elementary education ... more active supervision by the PRIs [*panchayati raj* institutions] can make a difference ... Civil society organizations can play a major role in assisting PRIs in this area' (Planning Commission 2006b: 102).[3]

While there may well be a need for some form of partnership with non-state actors, the rate at which PPPs in social sectors have been introduced as a feasible strategy for inclusive development prohibits a concerted examination of their consequences. Sarangi's analysis, though positive about PPPs generally, reveals that their introduction is linked to the fact that 'what ought [to] have been achieved incrementally over the years [has become] an almost impossible task' (Sarangi 2002: 267) due to persistently low government prioritisation and disinvestment. Thus, similar to the thrust behind the New Economic Policy, political expedience may be the main reason behind the push towards PPPs in social sectors. This is despite lessons emerging from countries with longer histories of PPP-friendly institutional frameworks that large-scale PPP arrangements are not only more risky for the public sector as there are fewer actors to bear the risk, but also that they operate with vested interests against those of the public, can lead to more complicated regulatory frameworks not fewer, and that they have the potential of becoming 'abusive' if the stronger partner dominates (Coulson 2005; van Marrewijk *et al.* 2008).

PPP strategies are not without controversy in the public debate in India. The Eleventh Plan Approach Paper seems to suggest a public-relations exercise to garner public support for PPPs: 'create credible PPP projects that evoke a positive public response ... The key to making PPPs acceptable is to create an environment where PPPs are seen to be a way of attracting private money into public projects, not putting public resources into private projects' (Planning Commission 2006b: 41). Perhaps this is why in education, interventions by the relatively less contentious NGOs, voluntary organisations, and community organisations is stressed, and that of private for-profit organisations is ignored, despite the wider acceptance in government circles that a slew of for-profit 'low-fee private' schools targeting disadvantaged groups have emerged in recent years because of inadequate government provision (Srivastava 2008).

The 'PPP mode' in education

The analysis of PPPs in education is complicated by a lack of clarification of the models proposed by the Government of India and the myriad of models in the literature. The most common in the literature on education are contracting models (LaRocque 2006; Patrinos *et al.* 2009). According to LaRocque (2006: 3), 'Contracting involves a government agency entering into an agreement with a private provider to procure a service, or a bundle of education services, in exchange for regular payments'. A slight variation of this is Patrinos *et al.*'s (2009: 9) definition from the World Bank as 'the process whereby a government procures education or education-related services of a defined quantity and quality at an agreed price from a specific provider'. This is distinct from the traditional design and build, operations and maintenance, lease–purchase, build–own–transfer, and build–own–operate models in the infrastructure literature on PPPs.[4]

Throughout the Eleventh Plan discussion on education, there is repeated reference to the vagaries of what is termed 'the PPP mode' in establishing and providing some facilities and services, without clear articulation of whether contracting, traditional, or other PPP models are proposed. Reference to the nebulous PPP mode is invoked in: establishing 2500 model secondary schools, providing incentives to upgrade the quality of government secondary schools and polytechnics, building 700 new polytechnics, upgrading and building 1000 new Industrial Training Institutes (ITIs), and providing 'useful' teacher training in District Institutes of Education and Training. Furthermore, perhaps for the first time in education in India, direct corporate-sector involvement is mentioned particularly in relation to ITIs and industry demand-led technical education, constituting a dramatic shift in the conceptualisation of education delivery and in direct response to India's technologically driven economic goals for the Eleventh Plan. However, the call for corporate involvement in establishing some of the model schools is most controversial, given regulations prohibiting private profit-making entities from running schools in most Indian states, and foreshadows a general penchant towards privatisation under the guise of PPPs with a decreased role for the state in education as discussed below.

Conceptualising the role of the state as financier, manager, and regulator

Given the insistence on redefining the role of the state in the Tenth and Eleventh Plans, and on PPPs as viable mechanisms to restructure its functions in the delivery of education, the primary focus of this analysis is to explicitly analyse the consequences for the state in light of proposed strategies and purported claims. Greenaway (1991) distinguishes three roles of the state in examining the delivery of merit goods such as education in a context of changing public and private arrangements. The basic assumption is that regardless of the type of private intervention in the delivery of merit goods, government intervention is desirable, as without it there will be inequities of access eventually leading to negative social consequences. Thus, in introducing private actors for the delivery of public goods, he asserts: 'Controversy then surrounds the appropriate form [of] intervention – should the state act as regulator, financier or provider?' (Greenaway 1991: 1254).

The distinction in state roles above is prevalent in the general literature on PPPs. However, for the purposes of this contribution, the roles of the state as regulator, financier, and *manager* were examined. This is a slight revision to Greenaway's articulation because, in addition to financier and regulator, the role of the state as manager has traditionally been prevalent in Indian policy documents and in the conceptualisation of education delivery in the bureaucracy.

The Eleventh Plan Approach Paper opens by articulating the need to: 'Redefin[e] the role of the Government to reflect the changed circumstances facing the economy [as] an important aspect of future strategy' (Planning Commission 2006b: 2). However, the beginnings of a redefined role for the state are visible in the Tenth Plan, which suggests a diminished role given private-sector development in India:

> *An all-pervasive Government role may have been necessary at a stage where private sector capabilities were undeveloped, but the situation has changed dramatically ... India now has a strong and vibrant private sector. The public sector is much less dominant than it used to be in many sectors and its relative position is likely to decline further as*

A Pocket Guide to Risk Assessment and Management in Mental Health

Risk assessment and risk management are top of every mental health organisation's agenda. This updated and expanded new edition provides an informative and practical guide to the process of undertaking a risk assessment, arriving at a risk formulation and developing a risk management plan.

Covering everything a practitioner may have to think about when undertaking risk assessments in an accessible, logical form, the second edition of *A Pocket Guide to Risk Assessment and Management in Mental Health* includes new and expanded content on: risk formulation; working in forensic settings; specific mental health disorders; models of suicide and self-harm; and triage. It features practice recommendations rooted in the latest theory and evidence base, clinical tip boxes, tables, diagrams and case examples, along with samples of authentic dialogue which demonstrate ways to formulate questions and think about complex problems with the person being assessed. A series of accompanying videos, professionally made and based on actual case studies, are available on a companion website, further illustrating key risk assessment and management skills.

This concise guidebook is designed for all mental health professionals, and professionals-in-training. It will also be a useful reference for all healthcare practitioners who regularly come into contact with people experiencing mental health problems.

Chris Hart is an independent nurse consultant, educator, facilitator and trainer, writer, film maker and academic. His specialist area of work now is risk assessment and risk management within the prison system, but he still works closely with mental health and non mental health NHS trusts and organisations to educate, train and develop staff in all aspects of risk assessment and management, as well as undertaking developmental work with senior nurses, clinicians and managers. He was previously a Senior Lecturer at Kingston University and St George's, University of London, UK and nurse consultant for South West London and St George's Mental Health NHS Trust.

ACHIEVING EDUCATION FOR ALL THROUGH PUBLIC-PRIVATE PARTNERSHIPS?

Government ownership in many existing public sector organisations is expected to decline substantially. (Planning Commission 2002a: 7)

Cognisant of the controversy surrounding such a position, the Planning Commission was quick to add: 'This is not to say that government has no role to play, or only a minimalist role, in promoting development. On the contrary, Government has a very important role indeed, but a different one from that envisaged in the past. There are many areas, e.g. the social sectors, where its role will clearly have to expand' (2002a: 7). While the assertion that achieving India's development goals in education 'requires a greatly expanded role for the state ... [and] deliberate public intervention' (Planning Commission 2006b:102) is echoed in the Eleventh Plan Approach Paper, the education working groups were mandated 'to wherever feasible, [make] suggestions for public–private partnership' (Planning Commission 2006a: 6).

This is taken one step further in the Eleventh Plan, where an adoption of privatisation as the preferred strategy for education is clearly visible: 'In the liberalized global economy where there is a pursuit for achieving excellence, the legitimate role of private providers of quality education not only needs to be recognized, but also encouraged' (Planning Commission 2008b: 8). This is despite the recognition that the ultra-poor are largely excluded from private schools: 'there is ... no evidence to show that enrolments in these schools are additional. Only those who can afford to pay apparently opt for these schools and their average enrolment is much lower than that in the aided and government schools' (Planning Commission 2008b: 15).

While privatisation may seem initially at odds with a position that purports to favour an expanded role for the state, it is consistent with the paradigm shift favouring such policy prescriptions since India's post-liberalisation boom of the 1990s. The government's iteration in successive Tenth and Eleventh Plan documents that India's economically favourable climate and more developed private sector means a changed but not necessarily smaller role for the state (Planning Commission 2002a: 7; 2006b: 90), is undoubtedly a response to alleviate fears that the post-liberalisation period led to a retreat of the state in social sectors including education (Chowdhury and Bose 2004; Kumar 2008). The Eleventh Plan Approach Paper is explicit about these concerns:

One concern that is sometimes expressed is that economic policy is moving in a direction that involves a dismantling or erosion of the role of the state in the development process ... the Paper explicitly recognizes that in particular circumstances, the objective of accelerating growth and making it more inclusive cannot be achieved without a very active, and in many respects expanded, role for the state in some areas. However, this does not mean an expansion of the state in every area, nor should it be interpreted as underplaying the role of the private sector. In fact the role of the government needs to be restructured. We need to reduce direct intervention in, and commitments of scarce public resources to, areas where the private sector operating under competitive markets can deliver. Public resources that would otherwise be absorbed in these sectors are best directed to the social sectors and rural infrastructure where expansion is sorely needed and which cannot be left solely to market forces. (Planning Commission 2006b: 90–1)

Given that education is a 'thrust area' for the Eleventh Plan and the well-versed arguments that its particularities as a merit good exclude it from being 'left solely to market forces' as noted above, it is reasonable to assume that education is an area in which we should see an expanded role for the state in proposed Eleventh Plan strategies, consistent with the government's own argument. Of course, the role of the state is not as clear cut as financier, manager, and regulator, with certain responsibilities falling between these areas and others outside them. However, the framework is nonetheless useful in examining whether proposed

PPP strategies in education indeed position the state in a strengthened role. The analysis will show that despite assertions to the contrary, the proposed strategies result in a diminished role in all three areas.

The state as financier

While there is a suggestion to increase public spending in education to 6 per cent of GDP in the Eleventh Plan Approach Paper (Planning Commission 2006b: 57) from the more typical 3 per cent, a benchmark set in 1968 by the Kothari Commission review of education, this target is merely mentioned in the Eleventh Plan, which states that current public expenditure is only 3.6 per cent of GDP (Planning Commission 2008a: 17). It is not unreasonable to question whether the target is unrealistic 40 years on when, as the Tenth and Eleventh Plan documents note, there are increasing numbers of children entering education (including those from poorer groups whose needs require additional funding), with twin goals of ensuring elementary education coverage under *Sarva Shiksha Abhiyan* (the government's national Education for All programme), and 'progressively rais[ing] the minimum level of education to high school or Class X level' (Planning Commission 2006b: 59).

Surely, aims to add two additional years of schooling as the minimum education level, improve quality with quantity, and increased enrolments necessitate funding beyond levels set in 1968. This is particularly so if we are to take seriously the government's commitment to schemes for inclusive growth under the Eleventh Plan, such as: residential schools for minorities and girls, targeted scholarships, expansion of existing school places, addition of new secondary places, upgrading facilities, and significant expansion of secondary, technical/vocational, and higher education. It is further questionable if the new Plan aims to compensate for the generally accepted claim that there has been underinvestment in education over the last few decades (Chowdhury and Bose 2004).

Tilak (2008) notes that while the increase to education in the 2008–09 Union Budget was five times higher than in the Tenth Plan in nominal terms, the actual increase of roughly Rs. 57 billion (approximately $1.36 billion)[5] from the 2007–08 budget is not that high given the expansion of priorities in all education sectors. While projected allocation to education from 7.68 per cent of the total allocation in the Tenth Plan is increased to 19.29 per cent in the Eleventh Plan (Planning Commission 2008a: 45), actual expenditure on education is another matter. Tilak (2008) finds a disturbing trend: public expenditure in education at the combined central and state levels *decreased* between 2000–01 and 2007–08 (see Table 1).

The commitment of the state to its role as financier is further questioned when the Eleventh Plan Approach Paper states that: 'In education we *may* need an increase of at least 0.5 per cent of GDP *by the end* of the 11th Plan period to cover the requirements of expanding secondary education, plus an additional 0.25 per cent of GDP for higher education' (Planning Commission 2006b: 87–8, emphases added). Both the tentativeness of this recommendation and the extremely low increase by the end of the five years, amounting to just 3.59 per cent of GDP

Table 1: Public expenditure in education

Expenditure in education (combined central and state levels)	2000–01	2007–08
Percentage of GDP	3.19	2.84
Percentage of total expenditure	11.3	10.2
Percentage of social-sector expenditure	50.8	45.3

Source: Tilak (2008: 50).

based on 2007–08 estimates (only 0.4 per cent higher than 2000–01 levels), falls well below the 6 per cent GDP expenditure target. Expenditure at the 6 per cent target is only possible if the combined 0.75 per cent of GDP above is allocated every year over the entire Eleventh Plan period. Thus, in practice, an expanded role of the state in education financing is not immediately apparent in the Eleventh Plan documents.

It may be that the aim is to partly fill the gap in government expenditure by large-scale PPPs in education as foreshadowed in the Tenth Plan Approach Paper, which noted that: 'An important channel for mobilising resources for development, particularly for social sectors, namely Externally Aided Projects ... and direct funding of projects (i.e. outside budgetary flows) by the NGOs has not been sufficiently integrated with our planning process ... an important source ... in the third world context, is not being adequately tapped' (Planning Commission 2001: 17). Perhaps mega-projects, similar to the relatively successful World Bank District Primary Education Project of the 1990s, are being considered. However, there are no associated recommendations on the amount of funding that would be required through large-scale external projects, or how they would be allocated.

The state as manager

Instead of a concerted strategy on strengthening or improving the role of the state in education management, the Tenth and Eleventh Plan documents stress the need to devolve further responsibility in areas such as quality assurance (particularly in elementary education) and monitoring to decentralised governance structures or *panchayats*, community-based organisations (without specifying what these are and how they would be involved), and undefined 'citizens' education committees', which we may assume are offshoots of village education committees already in existence. Given India's vast territory, regional differences, and differing levels of development, decentralisation is a relatively desirable strategy for education management if it is done in a planned manner to strengthen dysfunctional public institutions. However, the analysis here is in support of Tilak's assertion that:

> *some governments find it convenient to use decentralisation as a mechanism of abdication of its own responsibilities of educating the people. The methods of decentralisation we have adopted in the recent years aimed at mobilising more and more non-governmental resources for free elementary education on the one hand, and to dilute, if not completely to abdicate the responsibilities of the state – central and state governments in education. For example, the village education committees and the like are seen as a substitute to the school inspectorate system of the government, which is made to disappear.* (Tilak 2007: 3874).

It is difficult to dismiss Tilak's concerns when the Eleventh Plan Approach Paper is framed around a defeated acceptance that government management structures have failed to ensure quality, particularly regarding teachers' performance and absentee rates in elementary education. The Eleventh Plan Approach Paper suggests:

> *Empowering* panchayats *and citizens' education committees to oversee teacher performance will help increase accountability. The management of schools should move away from the highly centralized system of today to a more decentralized one based on local school management committees. These committees comprising of parents and other well-educated people from the neighbourhood will be accountable to the institutions of local self-government.* (Planning Commission 2006b: 59)

While the problem of absentee teachers – particularly in rural state schools – is well known, state inspectorates are conspicuous by their absence in the discussion. As Tilak (2007) notes above, this is at odds with what one would expect if the state is committed to strengthening its role. One may expect some discussion on the reinvigorated role of inspectorates and how they may be improved by cooperating with local governance structures and/or community organisations. Instead, throughout the Tenth and Eleventh Plan documents there is an insistence on devolving the monitoring and accountability of essential functions to private actors such as local citizens and NGOs, under the guise of empowerment, without any indication of how these actors would be supported in undertaking these responsibilities or what role the state would play. In fact, the seeds for increasing education-management responsibilities to the private sector were sown in the Tenth Plan in terms of monetary and material contributions, as well as its role in improving quality 'though effective management of the system' (Planning Commission 2002b: 39).

The neo-liberal belief that only the private sector can increase quality has explicitly manifested itself in the Eleventh Plan even at the elementary/basic levels of education as: 'A more liberal approach on the part of State Governments on allowing private schools to be set up to meet the large unmet demand for quality education' (Planning Commission 2008a: 17). In addition, the Planning Commission proposes the creation of 6000 model schools, 40 per cent of which would be managed through PPPs, without a clear indication of the PPP model proposed for the 2500 schools in question or the roles that public and non-state actors would play. The explicit mention of the corporate sector is particularly indicative of the greater paradigm shift:

> *about 2500 schools would be set up through PPP ... with emphasis on geographical, demographic, gender, and social equity. These schools will be managed and run by involving corporates, philanthropic foundations, endowments, educational trusts, and reputed private providers.* (Planning Commission 2008b: 17)

The Eleventh Plan acknowledged that there was increased private management of recognised secondary schools (Planning Commission 2008b: 8). Given aggravated equity effects of increased private provision, a disturbing trend is revealed in the Eleventh Plan: 'the share of government and local body schools ... has shown a declining trend with private unaided schools showing an increase from 15 per cent in 1993–94 to 24 per cent in 2001–02 and further to 30 per cent in 2004–05' (Planning Commission 2008b: 15). Despite calls for equitable and inclusive access to secondary education and the realisation that only those who can afford to pay enrol in private schools, the Eleventh Plan stresses that the 'massive expansion required in secondary education calls for an expansion in both public schools as well as private aided and unaided schools' (Planning Commission 2008b: 18). However, there are equity concerns about both types of private management in the literature.

Private-aided schools are a long-standing institutionalised form of PPPs in education from colonial times (Kumar 2008). They are privately managed, but the majority of their funding comes from state grants-in-aid and some through direct household fees to school committees. There is an emerging perspective that government funding of private-aided schools aggravates equity effects for two reasons (De *et al.* 2002; Kumar 2008; Panchamukhi and Mehrotra 2005). First, state budgets are further constrained by diverting funds into the private-aided sector which could be released to finance the state sector. In fact, certain states have discontinued establishing new private-aided schools because they cannot afford to support them. Second, since private-aided schools are not generally attended by the poorest children, states subsidise a sector that can otherwise be self-financed. Nonetheless, private management of schooling, particularly in secondary education, is encouraged:

ACHIEVING EDUCATION FOR ALL THROUGH PUBLIC-PRIVATE PARTNERSHIPS?

At present, private aided and unaided schools account for 58% of the total number of secondary schools and 25% of the student population. The 11th Plan will have to find sufficient resources ... and evolve strategies to significantly expand the number of places in secondary schools, including expansion of intake by private schools. (Planning Commission 2006b: 59–60)

However, as with private-aided schools, the rise of recognised and unrecognised privately managed unaided schools is a cause of concern in the wider literature (Kumar 2008; Srivastava 2008; Tilak 2007). Private unaided schools are privately funded and managed, include a heterogeneous array of fee structures (from elite, high-fee to modest, low-fee schools), and a wide mix of management bodies (philanthropic organisations, NGOs, private entrepreneurs). Although it is unconstitutional for schools to make a profit, many private unaided schools do (Srivastava 2008). The Eleventh Plan Approach Paper acknowledges that a number of families have 'voted with their feet' and exited the state system because they are dissatisfied: 'Clearly with state governments finding it difficult to fund public secondary education, the proportion of private schools has gone up and the relatively better off sections of the population have virtually stopped sending their children to public schools' (Planning Commission 2006b: 59).[6]

However, this assessment of the private schooling phenomenon in India is simplistic. First, it is not just 'better off' groups who have exited the public system. Low-fee private schools targeting disadvantaged communities have sprouted in rural and urban areas alike, particularly since the late 1990s, and are serving first-generation learners and daily wage earning households (De *et al.* 2002; Srivastava 2008). Second, it is not just in secondary education that we see this trend, but in elementary education as well (De *et al.* 2002; Srivastava 2008; Tilak 2007). Third, while recognised unaided schools should have gained recognition from central or state boards of education having met quality assurance norms, in practice many, particularly low-fee private schools, gained recognition through complex sets of informal rules and corrupt practices (Srivastava 2008; Tooley and Dixon 2005). The first two issues point to aggravated equity concerns and deficiencies in the government's otherwise glorified Education for All (EFA) achievements. The third seriously questions whether the government is truly 'Recognizing that the provision of good quality education is the most important equalizer in society' (Planning Commission 2006b: 99), when schools of comparable good quality for lower-income households do not exist.

Thus, it is not entirely clear why there is a policy preference that 'the expansion of private schools should be welcomed' (Planning Commission 2006b: 60) instead of actively increasing the quality of state provision. This seems to go against the spirit of EFA principles as well as the Government of India's strategy for inclusive growth. However, it does seem indicative of the general paradigm shift. While the Tenth Plan Approach Paper states that the introduction of user fees for essential public services is not desired (Planning Commission 2001: 17), the Eleventh Plan Approach Paper states on the one hand that 'A basic objective of the 11th Plan must be to extend essential basic services ... to those who are deprived of them' (Planning Commission 2006b: 99), and on the other that, 'It is also not possible for the Central and state governments to resist raising user charges and bear the burden of rising costs in a number of public services' (Planning Commission 2006b: 89). In short, favouring a policy of increased private management of schools in addition to the other management issues mentioned above are not indicative of a strong role of the state as manager of education.

The state as regulator

The commitment to an expanded or strengthened role of the state is seriously questioned when we examine its role in regulation – because of the silence on the issue. It is generally accepted that the myriad regulations governing education, and particularly private education, are regarded as inefficient and inappropriate. Thus, while one would not wish to see further regulation, it would be reasonable to expect some discussion on reforms of existing regulation that would lead to more comprehensive, efficient, and effective delivery of education to those who remain excluded from the current period of growth. Furthermore, given that PPPs in education are lauded with an expanded role for NGOs and voluntary organisations, it is surprising that there is no substantial discussion of creating an effective regulatory framework for transacting with them despite noted difficulties of working with them in the past. The Tenth Plan mid-term review noted particular difficulties related to the implementation of programmes by NGOs with Government of India funds. These were: (1) a lack of effective mechanisms for monitoring and evaluating their activities; (2) an apparent duplication of government activities in many cases; and (3) lack of information at the state level on activities conducted (Planning Commission 2005: 57).

Despite this, neither the working group reports nor the Eleventh Plan address how the regulatory framework may evolve to take these issues into consideration when working with an expanded array of private actors. The only regulatory recommendation for education appears in the Tenth Plan mid-term appraisal as: 'suitable taxation and land policies, concessional loan programmes ... to encourage the expansion of secondary schools by NGOs, trusts, and registered societies in the private sector' (Planning Commission 2005: 58). Particular regulatory issues relating to PPPs in education – such as protecting the public interest and the effective monitoring of non-state actors – are missing, even though they are normally considered in hard infrastructure-sector projects.

Other direct references to the regulatory framework for education in the Tenth and Eleventh Plan documents come in the form of expediting the opening of private schools, particularly in secondary education or in areas with disadvantaged populations including girls (Planning Commission 2001, 2006a, 2006c). This trend seems to have been set in the Tenth Plan Approach Paper: 'Laws, rules and procedures for private, cooperative and NPO [non-profit organisation] supply of education must be modernised and simplified so that honest and sincere individuals and organisations can set up universities, colleges and schools. Oppressive controls on fees, teacher salaries, infrastructure and staff strength must be eliminated' (Planning Commission 2001: 38). The desired expedience in these prescriptions somewhat explains the general increase in private schools and why, as previously mentioned, some low-fee private schools in particular are granted recognition without meeting set norms in the guise of meeting EFA targets (Srivastava 2008). Nonetheless, much like its role as financier or manager, these prescriptions do not point to a strengthened role of the state as regulator.

Concluding remarks

While on the one hand the Eleventh Plan Approach Paper asserts that there should be 'a greatly expanded role for the state' in education (Planning Commission 2006b: 101), the Eleventh Plan states that 'the legitimate role of private providers of quality education not only needs to be recognized, but also encouraged' (Planning Commission 2008b: 8). The aim of this contribution is not to make an *a priori* judgement for or against the role that non-state actors may play in meeting education targets in India. However, it is the 'schizophrenic' approach towards their exact roles and that of the state, and the lack of clarity on what is meant by delivering education 'in PPP mode' with which it takes issue. In particular, the lack of clarity on the role assumed by the state as a result of pushing forward ill-defined PPP strategies complicates a nuanced understanding of their potential effects on education delivery.

Burgos (2004: 56) reminds us that: 'The way in which partnership is construed has political and ethical consequences that may appear overlooked in the rhetorical construction of reforms'. Despite these concerns, the notion of partnerships with private actors has been uncritically absorbed in the Indian policy landscape, with little attention to the implications for education delivery. As this analysis on the role of the state as financier, manager, and regulator in education has shown, proposed strategies in the Tenth and Eleventh Plan documents are little more than modes of privatising education, and result in a diminished role of the state despite assertions to the contrary. Therefore, the challenge at the heart of the institutional context for education delivery lies in deconstructing the conception of 'partnership' as a justifying principle that is seemingly neutral, normatively correct, and a viable solution for severely resource-constrained countries to achieve EFA goals quickly. This marks a crucial disjoint if the rhetoric of resource constraint is uncritically applied to the rapid expansion of private actors in education in the Indian context.

India, by its own admission and economic analysis, is no longer a country under serious economic-resource constraint (Planning Commission 2005: 1; 2006b: 3–5), or at least the level of economic constraint that characterised its development trajectory until now. With an economic growth rate in GDP of about 8 per cent over the Tenth Plan period, a targeted average growth in GDP of 9–10 per cent over the Eleventh Plan period (Planning Commission 2006b: 11), and more than tripling its foreign reserves in just five years to $165.3 billion at the end of the Tenth Plan period (Planning Commission 2006b: 4), one must seriously question the impetus behind the acceptance of privatised strategies disguised as PPPs for education expansion as a monolith resting on the logic of scarce public resources for basic services, particularly when India simultaneously projects itself as one of the fastest growing and largest economies in the world.[7]

The economic optimism with which India projects itself internationally should translate into a firm commitment to meet the basic needs of its citizens. Thus, India's economic climate should favour higher levels of financing for education and other essential services, not stagnating levels or minimal increases. Furthermore, education management arrangements and regulation should be reassessed with a view to promoting sustainable and equitable access not only to basic, but increasingly, to secondary and higher education for groups that are most at risk from being excluded. While this does not necessarily mean full state control of all aspects of education, it also does not mean an uncritical acceptance of any strategy using the discourse of partnership as 'a universal – almost a neutral – value upon which all specific agents and governments in general, would agree' (Burgos 2004: 58). Sadly, there is little indication that sufficient analyses on the implications of such strategies for education delivery have been conducted in the Indian policy landscape.

Notes

1. Documentary data appear as references authored by the Planning Commission. With a change in government from the Bharatiya Janata Party to the Congress Party in 2004, the Planning Commission was reconstituted. All activities from the Tenth Plan mid-term appraisal onwards were conducted under the chairmanship of the new Prime Minister, Manmohan Singh. Changes for the Eleventh Plan were envisioned as a phased approach, beginning with the Tenth Plan mid-term appraisal conceived as laying the groundwork for the Eleventh Plan.
2. The working groups were: Development of Education of Scheduled Caste/Scheduled Tribe/Minorities/Girls and other Disadvantaged Groups; Technical Education; Higher Education; Language Development and Book Promotion; Secondary and Vocational Education; Sports and Physical Education; Adolescents' Development and Sports and Youth Affairs; Basic Education and Literacy; and Art and Culture. The steering committees were: Secondary, Higher and Technical Education; Youth Affairs

and Sports; and Art and Culture – see http://planningcommission.nic.in/plans/planrel/11thf.htm (retrieved 20 November 2008).
3. *Panchayati raj* is a system of self-governance at the village level. Under the 73rd Amendment Act, 1992, the Constitution of India provides a framework for this decentralised system of governance.
4. Because of space constraints, these are not discussed here. See Patrinos *et al.* (2009) for a review in education.
5. US$ 1 = approximately Rs. 42 (June 2008).
6. Since the time of initial writing, the Government of India passed the Right to Education Bill in August 2009 with a provision reserving 25 per cent of seats in private schools for socially and economically disadvantaged children. It remains to be seen whether schools implement this at the local level. Promoting further exit from the state sector, it is unlikely that there will be a positive quality effect on state schools.
7. Since the time of writing, initial estimates indicate that India was relatively insulated from the impact of the global recession of 2008–2009. The average estimate of national income by the Economic Advisory Council to the Prime Minister suggests that the GDP for the economy is likely to have grown by 7.2 per cent in 2009–10 (Government of India 2010: 5), and further, that the economy will likely grow by 8.2 per cent in 2010–11 and by 9 per cent in 2011–12 (Government of India 2010: 6).

References

Burgos, R. Buenfil (2004) 'Partnership as a floating and empty signifier within educational policies: the Mexican case', in Barry M. Franklin, Marianne N. Bloch, and Thomas Popkewitz (eds.) *Educational Partnerships and the State: The Paradoxes of Governing Schools, Children, and Families*, New York, NY: Palgrave Macmillan.
Chowdhury, Subhanil and Prasenjit Bose (2004) 'Expenditure on education in India: a short note', *Social Scientist* 32 (7/8): 85–9.
Coulson, Andrew (2005) 'A plague on all your partnerships: theory and practice in regeneration', *The International Journal of Public Sector Management* 18 (2): 151–63.
De, Anuradha, Manabi Majumdar, Meera Samson, and Clare Noronha (2002) 'Private schools and universal elementary education', in R. Govinda (ed.) *India Education Report: A Profile of Basic Education*, New Delhi: Oxford University Press.
Department of Economic Affairs (2007) 'Public Private Partnerships: Creating an Enabling Environment for State Projects', New Delhi: Department of Economic Affairs, Ministry of Finance, Government of India.
Gouri, Geeta (1997) 'The new economic policy and privatization in India', *Journal of Asian Economics* 8 (3): 455–79.
Government of India (2010) 'Review of the Economy 2009/10', New Delhi: Economic Advisory Council to the Prime Minister, Government of India, available at http://pmindia.nic.in/ReviewEconomy_2009-10.pdf (retrieved 6 April 2010).
Greenaway, David (1991) 'Markets and quasi markets in social services: editorial note', *The Economic Journal* 101 (408): 1254–5.
Kumar, Krishna (2008) 'Partners in education?', *Economic and Political Weekly* 43 (3): 8–11.
LaRocque, Norman (2006) *Contracting for the Delivery of Education Services. A Typology and International Examples*, Wellington: Education Forum.
Naib, Sudhir (2004) *Disinvestment in India: Policies, Procedures, Practices*, New Delhi: Sage.
Panchamukhi, P. R. and Santosh Mehrotra (2005) 'Assessing public and private provision of elementary education in India', in Santosh Mehrotra, P. R. Panchmukhi, Ranjana Srivastava, and Ravi Srivastava, *Universalizing Elementary Education in India: Uncaging the 'Tiger' Economy*, New Delhi: Oxford University Press.
Patrinos, Harry Anthony, Felipe Barera-Osorio, and Juliana Guáqueta (2009) *The Role and Impact of Public-Private Partnerships in Education*, Washington, DC: World Bank.
Planning Commission (2001) 'Approach Paper to the Tenth Five Year Plan (2002–2007)', New Delhi: Planning Commission, Government of India.

Planning Commission (2002a) *Tenth Five Year Plan (2002–2007), Vol. I: Dimensions and Strategies*, New Delhi: Planning Commission, Government of India.
Planning Commission (2002b) *Tenth Five Year Plan (2002–2007), Vol. II: Sectoral Policies and Programmes*, New Delhi: Planning Commission, Government of India.
Planning Commission (2004) 'Public Private Partnership: Report of the PPP Sub-Group on Social Sector', New Delhi: Planning Commission, Government of India.
Planning Commission (2005) 'Mid-term Appraisal of the Tenth Five Year Plan (2002–2007)', New Delhi: Planning Commission, Government of India.
Planning Commission (2006a) 'Report of Working Group on Elementary Education and Literacy for the 11th Five Year Plan', unpublished report, New Delhi: Planning Commission, Government of India.
Planning Commission (2006b) *Towards Faster and More Inclusive Growth: An Approach to the 11th Five Year Plan*, Yojana Bhavan, New Delhi: Planning Commission, Government of India.
Planning Commission (2006c) 'Working Group Report of the Development of Education of SC/ST/Minorities/Girls and Other Disadvantaged Groups for 11th Five Year Plan (2007–2012)', New Delhi: Planning Commission/Ministry of Human Resource Development, Government of India.
Planning Commission (2008a) *Eleventh Five Year Plan (2007–2012), Vol. I: Inclusive Growth*, New Delhi: Oxford University Press.
Planning Commission (2008b) *Eleventh Five Year Plan (2007–2012), Vol. II: Social Sector*, New Delhi: Oxford University Press.
Sarangi, Debendranath (2002) 'Infrastructure development: a public–private partnership in India', *International Social Science Journal* 54 (172): 267–71.
Sengupta, Mitu (2008) 'How the state changed its mind: power, politics and the origins of India's market reforms', *Economic and Political Weekly* 43 (21): 35–42.
Srivastava, Prachi (2008) 'The shadow institutional framework: towards a new institutional understanding of an emerging model of private schooling in India', *Research Papers in Education* 23 (4): 451–75.
Tilak, Jandhyala B. G. (2007) 'Inclusive growth and education: on the approach to the Eleventh Plan', *Economic and Political Weekly* 42 (38): 3872–7.
Tilak, Jandhyala B. G. (2008) 'Education in the 2008–09 Union Budget', *Economic and Political Weekly* 43 (28): 49–56.
Tooley, James and Pauline Dixon (2005) 'An inspector calls: the regulation of "budget" private schools in Hyderabad, Andhra Pradesh, India', *International Journal of Educational Development* 25 (3): 269–85.
van Marrewijk, Alfons, Stewart R. Clegg, Tyrone S. Pitsis, and Marcel Veenswijk (2008) 'Managing public–private megaprojects: paradoxes, complexity, and project design', *International Journal of Project Management* 26 (6): 591–600.

Madrasas as partners in education provision: the South Asian experience

Masooda Bano

Madrasas, *Islamic schools, are prominent non-state education providers in South Asia, especially for hard-to-reach children in Muslim communities. Recent attention on* madrasas *has, however, focused on their alleged links with militancy, overshadowing analysis of their role as education providers. Based on a comparative analysis of the state-led* madrasa-*modernisation programmes in Bangladesh, India, and Pakistan, which aimed to introduce secular subjects in the* madrasa *curriculum, this contribution argues that* madrasas *can be important partners to advance Education for All. The forging of such a partnership is, however, contingent on the state making a serious financial commitment to the reform programme and building a trusting relationship with the religious elite.*

Les madrasas *comme partenaires des services d'éducation : l'expérience de l'Asie du Sud*
Les madrasas, *écoles islamiques, sont parmi les importants prestataires non publics de services d'éducation en Asie du Sud, en particulier pour les enfants difficiles à scolariser des communautés musulmanes. Or, l'attention récemment accordée aux* madrasas *s'est concentrée sur leurs liens allégués avec le militantisme, ce qui a quelque peu éclipsé l'analyse de leur rôle comme prestataires de services d'éducation. Sur la base d'une analyse comparative des programmes de modernisation des* madrasas *menés par l'État au Bangladesh, en Inde et au Pakistan, qui visaient à introduire des sujets laïques dans le programme scolaire des* madrasas, *cette contribution soutient que ces dernières peuvent être des partenaires importantes dans les efforts vers la réalisation du but de l'Éducation pour tous. L'édification d'un tel partenariat dépendra, toutefois, de l'engagement sérieux de la part de l'État en faveur du programme de réforme et de l'établissement d'une relation de confiance avec l'élite religieuse.*

Madrasas *como parceiras na oferta de educação: a experiência sul-asiática*
As Madrasas, *escolas islâmicas, são importantes provedoras não-estatais de educação no sul da Ásia, especialmente para crianças de difícil acesso em comunidades muçulmanas. A atenção recente sobre as* madrasas, *porém, tem se concentrado em suas supostas conexões com a militância, obscurecendo a análise de seu papel enquanto provedores de educação. Com base em uma análise comparativa dos programas de modernização das* madrasas *coordenados pelo estado em Bangladesh, Índia e Paquistão, que visaram introduzir assuntos seculares no curriculum das* madrasas, *esta contribuição argumenta que as* madrasas *podem ser parceiros importantes para promover a Educação para Todos. A formação de tal parceria, porém, depende do estado assumir um compromisso financeiro sério para o programa de reforma e desenvolver uma relação de confiança com a elite religiosa.*

ACHIEVING EDUCATION FOR ALL THROUGH PUBLIC-PRIVATE PARTNERSHIPS?

Alianzas con las **Madrasas** *para la educación: experiencias del Sur Asiático*

Las escuelas islámicas o madrasas *son importantes proveedoras de educación no estatal en el Sur Asiático, en especial para jóvenes de comunidades musulmanas aisladas. En fechas recientes se ha hablado más de sus supuestos vínculos con corrientes militantes que de su rol como proveedoras de educación. A través de un análisis comparativo de diversos programas de modernización de las* madrasas *impulsados por el Estado en Bangladesh, India y Pakistán, consistentes en la incorporación de materias laicas en los planes de estudio, este ensayo sostiene que las* madrasas *pueden ser aliados importantes para lograr la Educación para Todos. Sin embargo, esta alianza implicaría que el Estado se comprometiera a adjudicar importantes recursos financieros para el programa de reformas y a forjar una relación de confianza con los líderes religiosos.*

Introduction

Since the terrorist attack on the World Trade Center on 11 September 2001, *madrasas*[1] (Islamic schools) in South Asia have been a focus of policy attention because of their alleged links with Islamic militancy (Blanchard 2005; ICG 2002). These concerns have deflected attention from the fact that *madrasas* remain important non-state providers of basic education in most Muslim countries (Hefner and Zaman 2007). South Asia – which hosts two largely Muslim countries, namely Pakistan (98 per cent) and Bangladesh (90 per cent), and an equally large Muslim population in the multi-religious India (12 per cent) – has been no exception: there are 16,000 registered *madrasas* in Pakistan, 9000 in Bangladesh and while no state-recognised data on India *madrasas* is available, all estimates place the figure at several thousand (Nair 2009; Sikand 2004).

Many *madrasas* cater for hard-to-reach children. While more recent studies contradict earlier assumptions that only the poor enrol in *madrasas* (Cockcroft *et al.* 2009; Nelson 2006), by providing free education and boarding, *madrasas* do increase education opportunities for children from low-income families. Further, *madrasas* are particularly effective in enrolling girls in schools in rural Muslim communities (Asadullah and Chaudhury 2007). They thus arguably have the potential to become important partners in helping the state meet Education for All (EFA) targets provided the *madrasa* curriculum incorporates a higher proportion of secular subjects. Despite efforts to introduce secular subjects into *madrasas*, state-led reform programmes have had different levels of success across the three countries. This contribution provides an analysis of the factors that can facilitate or hinder formation of a partnership between the state and *madrasas* to teach secular subjects through the *madrasa* platform.[2]

EFA challenges and potential of *madrasas*

Despite recording relative improvement in education indicators over time, progress towards EFA goals in the three most populated South Asian countries (India, Pakistan, and Bangladesh) remains slow (UNESCO 2008). The weakest performer is Pakistan, which together with Nigeria is expected to contribute one-third of the global total of out-of-school children by 2015, and also has particularly wide gender gaps in enrolment (UNESCO 2008). In all three countries, the inability of the state to ensure quality education for all has created room for non-state actors to play a prominent role, including private providers and NGOs. Development agencies have generally focused on successful NGO models, such as Bangladesh Rural Advancement Committee (BRAC) in Bangladesh, and have supported replication of these low-cost innovative models to reach marginalised groups. They are also increasingly directing attention towards the potential of low-fee private schools to reach the poor. However, little attention has been paid to *madrasas*, which remain prominent actors within the non-profit education sector in most Muslim communities.

Studies suggest that total student population in *madrasas* in India and Pakistan is relatively low, with estimates of 4 per cent of Muslim children in India (Sachar 2006) and less than 1 per cent of the school-age population in Pakistan (Andrabi *et al.* 2005). However, two considerations make *madrasas* significant for policy analysis. First, in terms of absolute numbers, these percentages reflect a large number: in Pakistan, for example, the officially recognised number of students in registered *madrasas* is 1.5 million (GoP 2006). In Bangladesh, according to Ministry of Education data, there are 1.77 million students within the *Aliya* (reformed) *madrasa* system alone, operating across the six divisions of the country. Second, their share in education provision in some instances, such as Pakistan, is larger than that of NGOs (Bano 2008; Cockcroft *et al.* 2009). It is therefore important to understand their potential to become partners in education provision.

Of these three South Asian countries, the *madrasa* education system features most prominently in the state education-sector plan in Bangladesh, where there are two types of *madrasas*: *Aliya* (reformed) and *Qoumi* (unreformed). *Aliya* (reformed) *madrasas* are ones that have registered to receive state support, in return for covering the same secular subjects as taught in secular primary, secondary, and post-secondary schools. They differ from secular schools by accommodating Islamic subjects, and so allocate less time for the teaching of secular subjects. There are over 9000 of these *madrasas* registered with the government's Bangladesh Madrasa Education Board, offering education from primary to Master's levels. The *Qoumi* (unreformed) *madrasas* primarily focus on religious subjects and work completely independently of the government, that is, they neither follow a state-approved curriculum, nor do they receive financial support from the state or are registered with it.

By contrast, in Pakistan, despite state actors debating plans to introduce a reform agenda for *madrasas* as early as 1960s, a *madrasa*-modernisation programme was implemented only in 2002 as a result of official support from the USA. In India, state support to *madrasas* for teaching secular subjects differs among states, with some states providing support through separate *madrasa* boards. The West Bengal Board of Madrasa Education presents one of the most developed *madrasa*-support programmes in India.

In all three countries, the majority of the *madrasas* continue to operate independent of government support and opt to register with *wafaqs* – umbrella organisations of *madrasas*, which can be established in the name of a specific school of Islamic thought. The *wafaqs* have an elected body of representatives and each country has more than one *wafaq*. In Bangladesh, there is estimated to be close to 15,000 *Qoumi* (unreformed) *madrasas*.[3] Wafaq-ul-Madaris Al Arabia, the biggest *wafaq* of *Qoumi* (unreformed) *madrasas* in Bangladesh, has 9000 registered *madrasas*.[4] In Pakistan, over 16,000 *madrasas* are registered with the five state-recognised *wafaqs*.[5]

The Wafaq-ul-Madaris Al Arabia, the largest *wafaq* in Pakistan, has 10,000 *madrasas* registered with it, while Rabata-ul-Madaris Al-Islamia, the most recent *wafaq* to be established there, has over 1000 registered *madrasas*. In West Bengal, Rabata-i-Madaris, the main umbrella organisation of *Kharzai* (unreformed) *madrasas*, has over 550 *madrasas*.[6] These collective platforms have been instrumental in strengthening the bargaining power of *madrasa* leadership *vis-à-vis* the state in each of the countries. It is important to situate the current working of *madrasas* in a historical context to enable a better understanding of the factors that shape the contemporary dynamics of state-led reform programmes. As the next section shows, attempts by the state to reform *madrasas* are not new – some dating back to the immediate post-Independence period.

History of South Asian *madrasas* and state-led reforms

The establishment of a formal *madrasa* education system in the Muslim world is attributed to Nizam-ul-Mulk, a Seljuk Wazir, who established Madrasa Nizami in Baghdad in the eleventh century (Hefner and Zaman 2007). *Madrasa* system in India started emerging from the twelfth century (Sikand 2004), and was consolidated under the Mughal Empire, when *madrasas* became the primary institutions for training the elite for the Muslim courts (Nizami 1983). The *madrasas*, however, remained largely informal in their method of teaching. Teaching was focused around the teacher rather than a fixed curriculum; the teacher chose the relevant text for the student based on the assessment of his interests and calibre (Nizami 1983). On completion of the education cycle, the students' competence was judged by the merit of the scholar who taught them rather than some certificate.

The curriculum had a combination of rationalist (such as mathematics, logic) plus transmitted subjects (those focused on the religious texts) and was very flexible. The establishment of British colonial rule, however, dramatically transformed the role of *madrasa* education in South Asia: by introducing Western educational institutions and replacing Persian with English as the official language, colonial rule made *madrasa* education irrelevant to the needs of the state and the economy. This period led to major shifts within *madrasas*, where the focus of the curriculum shifted from 'this-worldly' to entirely 'other-worldly' emphasis. This period saw the rise of Dar ul Uloom Deoband, a *madrasa* established in the nineteenth century, whose *ulama* (Islamic scholars) consciously responded to the changing context of Indian society under colonial rule by focusing primarily on inculcating personal piety among Muslims (Metcalf 1978). This puritanical school of Islamic thought soon led to the emergence of sister *madrasas* and today this school of thought has the largest number of *madrasas* in South Asia.

Deliberations on *madrasa* reforms were initiated soon after the creation of the newly independent states of India and Pakistan. The political leaders of these newly independent states were keen to follow the Western model of development and wanted the religious establishments to meet the demands of modernity. The state's ability to roll out a reform programme and the degree of acceptability of these reforms within *madrasas* has varied enormously. Under the political leadership of General Ayub Khan, who gained power in 1958, Pakistan was most vocal in its critique of *madrasa* education (Malik 1997). It is, therefore, ironic that it was the last of the three countries to roll out a reform programme. While the national government trialled a *madrasa*-reform programme under the auspices of the Ministry of Education in the early 1980s, a formal programme was only launched in 2001 with a provision of $225 million aid package made available by the USA under the banner of the 'war on terror' (Bano 2007c). Pakistan is also the country where the reforms have met the severest resistance from the religious elite: by 2007, only 250 of the 16,000 registered *madrasas* in Pakistan had accepted the state reform programme (Bano 2007c).

Despite its misgivings at intervening in a minority educational institution, the Indian government launched a *madrasa*-modernisation programme a decade earlier than Pakistan, with the inception of the Area Intensive Madrasa Modernization Programme in 1993–94. However, much older *madrasa*-reform programmes were already in place in some states of India (Nair 2009). The state of West Bengal had a *madrasa* board – West Bengal Board for Madrasa Education – in place as early as 1927 to manage state-supported *madrasas*. Although many prominent Indian Muslims were suspicious of the reforms (Nair 2009), the modernisation programme has had a higher level of acceptance within *madrasas* in India compared to Pakistan. While the seats of religious authority, namely the leading *madrasas* such as Dar ul Uloom Deoband and Nadwa tul Ulama, remain at a distance from the modernisation programme in most states, the West Bengal Board for Madrasa Education has been able to create a system of reformed *madrasas*. In terms of the number of the affiliate *madrasas*, these rival the *Kharzai* (unreformed) *madrasas*: by 2007, some 500 *madrasas* were reported to be registered with the Board and 550 with Rabata-i-Madaris (the board of *Kharzai madrasa*).[7]

The Bangladesh *madrasa*-reform programme differs from those in both India and Pakistan. The last country to emerge on the map of South Asia was paradoxically the first one to roll out a national-level *madrasa*-development programme. By 1978, the Bangladesh Madrasa Education Board was in place and the process of enrolling *madrasas* interested in joining the reform programme started the following year. Bangladesh is also the country where the reforms have had highest acceptability among *madrasas*: the *Aliya* (reformed) *madrasas* have recorded steady growth to 9000 in 2008,[8] which compete with an estimated 9000–15,000 *Qoumi* (unreformed) *madrasas*. Some *Aliya* (reformed) *madrasas* were established anew, while others are converts from *Qoumi* (unreformed) *madrasas*. The reforms have thus had different levels of success across the three countries.

Methodology

The purpose of this study is to understand the dynamics of the state–*madrasa* relationship across the three countries and the factors that have facilitated the acceptance of proposed inclusion of secular subjects by the *madrasas* in some contexts but not in others. An intensive three weeks of fieldwork was conducted in each of the three countries[9] with a focus on gathering a wide range of perspectives on the dynamics of the state–*madrasa* relationship. The study focused on identifying and interviewing the key respondents, including the government officials concerned with the *madrasa* reforms, the *madrasa* leadership, and the academic and journalist community that has observed this interaction over time.

The primary method of data collection was in-depth interviews. In the first stage, interviews were conducted with officials of the Ministry of Education in the three countries, particularly within the Bangladesh Madrasa Education Board in Dhaka, West Bengal Madrasah Board in Calcutta, Ministry of Minority Affairs in Lucknow, Uttar Pradesh, and Madrasa Reform Programme in Islamabad. These interviews were followed by in-depth interviews with prominent *ulama* from traditional and reformed *madrasas* across the three countries.

In Pakistan, these respondents included the leaders of the prominent *madrasas* who have chosen to stay outside the reform programme, as well as some of the smaller *madrasas* that have adopted the reform programme. In Bangladesh, the emphasis was on engaging with the prominent *Aliya* (reformed) and *Qoumi* (unreformed) *madrasas*. Since the Bangladesh Madrasa Education Board operates in the same manner across the six divisions of Bangladesh, the main focus was on *Aliya* (reformed) *madrasas* in Dhaka division (as Dhaka city hosts the head office of the Board), and the parent *Aliya* (reformed) *madrasa*. For insights into the *Qoumi* (unreformed) *madrasas* in Bangladesh, Chittagong division was most relevant given that it is the stronghold of these *madrasas*, including Dar-ul-Uloom Moin-ul-Islam Hathazari, Al-Jamia Al-Islamia Pattia, Al-Jamaat-ul-Islamia Al-Arabia Mozaher-ul-Uloom, and Jamia Dar-ul-Mar'arif Al-Islamia. In India, Uttar Pradesh and West Bengal were selected for the study. Uttar Pradesh is home to the oldest and most prestigious Indian *madrasas* such as Dar-ul-Uloom Deoband and Nadwat-ul-Ulama, which continue to be held as models of excellence by *ulama* in South Asia. West Bengal, on the other hand, hosts one of the oldest *madrasa* education boards, which has brought many *madrasas* within the reform fold.

Interviews were also conducted with prominent academics, journalists, and public intellectuals across the three countries who have been observing the evolution of the state and its relation with Islam, so as to get a neutral view of the political, economic, and social factors that have contributed to the state–*madrasa* relationship.

Factors shaping the relationships

What determines the state's ability to convince *madrasas* to become partners in imparting secular education? This section demonstrates that financial incentives, historical context, and establishment of a clear bureaucratic structure for engagement are critical for making faith-based organisations partners in development. However, the most crucial factor influencing the relationship is political will and a willingness to engage with the religious elites rather than to regulate them. In order to establish the significance of these factors, it is important to first establish that the difference in acceptance of the reforms does not rest in the design of the integrated curriculum proposed by the state, or the rigidity of the Islamic thought followed by the *madrasas* across the three countries.

Curriculum and rigidity of ideology

One proposition for the difference in the level of acceptance of the reform programmes across the three countries is that it is a result of the different natures of the curriculum reforms introduced by the state. This proposition does not hold, however, because the reform programmes across the three countries have had a similar objective, namely, to introduce modern subjects – English, mathematics, social studies, and general science – into *madrasas* alongside their religious teaching.[10] Across the three countries, the programme began by focusing on primary classes and then, during the second phase, shifting the focus to secondary education. What then explains the difference?

Nature of financial incentives

Analysis of the reform programmes reveals the importance of financial incentives in making *madrasa* leadership a partner in meeting EFA targets. Reforms have been mostly widely accepted in Bangladesh, where the state has provided most concrete financial incentives to the *madrasas*: the government pays for the salary of the core teaching staff within the *Aliya* (reformed) *madrasas* for secular as well as religious subjects – amounting to 72 per cent of total *madrasa* expenditure. By comparison, the financial incentives offered by the state in Pakistan and India have been more limited. In Pakistan, the reform programme provides for the training of 28,000 *madrasa* teachers for the teaching of secular subjects, and gives textbooks, stationary, computers, and furniture to the *madrasas*. However, in terms of core costs, it only provides for the salaries of the teachers of secular subjects and not the numerous religious-subject teachers who constitute the core of *madrasa* teaching staff.

The national-level reform programme in India similarly offers relatively weak financial incentives: the scheme includes 100 per cent support for two qualified teachers per *madrasa* on a salary of Rs. 3000 ($65) per month, less than half the salary of teachers appointed in government schools, a one-time lump sum grant for science and maths teaching kits, and another amount for the establishment of a book bank. As in Pakistan, it does not provide for the salaries of religious teachers (Nair 2009). In India, other very practical flaws in the design and implementation of the programme also restricted its impact. For instance, ignoring cultural constraints on women's mobility, female teachers were appointed to *madrasas* in remote places. The prolonged daily travel made these jobs physically taxing for these teachers and the transportation costs consumed a major share of their meagre remuneration (Nair 2009). In addition, many teachers did not know Urdu, making communication with the largely Urdu-speaking *madrasa* students difficult. In West Bengal, where the state *madrasa* board has succeeded in bringing many *madrasas* within the reform mould, the financial incentives matched those offered in Bangladesh, namely, coverage of all teachers' salary costs.

Given that in a *madrasa* the majority of teachers are engaged to teach religious subjects, in Pakistan and most states in India the reform programmes leave the main financial burden on the *madrasa* administration. Given that the governments were primarily concerned with the introduction of secular subjects into the *madrasa* curriculum, it is understandable why they have refrained from supporting salaries of religious-subject teachers. However, as a result the heads of the *madrasas* and the religious-subject teachers have had few incentives to accept the reform programme. The reform programmes have made greatest inroads in Bangladesh and West Bengal where the state did cover the salaries of the religious-subject teachers.

Trust in the reformer

The three-country comparison further shows that the level of trust that the state can establish with the religious community is another important factor for the implementation of state–*madrasa* reform programmes. The steady growth of the *Aliya* (reformed) *madrasa* system in Bangladesh is linked to the role of Jamaat-i-Islami (a prominent Islamic political party in South Asia) in Bangladeshi politics. Unlike some other Islamic political parties, the Jamaat-i-Islami in Bangladesh has supported *Aliya* (reformed) *madrasas* as opposed to the *Qoumi* (unreformed) *madrasas*. This connection was noted in interviews with the officials of the Bangladesh Madrasa Education Board, as well as in those with journalists, observers of the *madrasa* system, and heads of the *madrasas* themselves. The connection is not formal. As one of the *ulama* of the *Qoumi* (unreformed) *madrasa* explained: 'It is an ideological support. The teachers of the *Aliya madrasa* are of the Jamaat-i-Islami mindset'. Another added: 'Jamaat-i-Islami from the start developed close association within the *Aliya madrasas*. They have been able to cultivate the links in the *madrasas* by cultivating links with the teachers of the *Aliya madrasas*'. The Jamaat's philosophy is that religion has to be a way of life and the state has to be shaped by it. It does not believe in studying Islam just for the sake of becoming mosque imams (preachers) and religious teachers. Its leadership comes from educated middle-class professionals who believe that Muslim students should take a lead in all professions, but also have a good religious understanding. The *Aliya* (reformed) *madrasas*, with their emphasis on combining religious and secular education, thus found their support within a dominant religious force in the country.

In contrast to Bangladesh, the state in Pakistan and India did not have any active religious body supporting the reform programme. In Pakistan, the reform programme implemented since 2002 has suffered from serious distrust from the religious community, because of it being seen as part of US-led 'war on terror', where the objective is to control the *madrasas* rather than support them. As Maulana Naeemi, a senior Islamic scholar from the Brehlavi school of thought in Pakistan noted:

> *In the 1980s when the government made available some funds to support the* madrasas, *the impression was that the money is ours, now the impression is that the money is from outside. The* madrasas *are not letting the government come in because they feel that the government is engaging with the view to interfere in* madrasa *matters and to regulate*

the independent teaching of Islam. If you give money then you have a right to ask questions. Since the religious community does not have trust that the reform programme has been initiated out of a commitment to improving madrasa *education, the bigger* madrasas *want to protect themselves and stay outside the government reforms.*

There were often repeated objections by senior Islamic scholars on the use of the term 'reform'. The head of a Deobandi *madrasa* in Rawalpindi argued, 'The government use of the term "reform" implies that the government thinks that there is something wrong with the *madrasa* system, and the *madrasas* are understandably not very comfortable engaging with a government which is attempting to reform them rather than helping the *madrasas* support provision of better education'. In India, the minority status of Muslims has meant that all prominent Islamic groups associated with *madrasas* have refrained from developing reliance on the state to curtail influence of Hindu elements within the state on the Islamic education system. During interviews with Islamic leaders and Islamic scholars in India, a suspicion was voiced repeatedly that the Indian state is keen to support *madrasas* because it is a subtle way of eventually regulating the content of Islamic knowledge transmitted to the next generation of Muslims. Such concerns, frequently expressed by prominent Muslim personalities, were shared by Mahmood Madni, President of Jamaat-i-Ulama, the leading Muslim political party in India: 'The state does not support our efforts to establish secular educational schools for Muslim communities, so when the state repeatedly reiterates a commitment to supporting *madrasa* education it makes Muslims suspect the government motives'.

Local context

Local context and history also have a role to play in shaping the specific nature of the reform programmes and their acceptance within the religious community. One factor contributing to the rise of the *Aliya* (reformed) *madrasas* in Bangladesh was the significance of the Bengali language movement in the war of liberation. In 1948, the Government of Pakistan had declared Urdu as the official language. The Urdu language was viewed as the lingua franca of Indian Muslims. It had developed under Persian, Arabic, and Turkish influence in South Asia during the Delhi Sultanate and Mughal Empire. Having been developed on the basis of the Arabic script, Urdu was closely associated with the identity of Indian Muslims. By contrast, Hindi and Devanagari scripts were representative of the Hindu culture. Urdu developed most among the Muslims of north India, while, Bengali remained the dominant language of Bengal.

The declaration of Urdu as the national language led to strong resentment within East Pakistan (present-day Bangladesh) as it meant that Bengalis would be at a disadvantage in applying for any government positions, given that the government officials are required to be well-versed in the national language. This resentment turned into a popular movement when a protest organised by the students of the University of Dhaka met severe resistance from the police, resulting in the death of several students. This tragedy in 1952 resulted in the launching of a formal Bengali Movement and was sufficiently effective to get Bengali recognised as the second official language of Pakistan in 1956; it also became a forerunner of the Bengali nationalist movement.

The critical role of the Bengali language in the entire liberation movement placed the *Qoumi* (unreformed) *madrasas* in an awkward position. Despite the strong emphasis on Bengali in East Pakistan, *madrasas* were one place where Urdu had priority as the language of Indian Muslims. The senior *ulama* of the top *Qoumi* (unreformed) *madrasas* in Bangladesh had often studied at the most prestigious Jamias in Uttar Pradesh in India, the heartland of Urdu language. As noted by a teacher in Hathazari *madrasas* in Chittagong, 'Much of the scholarship on Islam was in Urdu too as the South Asian *ulama* had contributed much to Islamic publications, sometimes on issues not addressed in literature available in Arabic language'. The *madrasa* leadership was thus keen to preserve the Urdu language as the medium of instruction. However, after the 1971 war of liberation, which led to the creation of Bangladesh, Urdu became even less relevant for social and economic purposes in this newly established state.

The issue of language thus started to create pressure for reform within the *madrasa* community. In this setting, when the government in Bangladesh established the Bangladesh Madrasa Education Board and proposed *madrasa* reforms, including a switch to teaching in the Bengali language, the idea did not prove controversial. Even the bigger *Qoumi* (unreformed) *madrasas* like Hathazari, which up till then had placed heavy emphasis on learning Urdu, treat it as an additional language and not as the main medium of instruction, which is Bengali. For the smaller *Qoumi* (unreformed) *madrasas*, given resource constraints, even teaching Urdu as an additional language is not an option. Thus, Urdu has gradually been phased out of *madrasa* education in Bangladesh and the government financial incentive package which allows for salaries of core teachers for both secular and religious subjects has helped bring about that shift.

In the view of a prominent Bangladeshi academic:

> Madrasas *were financially weak in the 1980s. More importantly, they were giving education in Urdu and they were losing students as they were not getting jobs anywhere and the curriculum was also very biased towards certain kind of jobs. So there were structural issues that forced them to come to participate in the government reform. The Islamic elite had affiliation with Arabic but less so with Urdu, so it was an affiliation they could consider giving up.*

Political will

The three-country comparison reveals the great significance of political will in establishing partnership with *madrasas*. All the factors identified above that can facilitate a state–*madrasa* partnership are in reality conditional on this. What becomes clear across the three countries is that the state has placed verbal emphasis on *madrasa* reforms, but has only matched it with actual commitment in contexts where the proposed reforms have suited the political interests of the leadership of the time (Bano 2007a, b). In Bangladesh, due to the unique post-liberation context discussed above, the political interests of the elite were best served by supporting the reform programme, as society was open for a new public face of Islam compared to what had been promoted under West Pakistan rule. In India and Pakistan, by contrast, the political landscape made the national political elite less inclined to push for reform, because it disturbed the comfortable political alliance with the Muslim religious elite (Bano 2007a). In both these countries, the *ulama* influence electoral outcomes through the formation of Islamic political parties and through influencing the voting behaviour of their followers (Haqqani 2005; Yavada 1999).

The political will of the state affects the financial resources it is willing to commit to the programme; it also determines the establishment of bureaucratic procedures to implement the reforms. In addition to the state providing greater financial incentives, a formal Bangladesh Madrasa Education Board responsible for the administration of reformed *madrasas* was established in Bangladesh in 1979 as a department of the Ministry of Education. In Pakistan and India, the programme has been administered through *ad hoc* bodies.

Within Pakistan, the programme falls under a project director within the Ministry of Education and has been beset with numerous problems, including delays in release of approved funds and inadequate staffing. During interviews, officials across the four provinces responsible for the reform programme raised serious concerns about the design of the programme, the nature of incentives offered, and most importantly the inadequate number of staff appointments and lack of required facilities, such as vehicles to facilitate access to the *madrasas*. The officials also noted concerns about the basic conception of the programme: the programme was perceived to be facing resistance from the religious leadership because it was externally funded and adopted a language of 'reform' rather than 'support'.

Similarly in India, the *madrasa*-modernisation programme is under the supervision of the Ministry of Minority Affairs, rather than operating as an independent board. In West Bengal, however, where the state *madrasa*-support programme has expanded the most, the state has a separate *madrasa* board just like in Bangladesh. The history of *Aliya* (reformed) *madrasas* in this state – the first *Aliya* (reformed) *madrasa* was established by Warren Hastings in Calcutta in 1781 – and the strong presence of the Communist Party seems to have contributed to consolidation of the reform programme in West Bengal compared to other states.

Ideological commitment of the *ulama*

Last but not least, any full explanation for refusal of the *madrasa* leadership to accept government support to teach secular subjects has to take into account the ideological commitment of the *ulama*, especially in bigger *madrasas*. That the *ulama* were ideologically opposed to reform across the three countries is clear; the *ulama* and state officials clashed on the very conception of what knowledge is (Zaman 1999). For senior *ulama*, knowledge demands the pursuit of truth for its own sake with little consideration of employment matters, while the state is more concerned with education to produce a productive workforce. The walls of many *madrasas* visited during the fieldwork were engraved with quotations emphasising the pursuit of Islamic scholarship in the search for knowledge for its own sake. Interviews with leading *ulama* across the three countries revealed the perception that state reform programmes were aimed at secularisation and commercialisation of *madrasa* education rather than improving the *madrasas'* ability to train more learned *alims* (Islamic scholars).

The *ulama* also repeatedly highlighted the practical limitations of the proposed reform programmes: inclusion of secular subjects in the curriculum beyond matriculation level was argued to lead to *madrasa* graduates excelling in neither religious nor secular education. In the view of Maulana Jalandari, Secretary of Wafaq-ul-Madaris Al-Arabia in Pakistan, 'Today is the time of *takhassus* [specialisation]. Every teaching institution selects the curriculum according to its objectives. No one has said that why the doctor graduating from King Edwards College is also not an *alim*, the same should hold for the *madrasas*. Specialisation in religious subjects demands devoted scholarship which cannot sustain inclusion of secular subjects at the higher levels without seriously compromising the quality of religious education taught within the *madrasas'*'.

Additionally, the *ulama* repeatedly recorded concerns that acceptance of state funds could, in the long term, lead to compromises on core religious principles, even if in the initial phase the reforms were within acceptable limits. There was a recognition that, once the head of a *madrasa* becomes used to a regular income from the state, the comfort of that regular income can lead to compromise on religious beliefs; therefore, it is thought best not to get used to such comfort. To justify their resistance, senior Pakistani *ulama* quote examples of the relative secularisation of *madrasas* over time in states where they have accepted state money (Zaman 1999).

Further, during fieldwork in Bangladesh and West Bengal, *ulama* from orthodox *madrasas* repeatedly expressed the view that the reformed *madrasas* had lost their original purpose, namely to promote Islam, and become just another form of regular school. Maulana Abdul Razak Alhabadi from Rabata-ul-Madaris in West Bengal argued, 'Their name is *madrasas* but they are actually high schools. Hindu boys also study there'. Senior *ulama* in Bangladesh echoed similar concerns. In the words of the son of Sheikh-ul-Hadith, a prominent *alim* and political figure in Bangladesh, 'the real purpose of the *madrasa* is to impart the teachings of the Quran and Hadith [Prophet Mohammad's sayings] and not to primarily be worried about the degree. If a child wants the degree to secure a job he will go to *Aliya* (reformed) *madrasa*, if he only wants Islam he will come to *Qoumi* (unreformed) *madrasa*. In our country, one did not become a good *alim* in *Aliya* (reformed) *madrasa* nor did one become a good Master's graduate, one became a hybrid'. Here it is important to point out that the bigger *madrasas* across the three countries in general already impart secular education to the middle of secondary level, because this basic education is argued to be an important prerequisite for embarking on higher studies in Islamic theology. They differ with the reform programmes on introducing secular subjects beyond secondary level. Thus, while senior *ulama* across the three countries argued that the smaller *madrasas* that are finding it difficult to make ends meet should feel free to draw on government support, they found this dependence on the state to be an inferior option and preferred to stay independent of state support.

Conclusions

The three-country comparative analysis of state attempts to make *madrasas* a partner in imparting secular education shows that *madrasas* are not inherently opposed to teaching their students secular subjects – they *can* become important partners in meeting the EFA targets. The large *madrasas*, which provide education all the way to Master's level across the three countries, are already providing students secular education up to middle or secondary level; it is only after matriculation that they defend an exclusive focus on religious texts. These *madrasas* see their role as training specialists in Islamic education to cater to the spiritual needs of society. Smaller *madrasas*, by contrast, often lack the facilities to teach secular subjects. It is these smaller *madrasas* which often cater for children who might otherwise be excluded from schooling, and so are the ones that the state needs to support in particular if *madrasas* are to become a partner in meeting EFA goals.

Smaller *madrasas* are generally open to accepting state support. However, the success of these partnerships depends on the level of state commitment to the reform programme. Only a state with strong political will and acceptance of the value of religious teaching is likely to be committed to providing adequate financial incentives, putting in place an appropriate administrative structure, and developing a trusting rather than adversarial or controlling relationship with the religious elite. The *ulama* also need to take initiative to engage with the state. However, given their limited resources, the engagement is likely to be more conducive if the state makes an active effort to reach out to them. Thus, the prevailing view within some development agencies that faith-based organisations are less likely to enter development partnerships than NGOs because of being guided by dogmatic religious beliefs are exaggerated (Clarke 2007). Even a faith-based organisation like a *madrasa*, which is often associated with radicalisation of religious beliefs, can be open to entering into partnership with the state, provided the state shows a genuine commitment to the programme. The condition, however, is that the state views *madrasas* as a partner, and makes a serious financial and administrative commitment to implementing these reforms.

Acknowledgements

The author would like to gratefully acknowledge financial assistance from DFID Religions and Development Research Programme in support of this research. The contribution greatly benefited from detailed comments by Pauline Rose and two external reviewers.

Notes

1. Islamic teaching takes places through different platforms including mosques, *madrasas*, and *sufi khankas*. The *madrasa* education, which is one of the dominant models for following formal Islamic education, normally involves teaching of a set curriculum beginning with the process of *hifz* (memorisation of Quran) and leading to higher studies in Islamic theology.
2. This contribution attempts to assess the potential of *madrasas* to impart teaching of secular subjects. The objective is not to assess whether the religious education imparted in the *madrasas* is in need of reform.
3. Estimates provided by senior *ulama* and officials of the Madrasa Education Board during the fieldwork, as official data on *Qoumi* (unreformed) *madrasas* are not available.
4. Data provided by senior officials of the *wafaq*.
5. Data collected from the head offices of the five *wafaqs* in 2007.
6. Data secured from officials of Rabata-i-Madaris in West Bengal.
7. Source: Rabata-i-Madaris, West Bengal.
8. Source: Bangladesh Madrasa Education Board.
9. The analysis, however, benefits from the author's prior study of the *madrasa* system in South Asia, which involved over 18 months of fieldwork with *madrasas* across the four provinces of Pakistan.
10. For details of the reforms, the incentives offered, and the subjects introduced at each academic level see Bano (2007a, c) and Nair (2009).

References

Andrabi, T., J. Das, A. J. Khawaja, and T. Zajonc (2005) 'Religious School Enrollment in Pakistan: A Look at the Data', *Working Paper Series 3521*, Washington, DC: The World Bank.

Asadullah, Mohammad Niaz and Nazmul Chaudhury (2007) 'Holly [*sic*] Alliances: Public Subsidies, Islamic High Schools, and Female Schooling in Bangladesh', Royal Economic Society (RES) 2007 Annual Conference Paper, available at https://editorialexpress.com/cgi-bin/conference/download.cgi?db_name=res2007&paper_id=626 (retrieved 4 November 2009).

Bano, M. (2007a) 'Allowing for Diversity: State–*Madrasa* Relationship in Bangladesh', *Working Paper*, Birmingham, UK: DFID Religion and Development Research Consortium, University of Birmingham.

Bano, Masooda (2007b) 'Beyond politics: reality of a Deobandi *madrasah* in Pakistan', *Journal of Islamic Studies* 18 (1): 43–68.

Bano, M. (2007c) 'Competing for Authority: State–*Madrasa* Relationship in Pakistan', *Working Paper*, Birmingham, UK: DFID Religion and Development Research Consortium, University of Birmingham.

Bano, Masooda (2008) 'Non-profit education providers *vis-à-vis* the private sector: comparative analysis of NGOs and traditional voluntary organisations in Pakistan', *Compare* 38 (4): 471–82.

Blanchard, Christopher M. (2005) 'Islamic Religious Schools, *Madrasas*: Background', CRS Report for Congress, Washington, DC: Congressional Research Service, The Library of Congress.

Clarke, G. (2007) 'Agents of transformation? Donors, faith-based organizations and international development', *Third World Quarterly* 28 (1): 77–96.

Cockcroft, Anne, Neil Andersson, Deborah Milne, Khalid Omer, Noor Ansari, Amir Khan, and Ubaid Ullah Chaudhry (2009) 'Challenging the myths about *madaris* in Pakistan: a national household survey of enrolment and reasons for choosing religious schools', *International Journal of Educational Development* 29 (4): 342–9.

GoP (Government of Pakistan) (2006) 'Report on Deeni *Madaris* of Pakistan: Base-Line Information 2003–2004 & 2004–2005', Islamabad: Academy of Educational Planning and Management, Ministry of Education.

Haqqani, H. (2005) *Pakistan: Between Mosque and Military*, Lahore: Vanguard Books.

Hefner, R. W. and M. Q. Zaman (2007) *Schooling Islam: The Culture and Politics of Modern Muslim Education*, Princeton, NJ: Princeton University Press.

ICG (2002) 'Pakistan: *Madrasas*, Extremism, and the Military', *ICG Asia Report 36*, Islamabad and Brussels: International Crisis Group.

Malik, J. (1997) 'Dynamics among traditional religious scholars and their institutions in contemporary South Asia', *The Muslim World* 87 (3–4): 199–220.

Metcalf, B. D. (1978) 'The *madrasa* at Deoband: a model for religious education in India', *Modern Asian Studies* 12: 111–34.

Nair, P. (2009) 'The State and *Madrasas* in India', *Working Paper*, Birmingham, UK: DFID Religion and Development Project, University of Birmingham.

Nelson, M. J. (2006) 'Muslims, markets and the meaning of a "good" education in Pakistan', *Asian Survey* 46 (5): 699–720.

Nizami, F. A. (1983) '*Madrasahs*, Scholars, Saints: Muslim Response to the British Presence in Delhi and Upper Doab 1803–1857', unpublished DPhil dissertation, University of Oxford.

Sikand, Y. (2004) 'Reforming the Indian *madrasas*: contemporary Muslim voices', in S. P. Limaye, R. Wirsing, and M. Malik (eds.) *Religious Radicalism and Security in South Asia*, Honolulu, HI: Asia Pacific Centre for Security Studies.

Sachar, R. (2006) 'Prime Minister's High Level Committee, on Social, Economic and Educational Status of the Muslim Community of India', Delhi: Government of India.

UNESCO (2008) *Global Monitoring Report 2009: Overcoming Inequality: Why Governance Matters*, Paris: UNESCO.

Yavada, Y. (1999) 'Electoral politics in the time of change: India's third electoral system, 1989–99', *Economic and Political Weekly* 34 (34 & 35): 2393–9.

Zaman, Q. (1999) 'Religious education and rhetoric of reform: the *madrasa* in British India and Pakistan', *Comparative Studies in Society and History* 41 (2): 294–323.

Struggles for memory and social-justice education in Latin America

Lauren Ila Jones and Carlos Alberto Torres

Popular-education programmes conducted by social movements are reshaping politics and education in Latin America. Negotiating with governments, they promote social justice while educationally challenging 'neo-liberal' educational standardisation. Moving from a defensive towards an offensive strategy, some movements support themselves economically while developing new educational strategies. They encounter both support and opposition from the social democratic governments in the region. They are at odds with the international bilateral and multilateral organisations that promote neo-liberal top–down policies, and some of these new social movements have moved beyond social action in specific regions and national borders creating regional alliances for their struggle.

Luttes pour le maintien de la mémoire et l'éducation en justice sociale en Amérique latine
Les programmes d'éducation populaire menés par les mouvements sociaux latino-américains sont en passe de refaçonner la politique et l'éducation en Amérique latine. En négociant avec les gouvernements, ces mouvements promeuvent la justice sociale tout en mettant en cause, du point de vue de l'éducation, la standardisation « néolibérale » de l'éducation. Passant d'une position défensive à une position offensive, certains mouvements sont autosuffisants sur le plan économique et élaborent de nouvelles stratégies d'éducation. Ils se heurtent à la fois au soutien et à l'opposition des gouvernements sociaux-démocrates de la région. Ils sont en désaccord avec les organisations bilatérales et multilatérales internationales qui promeuvent des politiques directives néolibérales et certains de ces nouveaux mouvements sociaux ne se limitent plus à l'action sociale au sein de certaines régions et dans les limites des frontières nationales, mais ont commencé à créer des alliances régionales pour appuyer leur lutte.

Lutas para memória e educação sobre justiça social na América Latina
Programas populares de educação conduzidos por movimentos sociais estão reformulando as políticas e a educação na América Latina. Negociando com governos, eles promovem justiça social enquanto educacionalmente desafiam a padronização educacional "neo-liberal". Passando de uma estratégia defensiva para uma ofensiva, alguns movimentos apóiam-se economicamente enquanto desenvolvem novas estratégias educacionais. Eles encontram apoio e oposição dos governos democráticos sociais na região. Eles estão em disputa com as organizações internacionais bilaterais e multilaterais que promovem políticas de cima para baixo neoliberais, e alguns desses novos movimentos sociais têm ido além da ação social em regiões específicas e fronteiras nacionais criando alianças regionais por sua luta.

ACHIEVING EDUCATION FOR ALL THROUGH PUBLIC-PRIVATE PARTNERSHIPS?

La lucha por la memoria y la educación a favor de la justicia social en América Latina

Los programas de educación popular que nacieron dentro de los movimientos sociales latinoamericanos han logrado transformaciones a nivel nacional y mundial. En su trabajo con las personas que menos se benefician de los sistemas educativos formales, estos movimientos promueven la resistencia a la homologación educativa neoliberal a través de una "globalización desde abajo". En sus negociaciones con los gobiernos nacionales, estos movimientos fomentan la justicia social y, gracias a sus crecientes contactos internacionales, ejercen mayor presión a nivel mundial. Asimismo, estos movimientos se están autofinanciando al cambiar su estrategia defensiva por una ofensiva. Por tanto, en el ámbito de la educación encuentran tanto apoyos como obstáculos ideológicos provenientes de los gobiernos nacionales y de diversas alianzas internacionales.

Essay In Memoriam of Francisco de Souza and Carlos Nuñez Hurtado que en paz descansen[1]

Introduction

This essay – written within the spirit of the Theory of the South, about experiences of the South – develops a dialectical perspective of popular education within Latin America, both historically and, through discussion about three popular education efforts in Argentina, contemporaneously. We begin by describing the paradigm of popular education in Latin America. After describing our model of popular education, we explain how this becomes an antidote to neo-liberalism, providing a seminal perspective allowing for the development of theory, research, and praxis within the politics of education and culture. We contend that a struggle against neo-liberalism will become a struggle for the soul of Latin America. This essay speaks about how popular educators from a diverse range of political orientations practise a new sociological imagination of their memory of their struggle.

What we are trying to do through this contribution is to allow the voices and experiences of social movements,[2] communities, NGOs, and progressive intellectuals within the region to speak out loud and clear. We do not want to appropriate or reinterpret these voices and experiences as 'data'. Within perspective of Critical Theory, we believe that analytical and normative dimensions of research cannot be easily separated. In emphatic agreement with the tradition of popular education, and echoing the message of Karl Marx in the 12th thesis on *Feurbach*, we believe that we teach and research not simply to interpret, but to change the world. This was exactly the experience within these social movements that we want to share with our readers, in appreciation of them, as well as for the large number of anonymous heroes who have contributed towards causes for peace and justice within this region, risking and very often losing their lives in the process. Their message continues to resonate, not only within the walls of academia and the schooling system, but also within the experiences of non-formal and informal education. Their example enlightened us, so we might better understand our personal and political commitments, while trying to honour theirs.

Paulo Freire (1998: 44) recognised that 'even theoretical discourse itself, necessary as it is to critical reflection, must be concrete enough to be clearly identifiable with practice'. He was very specific when speaking about different forms of practice, or 'intervention', to be applied through education:

ACHIEVING EDUCATION FOR ALL THROUGH PUBLIC-PRIVATE PARTNERSHIPS?

> *When I speak of education as intervention, I refer both to the aspiration for radical changes in society in such areas as economics, human relations, property, the right to employment, to land, to education, and to health, and to the reactionary position whose aim is to immobilize history and maintain an unjust socio-economic and cultural order.*
> (Freire 1998: 99)

Therefore, we do not separate praxis from theory, and to that extent, we summarise, if sometimes briefly, three examples of Argentine education intervention that we believe to have implications for other parts of the region – namely, the Madres de Plaza de Mayo, the Cooperativa La Juanita, and the Barrios de Pie movement.

In this essay, we consider the need for reflection by institutions of higher education in the USA, arguing how important it is for international development and graduate programmes in international education to rethink Education for All curricula. By incorporating valuable alternative models for education, and by measuring potential contributions these models could make towards civil society alongside other larger efforts, graduate-level courses could be implemented that reflect a more heterogeneous conception of Education for All. Because interventions by the World Bank and other large donor agencies are not going to disappear from Latin American politics, a transformation within the education of young practitioners and researchers who will work for these agencies across this continent is an essential accompaniment to work being done on the ground in Latin America.[3]

In the conclusion of her four-country study of Latin American women popular educators, Jones (2009) argues that the incorporation of popular educators within interdisciplinary US and Latin American higher-education programmes could enrich students' academic trajectories and help them better understand education and development.[4] She cites, for example, the Nahual Institute for Global Studies programmes in Central America:

> *During the course in Guatemala, 'International Security and Conflict Resolution: The Impacts of Civil War in Guatemala 1954–present,' students met with a wide range of actors: including former guerrilla commanders and Guatemalan military personnel, liberation theologians and members of CEBs [Comunidades Eclesiales de Base (Christian-based communities)], Ex-government ministers and officials, Human Rights activists, Grassroots community organizers, Mayan Language Academy linguists, Maya priests/priestesses, CONAVIGUA (National Coordination of Widows of Guatemala), Repatriated refugee communities, and vendors in Indigenous marketplaces and villages. These courses filled disciplinary gaps that have often existed in, for example, ... the field of international security and conflict resolution. This program showed the complexity of the intersection of formal, non-formal, and informal actors in post-dictatorial development.*
> (Jones 2009: 212)

Here we see an intersection of formal, non-formal, and informal actors in an interdisciplinary Central American programme designed for US students. These courses offered by the Nahual Institute for Global Studies provide an innovative understanding of the role of popular educators in development of 'Education for All' by state and non-state actors. These courses would serve both foreign and domestic university students and reinvigorate this intersection.

To understand why we advocate for university students to have a deeper knowledge of the role of popular education, we need to better understand popular education within this region. We begin by discussing the legacy provided by Freire, and then discuss the challenges popular education has faced under neo-liberal educational policies.

Paulo Freire and popular education[5]

Popular education was born from radical models of education, many of which were linked to Paulo Freire's experiences in Brazil in the 1970s.[6] Characteristics common to popular education have been discussed by various analysts, and synthesised in other places (Gadotti and Torres 1993; Torres 1995a, b). Popular education rose from a political and social understanding of conditions endured by the poor, as evidenced by their most visible problems, including malnutrition, unemployment, and illness, with the intention of shedding light upon these conditions at both individual and collective scales of consciousness. These projects used an education intimately related to concrete abilities that could be taught to the poor (such as reading, writing, and arithmetic).

Popular education sought to inspire a sense of pride, dignity, and confidence in participants, so they might become autonomous both politically and socially. These projects could be integrated by governments into the process of rural development, as done in Colombia and the Dominican Republic (Torres 1995b); as done by Freire himself, from 1989 to 1991, when he was Secretary of Education for the Workers' Party (PT) within the Municipality of São Paulo (O'Cadiz *et al.* 1998); and as done by popular-education collectives in Nicaragua (Arnove 1986). These popular-education programmes could span all ages of students, from children to adults.

For Freire, the main problems within education were not methodological or pedagogical, but rather political. Educational programmes inspired by this model had earned a strong historical presence within the fields of adult and literacy education, by trying to constitute themselves within politico-pedagogical mechanisms of collaboration with socially subordinated sectors.

Yet, in considering the work of Freire, it is important to note Sondra Hale's (2007) astute critique:

> As we know, liberatory pedagogy has been associated with Paulo Freire, and is one of the inspirations behind some ethnic studies classrooms. However, Freire's neglect of gender and sexuality marginalizes women, lesbians, and gays as categories of people to be empowered, and has made him less attractive to Women's Studies. Feminists have, however, borrowed heavily from him and from others before him – sometimes without acknowledgement. (Hale 2007)

Freire continues to be read critically using these lenses described by Hale.

The neo-liberal agenda: the rationale of privatisation

It is worth noting that neo-liberalism is an agenda intimately linked to neo-classical economic principles that prevailed within a diverse group of regulatory capitalistic institutions, including the World Bank, the International Monetary Fund, and various foundations within the advanced industrial capitalistic world. Neo-liberalism had an 'elective affinity' – to use Weberian language – with positions held by neo-liberal governments within this region, the majority of which adopted features of this agenda. In the case of liberal tradition held by post-revolutionary Mexico, neo-liberalism of the governments of Carlos Menem and Salinas de Gortari (to name just two prominent experiences from this region), set the limits and possibilities of educational transformation within a country.

Analytical premises of hegemonic neo-liberal agenda, well represented within international organisations, could be labelled 'supply-side economics'. Two political premises guided this agenda – the notions of privatisation of public education, and of reduction of public cost. These political orientations were not incompatible, and privatisation could be considered an important strategy for reducting public-sector costs. These policies were crucial elements within reforms that promoted liberalisation of the market. Privatising public-sector businesses reduced pressure on public cost, a powerful tool to depoliticise regulatory practices of the state. Privatisation played a central role within the political arsenal of neo-liberalism, because:

> *Contracting of external services is on the one hand an administrative mechanism to solve some questions of social legitimacy of the state linked in the implementation of direct social services, and on the other hand an intent to borrow the business ethos and the conceptualization of private business (and the notion of business development, cost-benefit system analysis, and management by objectives).* (Culpitt 1992: 94)

Neo-liberals and neo-conservatives argued that the state and the market were two diametrically opposed social systems, and that both were real options for provision of specific services (Moran and Wright 1991). Why was there a preference for the market over the state? Neo-liberals considered markets more versatile and efficient than bureaucratic structures, for numerous reasons (Torres 1996). Markets responded more rapidly to technological change and to social demand within the state. Markets were seen as more efficient and effective, in terms of cost, than the public sector in the provision of services. Market competition would produce higher *accountability* for a social investment than bureaucratic policies. Together with these preferences was the question of neo-liberals linking privatisation of public businesses with solutions to the problem of external debt. In certain versions of neo-liberal ideology, the state's businesses 'were responsible for the creation of the external debt of Latin America and ... it's privatization can help to resolve the problem' (Ramamurti 1991: 153).

Many proponents of this generic philosophy of privatisation opted for a perspective that went further against the state than a realistic perspective drawn about privatisation would, without amplification of market competition. Did these policies generate real competition in diverse markets, or did they constitute a strategy to replace monopoly that state businesses had in specific areas of the economy, with a similar monopoly held by selected private businesses? In terms of specific educational policies, neo-liberal agenda opted for a mixture of guidelines, all of them represented by the World Bank.

Opting for school democratisation, by increasing participation of women and girls in education, was a credible objective rooted within the heart of liberal policies for equality, but what was given by one hand could be taken away by the other hand. There was a rhetoric for equality via educational policies that supported women's education, but these were the same women who had paid the highest cost for structural adjustment (Caufield 1996; Cavanagh *et al.* 1994; Emeagwali 1995). Two specific policies – a prioritising of basic education, and an emphasis on quality of that education – characterised educational agendas for the World Bank. As José Luis Coraggio (1999) showed, to the extent that the World Bank was composed primarily of economists and not of educators, the final objective of its educational policy was economic efficiency, liberalisation of markets, and globalisation of capital, all of which placed an overemphasis on quantitative methods to measure success of educational policy. Using strict economic criteria (such as rate of return based upon personal income), it was suggested that an additional year of private education within lowest levels of an educational system produced a higher increment of income at higher levels of the educational system. It was quickly concluded that investment in basic or primary education would more effectively lead to an increase in gross national product, than would investment at any other level (without bearing in mind the obsession of World Bank specialists with investment in higher education in Latin America – in particular, in subsidies for the elite).[7]

Applying an understanding of these connections between neo-liberal globalisation and education, we highlight interplay between various Latin American movements whose educative praxis was their resistance against these trends. Our methodology consisted of a combination of reflections upon personal experiences, along with texts that we acquired while working with, visiting, and/or learning from the movements. In other cases, we have attempted to analyse the movements' published literature and descriptions of their own work. Examples of their work were set along a continuum from private to public. The continuum started with those focused on remembrance (highlighting the importance of memory in the struggle for human rights); shifted towards those that focused on women's and workers' lives; and finished with those focused on negotiation of their role within public education. The latter challenged top–down approaches towards education with a bottom–up approach that truly worked towards providing education for all.

Popular education experiences

Remembering the world through writing the word: the Madres' collaborations – adult literacy and beyond

Connections between remembrance and popular education could be explored within spaces of women's movements within this region. Culture and resistance joined together through efforts of a social movement, the Madres de Plaza de Mayo, to become a global symbol of the power of human agency against dictatorship. The Madres recognised their unique role in Argentine civil society, a role that had evolved from their first steps taken on 13 April 1977, as mothers of some of the 30,000 students, activists, intellectuals, and others who had 'disappeared' at the hands of their country's repressive military government (supported clandestinely by the USA in its regional fight against communism). 'Disappearance' (*Desaparición*) was a manifestation of Gramscian concept of *liquidation*, or subjugation, that could be done by armed force, as was the case in Argentina (Gramsci 1971: 52–3; United Nations 1992). Jones highlights the interconnectivity of the liberatory work of the Madres:

> *Walking down Hipolito Yrygoyen street, the Madres' famous white kerchief emblem made it easy to locate building[s] that [housed] their various spaces for resistance, including the Universidad Popular de las Madres de Plaza de Mayo, the publishing house Ediciones Madres de Plaza de Mayo, the bookstore and coffee shop ..., a radio station, a library, and a video library. Inside the University, courses on documentary cinema and journalism connected students to a social justice-minded Argentine version of cultural studies. Literacy and housing programs based in satellite locations have, in the last few years, expanded the Madres' vision of resistance.* (Jones 2009: 165)

The Madres exemplified how a subaltern group had turned tragedy into many different victories now recognised by mainstream media, victories that the Madres share with other popular groups worldwide. With a message that had been amplified by various forms of mass communication, and a presence that had also benefited other 'Mothers' Groups', such as the Co-Madres in El Salvador, or the Mothers of the Disappeared in Ciudad Juarez, Mexico, the Madres offered an important example of critique and utopia. Gramsci (1971: 53) argues for the importance of critique, and for the development of alternatives, as carried out by critique of institutions and ideologies that legitimate them, along with development of counter-institutions and ideas that would produce alternatives to the existing system. By challenging the existing educational system, the Madres have provided support for international popular education, through diverse interventions that have occurred as a result of this aspect of their resistance.

Reclaiming space within public education has been a challenge that the Madres have tackled through various strategies; work for which they have been internationally recognised. On 20

June 1997, the Madres mobilised teachers – part of a long line of historic connections between the Madres and education. This history was honoured when the Madres received the 1999 UNESCO Education for Peace award (Vázquez 2007: 72). In the late 1990s, the Madres were awarded a Regents Lectureship in California.

Motherhood as a powerful source of strength resonated throughout domestic and international popular struggles that the Madres were involved with. Writing about their experience in Spain during International Women's Day, they noted that one of their conference sessions was titled, 'Madres mujeres, Madres maestras, Madres coraje' (Madres women, Madres teachers, Madres courage). This title reflected how their discourse connected the core role of motherhood with feminism, education, and the courage required for popular struggle. While participating in an activity with Rigoberta Menchú, this prominent Central American activist alluded to them as 'her teachers' (Vásquez 2007: 75), illustrating the transnational nature of connections within this struggle – from Buenos Aires to Guatemala City:

> *The ability of women in human rights groups such as the Mothers of the Plaza de Mayo in Argentina ... to unite across class, age, and ideological lines to protest repression and military dictatorships served as an inspiration and model for the broader democratic opposition that followed.* (Chinchilla and Haas 2006: 258)

Both the Madres and Rigoberta Menchú embraced their role as women, as they took this role into larger debates about civil society as a whole.

Creating a permanent space for higher education which reflected the principles of their movement was, for the Madres, an ongoing process. Even before their university opened, courses such as 'Critical Analysis of the Argentine Reality' were taught by the Madres within their bookstore. On 6 April 2000, their dream was realised, when the Universidad Popular was inaugurated. Connecting this new establishment to their long presence in Argentine civil society, in May 2000, the Universidad Popular began with a seminar entitled 'The History of the Madres de Plaza del Mayo' – the first of its kind (Vázquez 2007: 77). Along with their own experience, the Madres have also been instrumental in documenting other experiences of popular education (Korol 2004).

The Madres' paths crossed with the Zapatistas and the Movimento dos Trabalhadores Rurais Sem Terra (MST, Landless Workers' Movement), in meetings these groups held from 27 July to 3 August 1996 and 4–9 August 1996, respectively. The Madres attended the Primer Encuentro por la Humanidad y contra el Neoliberalismo in Chiapas (the First Meeting for Humanity and Against Neo-liberalism), where they participated in a panel, and spoke about various parts of their proposal to construct their own universities and free schools (Vásquez 2007: 49).

With the MST, the Madres visited one of that movement's camps in Matto Groso, Brazil, and talked with MST participants. In January 2004, the Popular Education team of the Universidad Popular and students from the Popular Education programme met with the MST, in a meeting documented in 'Encuentro con el Movimiento Sin Tierra de Brasil' (Meeting with Brazil's Landless Workers' Movement) (Bignani *et al.* 2004). Those who had come from the MST spoke about the goal of 'succeeding in having the militants of the movement themselves in settings like this, organizing functions, being educators ... making the schools fresh; as well as not being held prisoner by the institutional format of the schools' (Korol 2004: 161). These were concepts which the Madres, through their experiences in establishing permanent spaces for education, knew very well to be central to their own struggle.[8]

Collectives: defining work culture

The 2001 Argentine crisis displayed the failure of the neo-liberal economic policies implemented by the governments of Menem and De la Rúa. These policies had been advocated by international organisations as examples of the kind of progress that a country can achieve through neo-liberalism (Cavallo and Mondino 1995). Many cooperative experiences emerged after this crisis. Cooperatives responded to lack of employment and to the harshness of capitalist labour markets, and were often associated with the reformist character of socialist parties in this region. The Argentine collective La Cooperativa La Juanita focused specifically on work culture. It created a school bread workshop (Cooperative La Juanita 2009) that sold 3000 sweet breads in one month. With the money raised, it 'trained' more young bakers. Through this work to restore dignified working conditions, La Juanita – following the self-assigned name of the movement, Empresas Recuperadas (Recuperated Companies) – 'recuperated' work culture which allowed it to reject state-run assistentialist[9] plans. To examine the work of La Juanita, we should reflect upon popular education from the across-town popular movement of the Madres:

> *[these programmes] rise above mere assistentialist projects, 'to create popular power, combating, as a part of the cultural battle, some characteristics that come from the culture of survival,' including immediate satisfaction, pragmatism, short term thinking, and vulnerability. These factors favour co-opting processes, such as identification of the oppressed with the oppressor. Processes of popular education are seen to carefully break with policies that degrade human beings, instead favouring dignity, self-esteem, and forging of values born from resistance, while being 'antagonistic to those that sustain and reproduce domination'.* (Korol 2004: 13)

Work of La Juanita moved away from assistance projects, in order to create more sustainable work for this community. Dignity and self-esteem were reflected in the work of the students, who returned to bake the same bread that supported their programmes. Linking vocational education to social justice was an important instrument for moving towards being able to offer education for all. This case offers another example of how students gained unique knowledge, in this case culinary knowledge, that allowed transformation of work culture within their community.

Todos sabemos todo; nadie sabe más que nadie (We all know everything; no one knows more than anyone): Barrios de Pie

The Barrios de Pie Movement in Argentina began in 2001 as a struggle against hunger, poverty, and unemployment, and was in opposition to governments that have yielded to demands of the IMF:

> *we have demonstrated in public places to show the rest of the society the living conditions that millions of Argentine people have to suffer, demanding immediate solutions for our most urgent problems – such as lack of education, health security, and basic services which would enable us to live in dignity – and, above all, claiming our right to a proper nutrition, because Argentina is one of the most important producers of edible products in the world, so we (should not, and) will not let our children starve to death. Having taken the decision to struggle for what is ours, we are determined to solve the critical problems ourselves. In the various neighbourhoods where we are organized, Barrios de Pie has started community centres where thousands of adults and children receive daily meals. We also have community orchards and bakeries, juvenile work projects, scholastic support and literacy, popular education, popular libraries, health campaigns.* (Barrios de Pie 2009)

Barrios de Pie was determined to solve its own problems, by expressing its autonomy, as manifested in its programmes. This common element became essential in other movements, including bakeries, redefinition of the work culture, literacy, popular libraries, and health campaigns. For Barrios de Pie, democratisation of certain programmes, such as the *comedores populares* (community kitchens), was challenged by the fact that people within the community were conditioned to 'identify with the oppressor, the impossibility of carrying out autonomous actions, the naturalness of poverty, the shame of their class condition ... living in a constant present without projection as historical subjects; total and functional illiteracy' (Gónzalez Velasco 2004: 11). Considering praxis to be their path, they 'intervene to denaturalise the oppressor discourse' (Gónzalez Velasco 2004: 13), by participating in the World Social Forum, and by fighting for reversal of neo-liberal educational laws passed in the 1990s (Barrios de Pie 2009).

Gender arose as a key theme within the work of Barrios de Pie in 'La Participación de la mujer en los movimientos sociales (Seminario de Educación Popular)' (Women's participation in social movements [Popular Education Seminar]), a reflection upon work done from 2002 to 2004 by Barrios de Pie in popular education. This workshop focused specifically on participation of women, which according to leaders of this meeting (organised by the Red de Mujeres Solidarias [Women's Network of Solidarity]), resulted from 'detecting the necessity to include an additional meeting to tackle the question of gender from the point of view of popular education'. Three hundred women attended the meeting. Reflections on specific workshops could give young students of international studies, development, or education in the USA and Latin America a concrete example of how these movements moved from the defensive towards the offensive. Reading about how this workshop included celebration of neighbourhood conferences, and about the huge turnout (Gónzalez Velasco 2004: 107), students could see how these pedagogical strategies could become normative within practice of education, rather than 'alternative'. These Latin American movements should serve as an example for Northern movements struggling under many of the same neo-liberal conditions. The so-called Fourth World had conditions similar to those suffered within communities, such as parts of Los Angeles – communities that could benefit from learning about struggles against similar forces throughout the world.

Conclusion: towards a world beyond neo-liberalism

One of the longest-lasting teachings of Freire was his invitation to practise an epistemology of curiosity, one that was in no way naïve, yet respected popular knowledge and culture.

There are few certainties in these uncertain times. First and foremost is a need to challenge tenets held by neo-liberalism that have destroyed this region. It is not only important to react to how the establishment operates, but it is equally important to offer concrete proposals for social change. In reflecting upon the three Argentine cases reported above, we see how many people have committed their lives to creating new paths of transformation, based on new understandings of globalisation. Feminism and women's movements provide a backbone for those walking along this new path:

> *In this struggle for interpretative power and the creation of new cultural symbols and practices, in the strengthening of democracy and citizenship, and in the continuing daily effort to transform dominant institutions and political parties from inside out, ... feminism remains central to struggles for a 'world beyond neo-liberalism' in Latin America today.* (Chinchilla and Haas 2006: 275)

In addition, popular education movements represent a new perspective for radical democracy within this region. All of these programmes connect cultural memory with community knowledge, on a path towards utopia, through popular education. Through our discussion of the

ACHIEVING EDUCATION FOR ALL THROUGH PUBLIC-PRIVATE PARTNERSHIPS?

Madres de Plaza de Mayo, the Cooperativa La Juanita, and the Barrios de Pie movement, we have attempted to present a viewpoint useful to young practitioners and academics within this region, by emphasising successful programmes, regardless of their scale, since they represent pedagogical projects that can be reinvented and expanded in other contexts. University programmes developed around an understanding of these highly interdisciplinary community efforts will push these young practitioners and academics to expand their understanding of 'Education for All'.

Victory for these individual groups represents a potential victory for a larger group of grassroots organisations that form small popular-education movements ignored in international debate conducted by large donors. Solidarity among these movements creates a guiding light that could be used by progressive educators in the Americas, who have been left in the dark by neo-liberal education. Ultimately, as we have argued in this essay, work by these progressive educators must be used to consider possibilities for both state and non-state actors, since together their work leads towards a genuine 'Education for All'.

Notes

1. In the span of less than a month, the popular education movement lost two of its most important representatives. On 27 March 2008, the Brazilian sociology professor at the University of Recife and popular militant, Francisco de Souza, to whom Paulo Freire dedicated his last book, *Pedagogy of Autonomy*, was assassinated in a home invasion in the State of Bahia, perhaps by someone that he struggled throughout his life to defend and educate. Two weeks later, on 10 April 2008, the Mexican educator Carlos Nuñez Hurtado lost his battle with cancer. We dedicate this essay to their memory.
2. Numerous authors have focused upon the development of social movements in Latin America, including Alvarez *et al.* (1998), De la Garza Toledo (2005), and Escobar and Alvarez (1992).
3. Popular education is highly heterogeneous, and should not be seen as a static phenomenon. We are not able to properly represent all the different manifestations of popular education within the space available. While we recognise relationship between the World Bank and community-based education programmes such as the Escuela Nueva in Colombia, we do not have space to write about the complexity of these international efforts for support and, in some cases, institutionalisation of popular education programmes within the region. As the nature of such collaborations has unfolded, disclosure of critical reports has been questioned, challenging the supposed participatory nature of these community programmes. See Stiglitz (2003: 234).
4. For more on globalisation and higher education in the Americas, including social-movement activism within higher education, see Rhoads and Torres (2006).
5. This section is based on previous work of Carlos A. Torres.
6. Paulo Freire was born in Recife, capital of the state of Pernambuco, and cultural capital of north-eastern Brazil, on 19 September 1921. He studied law, but after his graduation he abandoned practice of this profession in order to dedicate himself to education. After working as a Portuguese teacher in secondary and private schools, he worked as the Literacy Director (1947–54), and then as the Superintendent (until 1957) of SESI (a labour-training service financed by Pernambucan industry). His research on adult education, especially that based on the cultural circles of Angiços, catapulted him towards becoming President Goulard's Director of the Popular Culture Commission. He had to go into exile from Brazil after the *coup d'état* of 1964, forcing his pilgrimage throughout the world, until he was able to return to Brazil in 1980 as a university professor and founder of the Worker's Party (PT). From 1989 to 1992, he served as Secretary of Education of the Municipality of São Paulo, in the first government that the PT won in an important urban area.
7. We recognise that the face of neo-liberalism is always changing, as is its relationship to education. For an in-depth historical and contemporary analysis of this topic, see Burbules and Torres (2000), Rhoads and Torres (2006), and Torres (2009).

8. Space does not permit complete explanation of relationships between shifting political geography of Latin America, processes of social movements, and processes of popular education; however, we wish to acknowledge that popular education of the 1990s and 2000s has continued to shift the definition of what constitutes popular education, and that it remains a heterogeneous and dynamic phenomenon.
9. 'Assistential' refers to the nature of a programme – often state led – that may lead to beneficiaries' dependency on said programme.

References

Alvarez, S., E. Dagnino, and A. Escobar (1998) *Cultures of Politics, Politics of Culture: Re-visioning Latin American Social Movements*, Boulder, CO: Westview Press.

Arnove, Robert (1986) *Education and Revolution in Nicaragua*, Westport, CT: Praeger.

Barrios de Pie (2009) 'Barrios de Pie', available at www.barriosdepie.org.ar (retrieved 25 May 2009).

Bignani, S., P. Zisman, L. D'Onofrio, D. Rodríguez, and D. Theis (2004) 'Encuentro con el Movimiento sin Tierra del Brasil', in Claudia Korol (ed.) (2004).

Burbules, N. C. and C. A. Torres (2000) *Globalization and Education: Critical Perspectives*, New York, NY: Routledge.

Caufield, C. (1996) *Masters of Illusion: The World Bank and the Poverty of Nations*, New York, NY: Henry Holt and Co.

Cavallo, Domingo F. and Guillermo Mondino (1995) 'Keynote Address: Argentina's miracle? From hyperinflation to sustained growth', in Michael Bruno and Boris Pleskovic (eds.) *World Bank Conference on Development Economics*, Washington, DC: The World Bank.

Cavanagh, J., D. Wysham, and M. Arruda (1994) *Beyond Bretton Woods: Alternatives to the Global Economic Order*, London: Pluto Press.

Chinchilla, Norma and Liesl Haas (2006) '*De Protesta a Propuesta*: the contributions and challenges of Latin American feminism', in Eric Hershber and Fred Rosen (eds.) *Latin America After Neoliberalism: Turning the Tide in the 21st Century?*, New York, NY: The New Press.

Cooperativa La Juanita (2009) available at http://www.helpargentina.org/en/node/1276 (retrieved 25 May 2009).

Coraggio, J. L. (1999) *Política social y Economia del Trabajo: Alternativas a la Política Neoliberal para la Ciudad*, Buenos Aires: Miño y Dávila.

Culpitt, Ian (1992) *Welfare and Citizenship. Beyond the Crisis of the Welfare State?*, London: Sage.

De la Garza Toledo, Enrique (2005) *Sindicatos y Nuevos Movimientos Sociales en América Latina*, Buenos Aires: CLASCO.

Emeagwali, Gloria T. (ed.) (1995) *Women Pay the Price: Structural Adjustment in Africa and the Caribbean*, Trenton, NJ: Africa World Press.

Escobar, Arturo and Sonia E. Alvarez (eds.) (1992) *The Making of Social Movements in Latin America: Identity, Strategy, and Democracy*, Boulder, CO: Westview Press.

Freire, Paulo (1998) *Pedagogy of Freedom: Ethics, Democracy, and Civic Courage*, Lanham, MD: Rowman & Littlefield.

Gadotti, Moacir and Carlos Alberto Torres (eds.) (1993) *Educación Popular: Crises y Perspectivas*, Buenos Aires: Miño y Dávila.

Gónzalez Velasco, Laura (ed.) (2004) *Nuestra Cabeza Piensa Donde Nuestros Pies Caminan*, Buenos Aires: Editorial La Fragua.

Gramsci, Antonio (1971) 'History of the subaltern classes' and 'The concept of "ideology"', in Quintin Hoare and Geoffrey Nowell Smith (eds. and trans.) *Selections from the Prison Notebooks of Antonio Gramsci*, New York, NY: International Publishers.

Hale, Sondra (2007) 'Invited Talk: Paulo Freire Forum', University of California – Los Angeles, Los Angeles, CA, 6 November.

Jones, Lauren Ila (2009) 'Individual Theologies, Community Pedagogies: Liberatory Praxes of Latin American Women Educators', unpublished doctoral dissertation, University of California, Los Angeles, CA.

Korol, Claudia (ed.) (2004) *Pedagogía de la Resistencia: Cuadernos de Educación Popular*, Buenos Aires: Ediciones Madres de Plaza de Mayo.

Moran, Michael and Wright Maurice (eds.) (1991) *The Market and the State: Studies in Interdependence*, Oxford: Blackwell.

O'Cadiz, M. d. P., P. L. Wong, and C. A. Torres (1998) *Education and Democracy: Paulo Freire, Social Movements, and Educational Reform in São Paulo*, Boulder, CO: Westview Press.

Ramamurti, Ravi (1991) 'Privatization and the Latin America debt problem', in Robert Grosse (ed.) *Private Sector Solutions to the Latin America Debt Problem*, New Brunswick, NJ: Transaction.

Rhoads, R. A. and C. A. Torres (2006) *The University, State, and Market: The Political Economy of Globalization in the Americas*, Stanford, CA: Stanford University Press.

Stiglitz, J. E. (2003) *Globalization and its Discontents*, New York, NY: W.W. Norton.

Torres, Carlos A. (1995a) *Estudios Freireanos*, Buenos Aires: Libros del Quirquincho (Conquena Grupo).

Torres, Carlos A. (1995b) 'Participatory action research and popular education in Latin America', in P. L. McLaren and J. M. Giarelli (eds.) *Critical Theory and Educational Research*, Albany, NY: State University of New York Press.

Torres, Carlos A. (1996) *Las Secretas Aventuras del Orden. Estado y Educación*, Buenos Aires: Miño y Dávila.

Torres, C. A. (2009) *Globalizations and Education: Collected Essays on Class, Race, Gender, and the State*, New York, NY: Teachers College Press.

United Nations (1992) 'International Convention for the Protection of all Persons from Enforced Disappearance', available at http://untreaty.un.org/English/notpubl/IV_16_english.pdf (retrieved 2 April 2008).

Vázquez, Inés (ed.) (2007) *Historia de las Madres de Plaza de Mayo: Luchar Siempre Las Marchas de la Resistencia 1981–2006*, Buenos Aires: Ediciones Madres de Plaza de Mayo.

Collaboration in delivering education: relations between governments and NGOs in South Asia

Richard Batley and Pauline Rose

Collaboration between governments and non-state providers of basic services is increasingly a focus of attention by international agencies and national policy makers. The intention of such collaboration is to support common goals for achieving universal provision. Drawing on research in Bangladesh, India, and Pakistan, the contribution shows that collaboration can be successful where NGOs do not depend on limited sources for their funding, and invest time in building an informal relationship with government officials. In such cases, not only can collaboration strengthen NGO service provision directly, but it also provides opportunities for NGOs to engage in broader policy advocacy through insider influence.

Collaboration dans la prestation de services d'éducation : relations entre gouvernements et ONG en Asie du Sud
La collaboration entre les gouvernements et les prestataires non publics de services de base suscite une attention croissante de la part des agences internationales et des décideurs nationaux. Cette collaboration cherche à soutenir des buts communs pour parvenir à une prestation de services universelle. En se basant sur des recherches menées au Bangladesh, en Inde et au Pakistan, cet article montre que la collaboration peut porter ses fruits lorsque les ONG ne dépendent pas de sources limitées pour leur financement et investissent du temps dans la construction d'une relation informelle avec les officiels gouvernementaux. Dans ces cas, non seulement la collaboration peut renforcer directement la prestation de services par les ONG, mais elle donne également l'occasion aux ONG de s'engager dans des activités de plaidoyer plus larges à travers l'influence qu'elles peuvent exercer de l'« intérieur ».

Colaboração para promover a educação: relações entre governos e ONGs no sul da Ásia
A colaboração entre governos e provedores não-estatais de serviços básicos é cada vez mais o foco de atenção de agências internacionais e formuladores de política nacional. A intenção de tal colaboração é apoiar objetivos comuns para se alcançar provisão universal. Baseando-se em pesquisa realizada em Bangladesh, Índia e Paquistão, o artigo mostra que a colaboração pode ser bem-sucedida quando as ONGs não dependem de recursos limitados para o seu financiamento e investem tempo no desenvolvimento de uma relação informal com representantes do governo. Nestes casos, não apenas a colaboração pode fortalecer a provisão de serviços de ONG diretamente como também oferece oportunidade para as ONGs engajarem-se em políticas e advocacy mais amplas através de uma influência interna.

ACHIEVING EDUCATION FOR ALL THROUGH PUBLIC-PRIVATE PARTNERSHIPS?

La cooperación en el sector educativo entre gobiernos y ONG en el Sur Asiático

Las agencias internacionales y quienes diseñan políticas nacionales cada vez prestan más atención a la cooperación entre los gobiernos y los proveedores de servicios básicos no estatales. El objetivo de esta cooperación es apuntar hacia metas comunes y así lograr una cobertura universal. Este ensayo demuestra, basándose en investigaciones realizadas en Bangladesh, India y Pakistán, que la cooperación puede lograr avances reales cuando las ONG no dependen de sus limitados recursos de financiamiento sino que dedican más esfuerzos a la construcción de relaciones informales con funcionarios gubernamentales. Estas relaciones de cooperación no sólo pueden fortalecer los servicios que proporcionan las ONG, sino que también generan oportunidades para su incidencia en la determinación de políticas públicas a través de sus contactos con funcionarios.

Introduction

The post-colonial ideal of universal state provision of basic services embraced in South Asia and elsewhere has not been realised. This has often left the poorest and most vulnerable households underserved by public provision of basic education, health, and sanitation. In such circumstances, non-state providers sometimes play an important role. A key question that emerges is whether and how these providers collaborate with the state to support common objectives for achieving universal provision.

This research round-up provides a summary of findings from a two-year research project that aimed to understand how relationships between governments and non-state service providers are organised, strategies that the actors use to manage the relationship, and what balance of influence emerges between them.[1] Among non-state service providers, the research focused on bodies describing themselves as 'not-for-profit', non-governmental, voluntary, or community organisations.

While the scale of non-state provision varies between countries and across service sectors, it can be sizeable. Surveys show that, in Bangladesh, 88 per cent of households seeking healthcare go to non-state providers – mainly traditional village doctors. Outside the core of the larger cities of India, Bangladesh, and Pakistan, the population largely depends on sanitation services organised by households, communities, and entrepreneurs (WHO and UNICEF 2008). While non-state provision in education is often not on as large a scale as observed for health and sanitation, it too can sometimes be sizeable. In Pakistan, up to one-third of school children are estimated to attend a private school (Andrabi *et al.* 2006). NGOs also play a crucial role in extending education provision to children living in particularly difficult circumstances who are unable to access formal government schooling. In Bangladesh and India, such non-formal education by NGOs caters for around 8–10 per cent of overall primary-education enrolment (Chowdhury *et al.* 2004; Government of India, Ministry of Human Resource Development 2002).

Most private-sector (commercial) providers operate independently from government, making up for gaps and deficiencies in public services. In some cases, NGOs or voluntary associations have adopted the same go-it-alone strategy, often supported by donor funding – Bangladesh is well known as a country where parallel systems of service delivery have developed since the 1980s. However, many NGOs work in collaboration with government, either to improve public services or to complement them. The case for 'partnership' of this kind is now widely promoted by donors and acknowledged, in principle, by governments and many NGOs. Even where formal partnership arrangements do not exist, there is usually a variety of ways in which NGOs and governments have to – or choose to – collaborate.

While collaboration is widely acknowledged, purists of NGO autonomy would prefer them to maintain a wholly independent stance, advocating policy change and exerting external pressure on government. Politicians and public officials may see threats to their nominal mastery of public policy in the involvement of NGOs in the delivery of public services. How are these relationships handled in practice, and what are their effects on the autonomy of non-governmental public action?

This contribution focuses on evidence from the education sector, drawing on analysis of in-depth research of the relationships between government and an established national NGO in each of Bangladesh, India, and Pakistan. The selected cases were complemented by interviews with other key NGOs involved in education and other basic services within each of the countries. In primary education, the NGOs included in the study were involved in direct provision to 'hard to reach' children (both in urban slums and in remote rural areas), or were indirectly involved in provision through support to improve the quality of government schools. Their programmes were not viewed by government or NGOs as permanent arrangements, but as ways of filling gaps in government provision, or of bringing new and improved practices into government services.

How relationships are formally organised: are governments in charge?

The degree to which NGOs maintain a sphere of autonomy in relationships with government depends partly on the explicit assertiveness of government policy, control of finance, and setting of the terms of agreements. In Bangladesh, India, and Pakistan, government policies for basic services include some commitment to collaboration with NGOs. In the health sector in Bangladesh, for example, the relationship was governed by a directive policy supported by coordinated flows of donor funding through government. However, such strong government authority is not apparent for education in any of the three countries.

For the education sector, there is marked variation in the visibility of NGOs in national plans, with limited attention to the formal development of relationships with NGOs. In Bangladesh, where NGOs are most active, their role is not even made explicit within the Primary Education Development Programme (PEDPII). By contrast, in India, the importance of 'alternative and innovate education' to reach those otherwise excluded from school has been a central part of the Sarva Shiksha Abhiyan (Universalisation of Elementary Education Programme) (Government of India, Ministry of Human Resource Development 2002). This includes some government funding for NGO programmes in some states, which requires a formal, contractual relationship. However, as indicated below, NGOs are not necessarily dependent on this funding, with most of their resources often coming from philanthropic and local corporate sources. In Pakistan, formal government recognition of NGOs has occurred primarily since the 1990s as part of a donor-driven policy approach.

Where NGO provision is increasingly recognised in national planning, there are usually expectations that funding of their programmes will rely on international (and other non-government) sources. The inclusion of NGO programmes in education plans in the three countries to a large extent reflects trends internationally. Until the late 1990s, international priorities focused on NGO provision as being an 'alternative', parallel system to government. It is only since that time that such provision has been increasingly viewed as complementary to government schooling. This shift is reflected in attempts to ensure that qualifications obtained through NGO provision are recognised by governments and employers, in order to provide a route for children back into the public education system and into the labour market (Rose 2009). The international focus on identifying complementarity between NGO and government provision has occurred in the context of broader trends towards advocacy for partnerships in basic service delivery (Batley and Larbi 2004).

Despite relatively weak formal recognition of NGO activities by the three governments, strong views were expressed by some NGO stakeholders of a tendency by governments to increasingly favour more formalised relationships in practice. The NGOs anticipate a shift towards donor funding being channelled via governments rather than directly provided to NGOs, as donors seek to fulfil the Paris Declaration pledges of coordination and country ownership. NGOs expect such arrangements to be accompanied by more hierarchical written agreements or contracts, placing governments more firmly in the driving seat. This has intensified NGO awareness and interest in trying to work more closely with government officials to build cooperative relationships.

What strategies do NGOs adopt to achieve influence?

One question that arose from the research was whether NGOs are subordinated to government agendas. The research found that relationships between governments and NGOs were usually not so unbalanced.

Relations with government have usually grown out of a history of informal relationships between government and well-established NGOs. These informal relations are often sustained as an important basis of trust. In most cases, NGOs have options about their sources of funding. They are therefore not dependent on government, and so not powerless in their relations with them. Rather, they pursue strategies that balance independence, financial survival, and commitment to their own goals. The research identified three patterns of such strategies by NGOs.

1. Avoiding dependence on government or donors, to collaborate on a voluntary and equal basis

Certain NGOs are able to build mutual (more-or-less equal) relationships with government. The ability of the Indian education NGO to exploit funding from independent (philanthropic) sources enabled it to decide whether, and for what purpose, to attempt to acquire government resources directly through the government's Alternative and Innovative Education programme. While not being dependent on government, the NGO's leaders recognised the importance of building a relationship of trust with government. As a result, the NGO was able to influence government policy to support its own activities.

Through negotiations with the municipal corporation, the NGO was able to persuade government officials to do away with the mandatory requirement of a birth certificate for admission to municipal schools. The requirement was a key deterrent for children living in the slums who were born at home or had migrated from other states and hence did not possess a valid birth certificate. The NGO was modest in its success, and did not seek to claim exclusive credit for the policy change. In addition, as a result of the NGO's efforts, the municipal corporation conducts examinations in mathematics, Hindi, and general knowledge, and issues certificates to graduates from the NGO centres. This is important in giving credibility to the programme, as well as offering children the opportunity to continue with their education in the formal school system or to access employment opportunities. In both examples, engagement with government was primarily aimed at ensuring success of the NGO's own provision.

2. Avoiding dependence on any one funding source, to retain capacity to shape relationships

Some NGOs managed their financial situation to ensure that they were not dependent on a single source – by combining donor, government, and their own funding. The availability of multiple alternative sources of funding left them relatively free to assert their own priorities and to shape their relationship with government and other funders. In the Pakistan education case, the NGO's director successfully established herself in the role of knowledge broker between government and external agencies. Through her contacts with international agencies, she is familiar with the idea and language of 'partnership' and with new approaches to public management. Indeed, unlike the other two education NGOs studied in Bangladesh and India, the Pakistani NGO's mission statement makes explicit its aim to influence public policy.

Thanks to her high level of technical expertise, the director has been able to explain and 'sell' new approaches to collaboration – and not only to support the NGO's own provision. The NGO has even taken on the role of drafting for government the framework of agreements between them. While the NGO enters into 'mutual agreements' with government (formally through 'memoranda of understanding', MOUs, outlining the roles and responsibilities of each party), in practice it manages to take control of the relationship. The NGO's leadership takes pride in its ability to draw up the MOUs on behalf of government, and that it was the first NGO to initiate the preparation of these. By doing this, it considers that it has helped to build the capacity of district government, which did not know how to prepare such documents.

As with others, the NGO was astute at giving government the impression that it was in control, while actually using strategies to manage the relationship. Overall, the NGO's approach has been to get its demands met by government through negotiation and skilful manipulation, rather than confrontation, which it recognises as being counterproductive to its aims.

3. Accepting dependence on one or a few sources of funding, and adapting the NGO to funders' requirements

Relying on fewer sources of funding often led NGOs to adapt to the requirements of hierarchical relationships with government. This was most apparent for the NGOs in Bangladesh. Here, the education NGO studied was particularly dependent on one aid donor. The relationship with the donor had been relatively relaxed, enabling the NGO to operate at a distance from government. However, as greater accountability was being demanded for aid delivery by the donor's own government, the conditions under which the NGO could receive funding were being tightened. One of the conditions was that the NGO should work more closely with government, given the ultimate aim of the donor was to strengthen the government's own programmes. This was challenging for the NGO, in part raising questions within the organisation about whether it saw this as its role, because over the two decades of its existence, it had focused on its own direct service provision.

With the danger of losing funding from its primary source, the NGO had to diversify to other available options. Paradoxically, the key alternative source available was funding through a government programme that involved direct contracting of NGOs. Without having an already established cooperative relationship with government, this risked compromising the NGO's independence. Given its resource dependence, however, it did not have much choice. Under the formal contractual relationship with government, with which it did not have a sufficient basis of trust, the government was able to break the terms of the contract (for example, related to procurement of teaching materials) without any possibility of come-back by the NGO. Moreover, the government was able to assert control when the NGO broke the terms of the agreement by using funds allocated under the budget for renting facilities so as to increase wages of teachers, which it considered to be too low. The government had the power to withhold funding. This situation of resource dominance, in which the government neither desired nor was required to build a cooperative relationship with the NGO, led to antagonism that effectively put service delivery to some of the most vulnerable children in danger. Ultimately, it led to compromise on the part of the NGO, for which confrontation would have been counterproductive.

What balance of influence emerges? NGO service providers as policy advocates on the inside

While the basic strategy of all the NGOs studied was ultimately to avoid confrontation with government, they have often been able to influence policy and its implementation by collaborating with government, sometimes demonstrating new approaches to service delivery that government can adopt. They are outsiders to government but, through contracts, agreements, or even unwritten informal processes, become insiders to a relationship whose structure gives them influence. Paradoxically, while playing the 'insider role' may put actors' independence at risk, it also gives them the necessary leverage to assert influence. Insiders have the opportunity to understand the constraints on and opportunities for change, and to develop convincing explanations for why change is necessary.

Examples were found in the research where such insider influence by NGOs was an explicit part of their agenda (in Pakistan, for example), as well as occurring more subtly (for example, in India). By contrast, the NGO in Bangladesh concentrated efforts on its own service delivery, and made little attempt to engage in advocacy. For the Pakistani NGO, the aim was to use its own service delivery as an entry point to have an effect on high-level policy directions. Thanks to the determination of the NGO's director and her connections with senior policy makers, this achieved some success. Ultimately, the Indian NGO was less ambitious, limiting advocacy for policy change to ones that supported its activities, and achieved the desired result of enabling disadvantaged children to go to school. In both the Indian and Pakistani cases, successful management of relationships by NGO service providers with government allowed them to engage in a form of 'soft advocacy' that may be as, if not more, influential on policy and practice than the 'hard advocacy' that external critics of government have to adopt.

Conclusion

NGO engagement in basic service delivery is often criticised on two somewhat contrary grounds. From one perspective, international support for NGO provision is seen as part of a 'neo-liberal' agenda, undermining the responsibility of government or marginalising it to a mere oversight role. From another perspective, NGO provision is seen as providing access to those who the government is unable to reach. However, from this perspective, the advantages of NGO independence in service delivery (in terms of offering greater flexibility and provision more responsive to local needs, for example) is viewed as being threatened where they are being encouraged to work in collaboration with government. Such collaboration is seen as potentially undermining both the flexibility of the provision that they are able to offer, and also their independent advocacy role. While at the extreme these two threats do exist, our research showed that there are more subtle possibilities that are more often the case in reality. Governments can maintain responsibility while benefiting from well-structured support by NGOs, in particular to provide education in difficult circumstances. Through this, NGOs can exert influence on both policy and service delivery where they take time to establish a reputation, show clear expertise, invest in building informal relationships with government, and ensure that they are not dependent on any one source of funding. As such, NGOs should not necessarily be seen as having to choose between being providers *or* advocates. Rather, this research finds that, under certain conditions, engagement in advocacy *and* service provision may exist simultaneously.

Note

1. This contribution is based on research funded by the Economic and Social Research Council under the Non-Governmental Public Action Programme (Project Number RES-155-25-0045). Besides the authors, the research team included Masooda Bano, Padmaja Nair, S. M. Nurul Alam, Kevin Sansom, Natasha Palmer, and Kelly Teamey. For further information, see http://www.idd.bham.ac.uk/research/service_providers.shtml.

References

Andrabi, T, J. Das, and A. I. Khwaja (2006) 'The Possibilities and Limits of Private Schooling in Pakistan', *World Bank Policy Research Working Paper 4066*, Washington, DC: The World Bank.

Batley, R. A. and G. A. Larbi (2004) *The Changing Role of Government: The Reform of Public Services in Developing Countries*, Basingstoke, UK: Palgrave Macmillan.

Chowdhury, Alamgir Farouk, Simon Delay, Naushad Faiz, Iftekher Haider, Brian Reed, Pauline Rose, and Ptitti Dave Sen (2004) 'Bangladesh: Study of Non-State Providers of Basic Services', London: DFID.

Government of India, Ministry of Human Resource Development (2002) 'Sarva Shiksha Abhiyan, A Programme for Universalization of Elementary Education', Delhi: Ministry of Human Resource Development.

Rose, Pauline (2009) 'NGO provision of basic education: alternative or complementary service delivery to support access to the excluded?', *Compare* 39 (2): 219–33.

WHO and UNICEF (2008) 'Progress on Drinking Water and Sanitation: Special Focus on Sanitation', New York, NY: United Nations Children's Fund, and Geneva: World Health Organization.

Working effectively with non-state actors to deliver education in fragile states

Chris Berry

This viewpoint uses evaluation reports from Nepal, Afghanistan, and Yemen in order to learn lessons about how donors and governments can work more effectively with non-state actors to deliver education in fragile states. The evaluation framework draws on the Development Assistance Committee principles for good international engagement in fragile states. The analysis concludes that a more effective partnership requires better regulation of non-state actors, increased efforts to build community capacity to hold schools and local government to account for the quality of services, and more upfront and systematic analysis of the conflict dynamics of investment in the education sector.

Collaborer efficacement avec les acteurs non publics pour fournir des services d'éducation dans les États fragiles
Ce point de vue a recours à des rapports d'évaluation provenant du Népal, d'Afghanistan et du Yémen pour tirer les leçons de la manière dont les bailleurs de fonds et les gouvernements peuvent travailler plus efficacement avec des acteurs non publics pour fournir des services d'éducation dans des États fragiles. Le cadre d'évaluation se base sur les principes du Comité d'aide au développement relatifs au bon engagement international dans les États fragiles. L'analyse conclut que, pour être plus efficace, un partenariat requiert une meilleure réglementation des acteurs publics, des efforts accrus pour renforcer la capacité communautaire à exiger des comptes aux écoles et aux autorités gouvernementales locales sur la qualité des services, et une analyse plus opportune et systématique de la dynamique de conflit des investissements dans le secteur de l'éducation.

Trabalhando efetivamente com agentes não-estatais para implementar a educação em estados frágeis
Este ponto de vista utiliza relatórios de avaliação do Nepal, Afeganistão e Iêmen para aprender lições sobre como doadores e governos podem trabalhar mais efetivamente com agentes não-estatais para implementar a educação em estados frágeis. A estrutura de avaliação baseia-se nos princípios do Comitê de Assistência ao Desenvolvimento para um bom engajamento internacional em estados frágeis. A análise conclui que uma parceria mais efetiva requer uma melhor regulação de agentes não-estatais, maiores esforços para desenvolver a capacidade da comunidade de manter as escolas e o governo local responsáveis pela qualidade dos

serviços e uma análise mais honesta e sistemática das dinâmicas de conflito de investimento no setor da educação.

Cómo los programas de desarrollo pueden trabajar con entes no estatales para proporcionar servicios educativos básicos más eficaces en Estados frágiles
Este ensayo se vale de evaluaciones realizadas en Nepal, Afganistán y Yemen para documentar cómo los donantes y los gobiernos pueden trabajar con entes no estatales y lograr mejores servicios educativos en Estados frágiles. El marco evaluativo se basa en los principios de buena conducta internacional en Estados frágiles adoptados por el Comité de Ayuda para el Desarrollo. El ensayo concluye que para conseguir alianzas más eficaces se necesita una regulación más adecuada para los entes no estatales, mayor vigilancia comunitaria sobre la calidad de los servicios escolares y gubernamentales, y un análisis más transparente y sistemático de la difícil dinámica de inversión en el sector educativo.

Introduction

The aim of this contribution is to understand how development programmes can better work with non-state actors to improve the effectiveness of the delivery of aid to primary and secondary education in fragile states. For the purposes of this contribution, non-state actors in education encompass NGOs, community organisations, private-sector organisations, and faith-based groups (see Rose 2007).

The fragile-states agenda has become increasingly important for donor agencies (for example, DFID, US Agency for International Development, World Bank) since the early 2000s. While precise definitions vary, and it is difficult to categorise countries, fragile states generally have low income, are prone to conflict, have weak governance structures, and are frequently regarded as difficult environments to live and work in. They are also the countries which will be least likely to attain the Millennium Development Goals (MDGs), and are also regarded as potentially destabilising to their neighbours (and possibly globally, hence the increasing attention that they have been receiving from donors). Within many of these countries, the education sector is regarded as potentially both part of the problem and part of the solution (Smith and Vaux 2003). For example, education can be used to fuel social exclusion, or it can build a more cohesive society.

Non-state actors play an important role in the education sector, especially in situations where access to education services is low, as is often the case in fragile-state contexts (Rose 2007). NGOs may step in to deliver education services for excluded or underserved groups, communities themselves may spontaneously join together to build and even staff schools, private schools proliferate where state provision does not reach or is perceived as irrelevant, and faith-based organisations may seek to find ways to reach the poor and marginalised. In fragile states, where education services tend to break down, it can be assumed that conditions generally exist for high levels of non-state actor involvement, although data either does not exist or is highly unreliable.

Typical donor engagement with education non-state actors in fragile-type environments tends to lead to the development of parallel, fragmented systems, which can weaken state authority and visibility, and make it difficult to rebuild a coherent education system when conditions become more favourable. It is important, therefore, to find ways to develop programmes that engage non-state actors but reduce these adverse effects.

Cases and framework for the analysis

The three country contexts chosen as the focus of this paper are Afghanistan, Yemen, and Nepal. The contexts were chosen because they broadly represent different types of fragility, and the aid instrument used to support them was different in each case. At the time of analysis (in 2006), Nepal was in conflict, Afghanistan was classified as recovering from conflict, and Yemen had been in a state of constant instability since its independence in the early 1960s. Table 1 summarises the programme approach used in each of the three contexts and the period for which evaluation data were available in each case.

In Nepal, a Sector-wide Approach (SWAp) with the government was supported by five donors (Denmark, DFID, Finland, Norway, and the World Bank) during the Maoist insurgency (the programme was agreed in 2004 when only 10–20 per cent of Nepal's territory was within government control). The programme, 'Education for All', focused on pre-primary, primary, and adult literacy. Approximately 25 per cent of the government's annual sub-sector budget was provided from this fund – typically in the region of $40 million per annum. During the period under review (2004–2006), net enrolment in primary education increased from 84.2 per cent to 86.8 per cent, and for girls from 78 per cent to 83.4 per cent (DFID 2006).

In Afghanistan, after the international community intervened to oust the Taliban in 2001, it was clear that large-scale assistance would be needed to address the physical damage and the years of neglect that the country had suffered (Scanteam 2005). The Afghanistan Reconstruction Trust Fund (ARTF) was set up in March 2002 to serve as a coordinated financing mechanism for the transitional government's recurrent budget (the Recurrent Cost Window), and priority reconstruction programmes and projects identified by government (the Investment Window). Between 2002 and 2007, the ARTF successfully mobilised $1.45 billion in grant contributions from 25 donors. In the education sector, much of the budget was used to pay teachers' salaries – the equivalent of around $109 million per annum. Enrolment of children in grades 1–12 increased across the country from 3.1 million in 2002 to just over 5 million in 2006. Enrolment of girls more than doubled over same period, from 839,000 to 1.75 million (World Bank 2007).

The Yemen Social Fund for Development (YSFD), which was established in 1997, was designed to improve access to basic social services for low-income groups, and also to provide an example of an effective, efficient, and transparent institutional mechanism for providing social services in Yemen. The third phase of YSFD (2005–2008) was supported by 15 donor agencies who contributed a total of $300 million. In addition, International

Table 1: Approaches to and examples of education aid in three fragile states

Approach	Data source
Sector-wide approach (SWAp) (working within a government-led framework)	Nepal Education for All Programme 2004–2006
Trust Fund (working towards a government-led framework)	Afghanistan Reconstruction Trust Fund (ARTF) 2002–2006
Social Fund (working alongside a government-led framework)	Yemen Social Fund for Development (YSFD) 1997–2006

Development Assistance provided $60 million, and the Yemeni government $40 million. Over 50 per cent of the investment was absorbed by the primary education sub-sector. From its establishment in 1997, up to the time of evaluation at the end of 2006, the fund contributed to building 12,978 classrooms, and the number of students enrolled increased by 38 per cent. The increase in enrolment of girls was particularly impressive – up by 122 per cent in rural areas (ESA Consultores Internacional/Environmental Resources Management 2007: 36–58).

This contribution examines non-state involvement in these programmes with respect to three of the 12 Principles for Good International Engagement in Fragile States developed by the Organisation for Economic Cooperation and Development Development Assistance Committee (OECD DAC 2007) – coordination, state building, and do no harm. These three principles of effectiveness were selected on the basis of their particular relevance to the education sector. They are used as a basis for analysing the extent to which donors were able to work with non-state actors to effectively deliver education aid in each of the three selected fragile-state contexts. Lessons learned from these three examples are also presented.

Coordination

The aim of DAC Principle 7 is to encourage international actors to agree practical coordination mechanisms for aid delivery. The principle suggests that, where possible, international actors should work together with reformers in government and civil society to develop shared analysis and priorities. Working on coordination frameworks with international and local NGOs in the education sector is important because of the risks of fragmentation of efforts, and the need for planning to strategically build the capacity of NGOs to engage in the longer term. All three of the selected examples point to challenges for donors in working effectively with partner governments to coordinate with NGOs and to develop coherent strategies for their engagement in the sector.

In Nepal, twice-yearly review meetings steered the direction of the Nepal SWAp, but NGOs were not represented in these meetings, even though they had become increasingly important in helping the government to deliver education services, especially in contested areas of the country (Berry *et al.* 2004). In their study of the SWAp and conflict, Vaux *et al.* (2006: 36) point to the difficulties that NGOs faced when engaging with a government that tended to operate in a top–down way. They also refer to a 'contracting' culture among many NGOs that led to suspicions on the part of government that NGOs were only in it for the money. Vaux *et al.* (2006: 37–41) conclude that more needs to be done by donors to persuade government to include NGO representation in SWAp consultations.

According to a joint evaluation of aid to Afghanistan (DANIDA Evaluation Department 2005), there was a history of NGOs filling the gap in education provision left during the Taliban regime. After the fall of the Taliban, ARTF helped support the Ministry of Education to take a leadership role in the sector. The Ministry of Education (MoE) has included NGOs in its consultative and technical groups, and these have worked to various degrees. However, more general government suspicions of the motives of NGOs led to discussions about their future in the sector. They were perceived by some in the government as lacking qualifications to provide proper education services. The joint evaluation concludes that NGOs are crucial to the development of the sector, but that donors should work with other stakeholders to find ways to regulate them and thereby avoid misuse of the NGO concept.

YSFD has mainly supported NGOs in the education sector on service delivery, focusing particularly on special needs. For example, it supported a project to enhance the capability of instructors at the Al-Hodeidah Association to deal with mentally disabled children. Another project supported the integration of deaf children into public schools (ESA Consultores

Internacional/Environmental Resources Management 2007). However, an institutional assessment of YSFD (Jennings 2006) highlighted the problem of large numbers of welfare-oriented NGOs, often highly dependent on external financing and temporary in nature. Both reports conclude that YSFD should invest more in the institutional development of NGOs and develop a framework for working with NGOs to reduce the risks of fragmentation in the sector. Jennings (2006: 26) recommended that YSFD conduct an assessment of NGOs to assess their strengths and weaknesses, develop a capacity-building strategy, and coordinate the respective roles and responsibilities among NGOs with a view to developing joint funding proposals.

State building

DAC Principle 3 focuses on state building as a central objective, including improving governance and capacity in core service-delivery functions. In all three of our country examples, the education sector is a priority area for engagement because it is perceived to contribute to longer-term state-building objectives, such as citizenship and skills development, and because community demand for education services remains high even in difficult circumstances. This section examines the extent to which the approach taken was effective at building community structures that hold schools and teachers to account and at strengthening the link between community and government policy makers.

The Education for All programme in Nepal supported decentralised school management through the strengthening of school management committees. Vaux *et al.* (2006) report that these committees frequently had only tokenistic representation from minority groups, and were forced to charge informal fees to students in order to make up for a lack of government financing. Where schools were started spontaneously by local communities, they were only allowed to register on payment of Rs. 50,000 (about $500) – a huge sum for a small community. These schools were also only entitled to one teacher for 60 students, compared with the national norm in government schools of one teacher for 50 students. School management committees were reported to lack confidence in the decision-making process of the ministry, and considered that resources were allocated mainly to schools favoured by the government. Teachers in these schools were also reported to worry that their terms and conditions would not be protected by communities, and to have encouraged Maoists to close the schools down. The report recommends increased transparency in budget allocation to schools, further increasing their autonomy through strengthened management councils, and ensuring adequate consultation on the community school model with teachers and teacher unions.

In Afghanistan, one of the ARTF's vehicles for investment financing was the National Solidarity Programme. This programme deliberately sought to build community-level structures, called Community Development Committees, on the basis of demand for services. At the time of the Scanteam (2005) evaluation, over 300 schools had been built using a community-led approach. Four issues were emerging, however. The first was that the community structures that the programme was seeking to develop were fragile, and not yet capable of making the links between communities and national government. Second, there was no gender policy underpinning participation in, and management of, the Community Development Committees. Third, the demand for services generated by the capital investment through the Community Development Committees could not be met on the supply side (that is, provision of teachers) by the Ministry of Education. Fourth, the sub-national level of governance, on which the success of a community-driven approach rests, was not being given adequate attention. One of the recommendations was to develop a more programmatic approach to Community Development Committees and focus more on the sustainability of investments (Scanteam 2005: 41–4).

YSFD has made a substantial investment in school and classroom building, as much as 12 per cent of the total stock (ESA Consultores Internacional/Environmental Resources Management 2007: 36), using a community development approach. Jennings' (2006: 18–19) institutional evaluation of YSFD identifies two best-practice projects in the education sector for introducing participatory approaches and transforming the relationship between parents and schools (the Quality of Education Programme and the Girls' Education Pilot Project). In the case of the Girls' Education Project, women have become active in promoting girls' education on a house-to-house basis. An unanticipated outcome of the projects is that parents and teachers considered that education is a shared responsibility between the community and the Ministry of Education. Parent Councils were taking a leading role in taking education beyond the classroom and out into the community. The challenge for YSFD was how to work with government to scale up these projects in a cost-effective and sustainable way.

Do no harm

DAC Principle 8 states that the international community should seek to avoid activities that undermine national institution building. Education has been identified as an important positive force with respect to promoting social cohesion, but there are also instances of state using the education system for political or ideological ends, and this may have the opposite effect (Smith and Vaux 2003). The three cases examined here illustrate how working with non-state actors in the education sector may have both positive and negative consequences.

In Nepal, private schooling expanded rapidly between 1995 and 2006, with as many as 20 per cent of children enrolled in private schools (Vaux *et al.* 2006). Initially, Maoists targeted private schools on ideological grounds, and many were closed down. Over time, however, they were reported to have increasingly tolerated them, possibly because they were a source of revenue. Problems with improving the quality of government schools – for example, in getting textbooks delivered in a timely fashion – were reportedly increasing the risk of elites disengaging from government schooling. Private schools, with a focus on English as the medium of instruction, and far higher chances of passing the examinations, were reported to lead to a division in Nepali society between those who can afford private schooling, and those who continue to be failed by the government system. Vaux *et al.* (2006: 19–22) concluded that this divide was not conducive to resolving the conflict, and urged for more policy thinking around the issue.

In Afghanistan, one of the issues that emerged from the support for NGO provision through ARTF was that of differential terms and conditions for those employed by NGOs and those employed by the government. The Scanteam (2005) evaluation pointed out that more favourable packages offered by the NGO sector were in some cases sucking skilled workers out of the civil service and undermining longer-term development objectives. While this problem was not restricted to the education sector alone, it had resulted in serious government suspicion about the motives and effectiveness of NGOs in the sector (as mentioned above). One recommendation emerging from the joint evaluation (DANIDA Evaluation Department 2005) was for donors to look more seriously at reform efforts to mitigate the capacity and resource gap between the public administration and the international humanitarian and development assistance. The same report also concluded that 'the aim should be to develop voluntary synergies and constructive synergies between NGO and state interventions, while avoiding the creation of a local NGO elite which out-competes the public sector for staff because of its better remuneration' (DANIDA Evaluation Department 2005: 167).

The YSFD experience highlights some of the risks of using community-driven approaches to support development in the education sector. The impact-evaluation study (ESA

Consultores Internacional/Environmental Resources Management 2007) highlights cultural barriers to getting females involved in decision-making processes because of traditional male dominance. Consequently, there are reported problems with getting girls into school, and hiring female teachers (often a prerequisite for getting and keeping girls in school in Yemen). The same evaluation recommends that YSFD put increased efforts into ensuring the participation of women in community groups, and related efforts to close the gender gap in education.

Lessons for developing programmes

The key lessons for the design and implementation of development programmes are as follows.

- *Coordination:* in all three cases, NGOs play an important role in the provision of education. However, they are also diverse and differ in terms of their capacity and intentions. Governments may be suspicious of their motives, and donors too quick to support them outside of agreed coordination structures. This review points to the need for some way of regulating NGOs, as well as including them more systematically in dialogue and planning.
- *State building:* the cases show that demand for education is extremely resilient and this makes the education sector a good entry point for community-driven approaches. However, programmes need to ensure that the capacity of community groups is given sufficient support (training and resources) in order to hold schools to account effectively. They also need to be aware of the risk that demand-side efforts may outstrip capacity to supply inputs such as teachers and learning materials.
- *Do no harm:* the way development programmes work (or don't work) with community groups, private schools, and NGOs can all make things worse. They can, of course, also make things better. The evaluations reviewed here point to the need to do some serious upfront analysis of the stakeholders involved in the sector, and the possible dynamics and adverse consequences of donor and government actions.

References

Berry, Chris, Debbie Duncan, and Jeremy Armon (2004) 'Service Delivery in Difficult Environments: The Case of Nepal', unpublished report, London: DFID.
DANIDA Evaluation Department (2005) 'A Joint Evaluation of Humanitarian and Reconstruction Assistance to Afghanistan 2001–2005', Copenhagen: Ministry of Foreign Affairs.
DFID (2006) 'Education for All', unpublished report, London: DFID.
ESA Consultores Internacional/Environmental Resources Management (2007) 'Yemen Social Fund for Development: 2006 Impact Evaluation Study', unpublished report, London: DFID.
Jennings, Mary (2006) 'Institutional Evaluation of Social Fund for Development, Republic of Yemen', unpublished report, London: DFID.
OECD DAC (Organisation for Economic Cooperation and Development Development Assistance Committee) (2007) 'Principles for Good International Engagement in Fragile States & Situations', [Paris]: OECD, available at http://www.oecd.org/dataoecd/61/45/38368714.pdf (retrieved June 2007).
Rose, Pauline (2007) 'Supporting Non State Providers in Basic Education Service Delivery', *Research Monograph No. 4*, Brighton, UK: University of Sussex Institute of Education.
Scanteam (2005) 'Assessment, Afghanistan Reconstruction Trust Fund', unpublished report, Oslo: Scanteam Analysts and Advisers.
Smith, Alan and Tony Vaux (2003) 'Education, Conflict and International Development', London: DFID.

World Bank (2007) 'Expanding Access to Education in Afghanistan', available at http://web.worldbank.org/WBSITE/EXTERNAL/EXTABOUTUS/IDA/0,,contentMDK:21289161~menuPK:3266877~pagePK:51236175~piPK:437394~theSitePK:73154,00.html (retrieved June 2007).
Vaux, Tony, Alan Smith, and Sirjana Subba (2006) 'Education for All – Nepal: Review from a Conflict Perspective', unpublished report, London: International Alert.

Non-state providers, the state, and health in post-conflict fragile states

Stephen Commins

Relations between states and non-state providers in fragile states occur within specific complex political and economic contexts. Moreover, donor approaches to specific fragile states shape the flow and priorities of aid resources. In the health sector, fragile states have dramatically poor health outcomes, with higher mortality and morbidity rates than other low-income, relatively stable states.

Les prestataires non publics, l'État et la santé dans les États fragiles post-conflit
Les relations entre prestataires publics et non publics dans les États fragiles ont lieu dans le cadre de contextes politiques et économiques complexes précis. De plus, les approches des bailleurs de fonds concernant les États fragiles influencent le flux et les priorités des ressources d'aide. Dans le secteur de la santé, les États fragiles affichent des résultats extrêmement mauvais en matière de santé, avec des taux de mortalité et de morbidité supérieurs à ceux d'autres pays à faible revenu relativement stables.

Provedores não-estatais, o estado e a saúde em estados frágeis após conflito
As relações entre provedores estatais e não-estatais em estados frágeis ocorrem dentro de contextos políticos e econômicos complexos específicos. Além disto, abordagens de doadores para estados frágeis específicos influenciam o fluxo e as prioridades dos recursos de ajuda. No setor da saúde, estados frágeis apresentam resultados de saúde incrivelmente ruins, com taxas de mortalidade e morbidade maiores do que outros países relativamente estáveis de baixa renda.

Proveedores no estatales, el Estado y la salud en Estados frágiles durante el posconflicto
Las relaciones entre el Estado y los proveedores no estatales se dan en contextos políticos y económicos especialmente complejos en Estados frágiles. Además, en ciertos Estados frágiles son los donantes quienes diseñan las estrategias que establecen el flujo y las prioridades de los recursos humanitarios. En el sector salud, los Estados frágiles tienen los indicadores más negativos, con tasas de mortalidad y morbilidad más altas que en Estados de bajos ingresos pero relativamente más estables.

This contribution looks at some of the roles of non-state providers (NSPs) in providing health services in fragile states that are coming out of conflict, and the relationships of NSPs with state agencies. The most significant issue for both NSPs and donors in fragile states is the challenge of delivering services effectively while also strengthening the capacity of public institutions, where feasible, so that the state will have both the capacity for service delivery (even if not direct provision) and the willingness to be accountable to its citizens. This can be described as the 'two-track problem': balancing the urgent need for services with the long-term process of building effective and accountable public institutions. Two examples of the role of health NSPs are given in summary: contracting out basic health provision in Afghanistan, and financing health provision via the Multi-Donor Trust Fund in Southern Sudan. The contribution concludes with a few observations on ways to address the balance between state and NSP roles in fragile states.

In assessing the connections between health services and the roles of the state in fragile states, some of the key issues include:

- Dynamics of the political settlement
- Approaches to connecting health services to health-system strengthening
- Donor aid instruments
- Pre-existing and evolving roles of NSPs.

Health in fragile states

The primary work on defining fragile states has been done by DFID (2005), with additional work by the World Bank (2009), USAID (2005), and the Fragile States Group of the Development Assistance Committee (DAC) at the OECD (2005a, b).[1] The DAC Fragile States Group used a concept of fragile states as suffering 'deficits in governance' creating 'conditions that make development difficult' (OECD 2005b). In such states:

- There is a lack of ability or willingness to establish preconditions for long-term development;
- Prevailing conditions are 'too fluid and too risky to make savings and long term investment attractive';
- 'Society focuses on the near term and securing its most basic needs', sometimes through 'creative local solutions' (OECD 2005a: 4).

This conception builds on the efforts of several donor agencies (drawing on scholarly work), each of which has advanced a definition of troubled states that responds to its own mission and programmatic strategies:

- Deterioration (conflict/risk of conflict; declining capacity and/or willingness to provide services)
- Arrested development (lack of will, may have moderate or high capacity)
- Post-conflict (may be post-conflict or not; high will but low capacity)
- Post-conflict (transitional phase, with risk of return to conflict; low capacity of government, political will may be high or low) (OECD 2005b).

Fragile states are all distinct in their histories, the nature of the political fragility, and the obstacles to effective service delivery. At the same time, they share common characteristics. Notably, in terms of services, they are among the countries least likely to meet the Millennium Development Goals (MDGs). For example, they contain a third of those people globally living on less than a dollar a day and half of all children who die before the age of five years (HLF

2004). They also share examples of poor governance, which can be the result of a lack of capacity or lack of interest in the well-being of their citizens.

According to the High Level Forum (HLF) on the Health MDGs (HLF 2004), fragile states contain approximately 15 per cent of the world's population, but have notably poor health indicators. For example, 30 per cent of maternal deaths, 50 per cent of the children who die before the age of five, and a third of those affected by HIV and AIDs in developing countries occur in fragile states. The HLF (2004) noted that (then) current approaches to reaching the health MDGs were not feasible without new ways of addressing health services in fragile states.

There are significant obstacles to establishing effective, coherent, and sustainable health-delivery systems in fragile states, as donors often find it necessary to by-pass state systems in post-conflict settings. The health sector has greater complexities in terms of the factors that influence health outcomes (many of which are outside of 'health', such as nutrition or clean water). Health provision requires more diverse technical skills and a greater use of technical inputs (notably drugs) than either education or water systems do. This means that the structure and development of government functions is likely to involve a different set of capabilities and roles than in other sectors.

The use of NSPs and other agencies in the delivery of social services has been the option of choice for many donors in situations of humanitarian emergencies and/or poor governance. Bilateral and multilateral donors have, for a variety of reasons, by-passed state institutions with an emphasis on non-public (NSP, social fund, private for-profit) provision of services. NSPs have had to struggle to find ways to work effectively in situations where there has been a history of proliferating donor funding approaches in fragile states. This relates to the longer-term question of how NSPs can strengthen or undermine the capacity of state agencies.

Relations between states and non-state providers of health

In dealing with a post-conflict fragile state, donors have frequently adopted a strategy that substitutes an international agency or NGO for the state. This is particularly the case in humanitarian emergencies, where there is a short-term urgent need to provide access to certain services. Internationally recognised bodies then take on some, or all, of the policy-making tasks, including identifying the level and quality of services to be delivered. Contracts for services to NSPs may produce short-term benefits in terms of enhanced service delivery, but there are problems in terms of building sustainable service-delivery systems for the long term. This 'two-track problem' poses a real dilemma between mitigating immediate humanitarian needs and delaying the establishment of durable, local service delivery.

While the growing emphasis on fragile states in the period after 2002–03 has allowed donors to address common problems of aid allocations in difficult contexts, other problems remain. These include the need to rebuild state capacity alongside of delivering services, often under the problematic term of 'state building'. The role of NSPs in relation to state building remains unclear, as there are only evolving frameworks for who is responsible to build the public-sector capacity to regulate, finance, monitor, or provide different services. The various donor programmes are often inconsistent and do not have the information necessary for detailed operational planning linked with policy oversight.

Country experiences of the relationship between non-state provision and the state in the health sector[2]

In practice, NSPs have been engaged in state building in terms of supporting state capacity in the health services. However, there are quite specific country relationships, often complex, between NSPs and states. Commins' (2006) study for OECD/DAC reviewed several dozen NSP reports, which consistently showed that there were more formal relations or contracts between NSPs and states than might have been anticipated. Interviews with NSP staff working in Afghanistan, Liberia, Sierra Leone, Sudan, and other countries have shown that many NSPs invest time and resources in working with state agencies. In addition, despite the image of NSPs operating separately from state agencies, the greater problem is not NSPs acting without any relationship with the state, but rather the lack of any overall policy or coordination framework, both among donors themselves, and among donors, governments, and NSPs. Examples are explored here in the fragile-state contexts of Afghanistan and Southern Sudan.

Afghanistan and Southern Sudan have both experienced several decades of civil war. Following the Soviet invasion in 1979, Afghanistan's health system was devastated by the war between various Afghan militias and the Afghan government plus Soviet forces. The withdrawal of the Soviet forces led to new conflict between different militias and the eventual emergence of the Taliban, a Pushtun-based Islamic movement that sought to end the corruption of the warlords. The overthrow of the Taliban because of their support for Al Qaeda in 2001 led to the establishment of a new coalition government, which was a patchwork collection of local powerbrokers and political exiles. Meanwhile, Southern Sudanese fought against the Khartoum-based national government in two long civil wars, 1955–1972, starting again in 1983 until the Comprehensive Peace Agreement (CPA) in 2005.

Among the differences in the political dynamics and NSP experiences between Afghanistan and Southern Sudan are two key points: the Government of Southern Sudan was a relatively unified political movement, the Sudanese People's Liberation Army, while the Government of Afghanistan was a new creation after 2001; international NSPs had minimal presence in Afghanistan during the Taliban period, while NSPs were widespread in Southern Sudan throughout the civil war. This meant that both the dynamics of the political settlements (and push for state legitimacy) and the pre-existing roles of NSPs were quite distinct. Both countries illustrate some of the challenges of providing health services in a fragile-state context, and both provide examples of the difficulties in ensuring that both services and systems are developed in a coherent manner. As of 2008, despite the greater problems of insecurity and political fragility, the results in Afghanistan appear to offer a more positive set of outcomes in the health sector.

Afghanistan

In Afghanistan, the Ministry of Public Health in conjunction with the major donors developed a Basic Package of Health Services that sought to set out specific guidelines for priority service delivery, health infrastructure, and staff capacity. The government and donors also concluded that, with a lack of government capacity, the Basic Package would be better carried out through contracts with NSPs. The establishment of the Basic Package sought to address four obstacles to an effective health system in Afghanistan highlighted in a study on the country's health system (Waldman *et al.* 2006): (i) lack of managerial and service-delivery capacity within the Ministry of Public Health; (ii) lack of physical infrastructure and qualified personnel; (iii) poor distribution of financial and human resources; and (iv) uncoordinated and undirected efforts of the NSPs.

The Ministry began contracting out provision of the Basic Package through NGOs with funding and technical support from donors in 2003. Studies of the Basic Package (Waldman *et al.* 2006) have highlighted some of the specific issues facing the Government of Afghanistan in moving forward with a country-wide contracting system. The Ministry has had to address issues of insecurity, the size and diversity of the country, and the role of local government. It has sought to balance out NSP roles through the structure of the service contracts, as well as the improvement of the capacity of the Ministry to oversee the health sector through the Basic Package. Among the results that have been documented in Afghanistan are a substantial reduction in child mortality, increased immunisation coverage, and higher coverage in reproductive-health services. This has been attributed to a clear focus in the Basic Package on delivery by NSPs and oversight by the Ministry. While the Basic Package has had success in areas where security has allowed for NSP operations, questions remain over whether it can contribute to state building and state legitimacy given the larger political factors and ongoing level of violence.

Southern Sudan

In Southern Sudan, the particular politics of the Comprehensive Peace Agreement and the looming deadline of a vote on the future of the Sudanese state elevated the pressure on the Government of Southern Sudan (GoSS) to take a central and visible role in the health sector. This has at times meant a push for more direct government services, even when there has been a lack of state capacity, so that the prioritising of state building has created potential problems for ensuring improved service delivery. There is less clarity on roles and responsibilities than in Afghanistan, which is partly due to the limited time that donors and government had to put the 'within the state' system in place. NSPs have had serious problems with the Multi-Donor Trust Fund (MDTF) that was supposed to serve as an effective financing mechanism by co-ordinating donor funding. MDTFs are supposed to provide a central funding mechanism for the distribution of donor funds to improve coordination and tracking of resources, but this has not been the case in Sudan.

Many NSPs had existing relations with officials in the GoSS during the civil war, which helped smooth some of the initial planning processes. Indeed, one of the major differences in the relations between NSPs and state authorities in Afghanistan and Southern Sudan is the long-standing presence of NSPs in Southern Sudan, whereas most of the NSP programmes in Afghanistan did not begin until 2002 at the earliest. Prior to the peace agreement, NSPs had extensive relations with the Sudanese Relief and Rehabilitation Association, the humanitarian arm of the Sudanese People's Liberation Army. Thus, NSPs had both extensive community-level programming and a working relationship with officials in the new GoSS. However, difficulties with the MDTF have spilled over into state–NSP relations.

The expectation was that the MDTF would provide a suitable instrument for donor co-ordination, and would simplify financing and contracting arrangements for the GoSS and NSPs. However, in practice, slow disbursements and log-jams within the MDTF for Southern Sudan have been consistent problems. Some of the difficulties were due to tensions between NSPs and officials of the GoSS. The government wanted to be in the lead for reasons attributable to the ongoing political settlement issues between the national government and the new government in the south, as well as for issues involving ethnic tensions in local politics. NSPs had access to direct donor support outside of the MDTF, and the government was concerned about the lack of oversight of NSPs by GoSS authorities. There have been ongoing debates about NSP roles in the MDTF, and whether and how Sudanese civil society has a voice either about NSP services or the MDTF. Sudanese civil-society organisations have criticised the donors, the GoSS, and the NSPs for the apparent lack of community-based engagement on health policies and government priorities.

The slowness and inefficiency of the MDTF has been widely criticised by the GoSS, by donors other than the World Bank, and by NSPs. The concern most loudly voiced is that in the first few years of operation, the MDTF had minimal impact compared to need and compared to the resources available. Reviews of the MDTF have noted that the fund was hampered by potentially contradictory objectives, as it was supposed to support quick-impact projects while building state capacity and ownership, and work within the different donor interests. In addition, the very limited capacity of the newly established GoSS also contributed significantly to the delays and inefficiencies associated with the MDTF.

However, not all the responsibility resides with the MDTF or the GoSS. As Fenton noted in her study for Save the Children UK on Southern Sudan:

> *NGOs themselves also bear some responsibility for the lack of engagement with the MDTF. Two years after the CPA signing, a number of key NGOs – including Save the Children – are still in the process of relocating their offices and decision-makers to Juba from Nairobi. There are many reasons for these delays, including difficulties in finding suitable and affordable office space and accommodation, shortages of qualified and experienced Southern Sudanese staff, challenges associated with attracting and retaining staff given the difficult working and living conditions in Juba, and problems with accessing sufficient funding to support the move. Those NGOs who were able to move quickly into Juba either already had an office there which had been managed from Khartoum or were able to access sufficient internal unrestricted funding quickly. In addition, NGOs lacked knowledge and experience of dealing with MDTFs at both country and head office levels, which limited their ability to take up opportunities for engagement and advocacy.* (Fenton 2007a: 17–18)

State–NSP relations: a two-track approach of service delivery and state building

The experiences in Afghanistan and Southern Sudan indicate that a number of factors – including the political settlement dynamics, donor aid instruments, and roles of NSPs – all affect how well the two tracks can be connected (Fenton 2007a, b; Zivetz 2006). While there are trade-offs between NSP and government services, the distinction should not be overplayed, as 'state' and 'non-state' presents too sharp a dichotomy. State agencies have the responsibility to regulate, finance, monitor, evaluate, and contract NSPs for service delivery. For example, while NSPs may provide most of the delivery on the ground, the management of contracting out services and monitoring results are key functions of the state, which retains responsibility for the quality or delivery of the services. The central role of state responsibility can help guide donor decisions as they address state-building processes, timeframes for strengthening public institutions, and the accountabilities of both NSPs and donors in contexts of state failure or difficult partners. In the case of the Southern Sudan MDTF, the experiences indicate that the problems affect both services and state-building goals. Beyond the necessity of integrating an overall institutional perspective, which is currently uneven, there are many areas of the donor's work that would benefit from developing an NSP framework as it relates to the balancing of short-term service goals with state-building priorities.

A number of serious challenges remain for NSP involvement in health-service systems, including financing, the coherence of the health system, the sometimes problematic role of vertical funds (that is, those with specific sub-sectoral designations, such as the Global Fund on AIDS, TB and Malaria, or the Global Alliance for Vaccines and Immunization), and staff capacity. Vertical funds have been particularly questioned in terms of the potential fragmentation of health systems' coherence and the skewing of funds towards 'favoured' diseases (Commins 2006; Waldman 2006). In addition, issues continue in terms of accountability to local communities and local community-based organisations.

The goal of building state capacity while delivering services requires linking two tracks of programme goals: one track focuses on state building, the other on delivering services as quickly as possible. In order to connect the tracks, it is vital to develop a long-term vision of a pro-poor health system from the start, even when donor and government efforts are focused on short-term measures to keep the health system going. Work by the Health and Fragile States Network (2009) has demonstrated the value of developing a strategic framework and policies for the health sector as early as possible. Fragile states face specific difficulties in financing health systems and retaining health workers. The health sector is likely to be more expensive in fragile states than in other low-income states. Donors need to respond to this. There are many challenges, such as how to make best use of all service providers (state and non-state), and how to generate demand in environments where the health sector has performed poorly. One approach is through creating islands of dependability to help retain health workers and maintain trust in the health system.

Different country experiences with health-service delivery in fragile states provide some basic guidance for donors and governments for incorporating NSPs into both health-service delivery and health-systems strengthening:

- Support oversight mechanisms on NSPs working in fragile states to ensure coherence with other programmes (Commins 2007);
- In improving contexts, require NSPs to coordinate and share information with appropriate government ministries, and with district and local government;
- In deteriorating contexts, NSPs should share information and coordinate with local government agencies when feasible; donors need to ensure that their funding instruments are coherent and allow for adjusting to changes in how fragility affects health services and government capacity (Canavan *et al.* 2008).

Governments and NSPs work across a wide range of programmes and projects in the health sector. The question for long-term planning concerns the ways in which these various actions contribute to strengthening the public sector's roles and capacities in the longer term.

Conclusions

Country examples indicate that it is possible and practical to link the roles of NSPs in the health services with improving the capacity of the state, but also that there are underlying political issues of state formation that may hamper cooperation between NSPs and state agencies (Eldon *et al.* 2008). It is possible to contribute to both 'tracks', and NSP relationships with state agencies in fragile states that are seeking to build political legitimacy can contribute to the strengthening of the capacity of public institutions. This requires continued assessment by donors of how funding instruments, such as trust funds or vertical programmes, may bypass the task of rebuilding health systems. The challenges that exist in low-income non-fragile states are amplified in fragile states, in such areas as state capacity, human resources in health, and availability of funding.

Reviews of health-sector strengthening in countries such as Afghanistan (and previously Cambodia and Mozambique, see Commins 2006; Waldman 2006; Zivetz 2006) show the potential benefits of giving attention to national health systems. Three potential lessons are notable: (1) the approach is part of a larger focus on services and public-sector strengthening; (2) it is financially realistic and has sustained support; and (3) it is sound in terms of capacity and capacity-building options. Another important lesson involves the need to address local-government roles, as different levels of government need capacity for contracting with NSPs. In this work, NSPs could be key bridges between local communities and the public sector.

In the health sector, because of the particularly broad and complex mix of factors in the delivery of health services, as well as the diverse roles assigned to NSPs, the strengthening of the public sector requires a particular set of approaches, compared to other services. Among the factors necessary are the training and retention of a competent health workforce, the oversight of the procurement and delivery of essential drugs, disease surveillance, and the mechanisms for financing service delivery to people without the means to pay for services or drugs. A key for building competent and accountable public health institutions resides in ensuring that the state has a broad and effective oversight of the health sector. Given the difficulties with the different instruments and organisations aligning in Southern Sudan, a key point is that in most fragile states there will be a continuing dynamic between reducing immediate vulnerability; achieving specific health outcomes; building a more lasting and equitable health system; and building the capacity of civil society to monitor services, holding both NSPs and government service providers to account.

Notes

1. In 2009, the Fragile States Group merged with the Network on Conflict, Peace and Development Cooperation to form the International Network on Conflict and Fragility (INCAF).
2. This section benefits from discussions held at the conference organised by Merlin and the London School of Hygiene and Tropical Medicine in 2007 (see Merlin and the London School of Hygiene and Tropical Medicine 2007) and research done by Wendy Fenton (2007a, b) on fragile states experiences for Save the Children UK. See also reports on the website of the Health and Fragile States Network (www.healthandfragilestates.org).

References

Canavan, Ann, Petra Vergeer, and Olga Bornemisza, with Jacob Hughes and Nadine Ezard (2008) 'Post-Conflict Health Sectors: The Myth and Reality of Transitional Funding Gaps', [London]: Health and Fragile States Network, and [Amsterdam]: Royal Tropical Institute.
Commins, S. (2006) 'Synthesis Paper on Good Practice: the Challenge for Donor', [Paris]: OECD/DAC Workstream on Service Delivery.
Commins, S. (2007) 'Treading a Delicate Path: NGOs in Fragile States', draft report, London: Save the Children UK.
DFID (2005) *Why We Need to Work Effectively in Fragile States*, London: DFID.
Eldon, J., C. Waddington, and Y. Hadi (2008) *Health System Reconstruction: Can it Contribute to State-building?*, London: HLSP Institute, for the Health and Fragile States Network.
Fenton, W. (2007a) 'Treading a Delicate Path: NGOs in Fragile States – Case Study Southern Sudan', draft report, London: Save the Children UK.
Fenton, W. (2007b) 'Treading a Delicate Path: NGOs in Fragile States – Case Study Afghanistan', draft report, London: Save the Children UK.
Health and Fragile States Network (2009) 'Health Systems Strengthening in Fragile Contexts: A Report on Good Practices and New Approaches', [London]: Health and Fragile States Network.
HLF (2004) 'Achieving the Health Millennium Development Goals in Fragile States', Geneva and Washington, DC: High Level Forum on Health MDGs.
Merlin and the London School of Hygiene and Tropical Medicine (2007) 'Health Services in Fragile States for $5 Per Year: Myth or Reality', London: Merlin.
OECD (2005a) *Principles for Engagement in Fragile States*, Paris: OECD.
OECD (2005b) *Service Delivery in Fragile States: Advancing Donor Practice*, Paris: OECD.
USAID (2005) *Fragile States Strategy*, Washington, DC: USAID.
Waldman, R. (2006) *Health Programming in Post-Conflict Fragile States*, Arlington, VA: BASICS, for USAID.
Waldman, R., L. Strong, and A. Wahid (2006) 'Afghanistan's Health System Since 2001: Condition Improved, Prognosis Cautious', *AREU Briefing Paper Series*, Kabul: Afghanistan Research and Evaluation Unit.

World Bank (2009) *Effective Poverty Reduction Strategies in Fragile and Conflict Affected Countries*, Washington, DC: The World Bank.

Zivetz, L. (2006) 'Health Service Delivery in Early Recovery Fragile States: Lessons from Afghanistan, Cambodia, Mozambique and Timor Leste', Arlington, VA: BASICS, for USAID.

Free primary education still excludes the poorest of the poor in urban Kenya

Moses Oketch and Moses Ngware

The Kenyan government introduced free primary education in 2003 in order to universalise access to primary education. Although the policy allows universal coverage, it ought to benefit the poor most as they are the ones who were excluded from the education sector before the policy was introduced. Using household-survey data collected in Nairobi, this contribution assesses the impact of the policy on schooling outcomes of the poor. The findings reveal that the free primary-education policy in Kenya still excludes the poorest of the poor.

L'éducation primaire gratuite exclut encore les plus pauvres des pauvres dans le Kenya urbain
Le gouvernement kényan a introduit l'éducation primaire gratuite en 2003 afin d'universaliser l'accès à l'éducation primaire. Bien que la politique générale stipule une couverture universelle, elle devrait surtout profiter aux pauvres puisque ce sont eux qui étaient exclus du secteur de l'éducation avant l'introduction de la politique. À l'aide de données d'une étude sur les ménages recueillies à Nairobi, cet article évalue l'impact de la politique sur les résultats en termes de scolarisation parmi les pauvres. Les conclusions révèlent que la politique d'éducation primaire gratuite au Kenya continue d'exclure les plus pauvres des pauvres.

Educação primária gratuita ainda exclui os mais pobres dos pobres na zona urbana do Quênia
O governo queniano introduziu a educação primária gratuita em 2003 para universalizar o acesso à educação primária. Embora a política permita uma abrangência universal, ela deve beneficiar mais os pobres uma vez que são eles os excluídos do setor da educação antes da política ser introduzida. Utilizando dados de pesquisa sobre famílias coletados em Nairóbi, este artigo avalia o impacto da política sobre os resultados escolares dos pobres. Os resultados revelam que a política de educação primária gratuita no Quênia ainda exclui os mais pobres dos pobres.

La educación primaria gratuita sigue excluyendo a los más pobres en las ciudades de Kenya
El gobierno de Kenya estableció la gratuidad de la educación primaria en 2003 a fin de que fuera accesible para todos los niños. Al instaurarse la cobertura universal, esta política debió haber beneficiado más a los pobres al ser ellos los más excluidos del sector educativo. Este ensayo analizó el impacto de esta política sobre los resultados escolares de los pobres utilizando datos de encuestas aplicadas en hogares de Nairobi. Las conclusiones muestran que la política de educación primaria gratuita en Kenia sigue excluyendo a los más pobres.

Introduction

The Kenyan government decided to implement a policy of free primary education in 2003. For many years, Kenya had made impressive attempts to universalise access to primary education: first in 1974, through policies that targeted those from semi-arid and arid areas and in lower grades (1 to 4); and later, in 1979, through elimination of tuition fees and other related charges. Despite these efforts, universal access has not been realised in Kenya. However, the national and international commitment since 2003 has yielded some impressive enrolment numbers, but the quality of education offered and the confidence in the public school system is becoming rapidly eroded (Oketch and Rolleston 2007).

African Population and Health Research Center, an international research centre with its headquarters in Nairobi, has been assessing the impact of Kenya's free primary education (FPE) policy. The research design involves four sites: two slums and two non-slum sites. With donor funding, the initiative recorded the schooling history of individuals aged 5 to 19 years who live in or migrate to these sites. This provided a dataset for a cross-section of the population over time, which has enabled analysis of how different groups of urban dwellers experience and respond to the removal of the cost barrier to the education of their children. This dataset has been used as the basis of several working papers capturing the following themes:

1. Why are there proportionately more poor pupils enrolled in non-state schools in urban Kenya in spite of FPE policy?
2. Pupil school mobility in urban Kenya.
3. Do household characteristics matter in schooling decisions in urban Kenya?
4. What quality of primary education are children in urban schools receiving? (Evidence from Nairobi.)

This contribution summarises the key findings from our research work on the assessment of the impact of FPE on various aspects of school participation, and outlines the policy messages from these findings.

Why are there proportionately more poor pupils enrolled in non-state schools when there is free primary education?

Many pupils residing in urban informal settlements are still enrolled in fee-paying non-state schools (what some refer to as 'private schools for the poor') in several countries in Sub-Saharan Africa that have an FPE policy. The question asked by those who have become interested in this issue is whether FPE meets the needs of the poor when many poor parents who live in the informal settlements are still paying for 'poor-quality education', when they could be getting free schooling in the state sector? In an attempt to answer this question, our analysis (Oketch *et al.* 2010) contributes to this debate using the 'excess demand' and 'differentiated demand' theory (see James 1993).

Proponents of private schools argue that, due to insufficient public provision of education in low-income countries, the private sector is one means to achieving universal enrolment, as it expands supply while shifting costs away from government (Chubb and Moe 1990, cited in Lincove 2007). Private-sector involvement in education increases education revenue, enabling expansion of supply and redistribution of educational opportunities.

On the contrary, opponents of private schools argue that private-sector education relies on strong demand and the ability and willingness of parents to pay (Gordon and Whitty 1997, cited in Lincove 2007). Consequently, private schools tend to have incentives attracting those with both the ability and the willingness to pay, which exclude students from poor households and remote areas. In developing countries, public supply is limited; so, private

Table 1: Number of children enrolled in private schools by study site and wealth index

Variable	Private	Total	Percentage private
Site: Slum	2415	6156	39.2
Non-slum	209	1127	18.5
Wealth Quintile: Slum			
Poorest 20 per cent	529	1232	42.9
2	490	1231	39.8
3	504	1231	40.9
4	485	1233	39.3
Least poor 20 per cent	407	1229	33.1
Wealth Quintile: Non-slum			
Poorest 20 per cent	12	227	5.3
2	25	224	11.2
3	39	227	17.2
4	55	228	24.1
Least poor 20 per cent	78	221	35.3

Source: *Oketch* et al. *(2010).*

schools meet excess demand from parents who are willing to pay for education but are excluded from public schools by supply constraints. Where public supply is low, private markets provide lower-quality second-chance schools for students who cannot access selective public schools. When public-school capacity can accommodate all students, private schools emerge to provide competition and offer differentiated education services (Lincove 2007).

Table 1 shows who is using private schools in urban informal (slum) and formal (non-slum) areas. There is generally a high level of use of private schools in the slums by the poorest. Since there is inadequate public spending on education in the slums, the poor are crowded out by the wealthier segments in the public system and pushed to using low-fee 'private schools for the poor' – this is attributed to 'excess' demand.

The converse is the case in the non-slum areas, where the wealthy are more likely to use high-fee private schooling, which they prefer to the available public system. This we attribute to 'differentiated' demand. The non-slum wealthy quintiles are looking for something better for their children that is different from what is available in the public system. To this group, public schools are imperfect substitutes for private schools. For the wealthy in the non-slums, private schools offer them choice. In the slums, the 'mushrooming' of low-fee 'private schools' merely fills the gap left by insufficient supply of school places in the public system. For this group, private schools substitute for public schools.

Our analysis of why children from poor populations continue to attend fee-charging low-quality private schools concludes that 'excess demand' explains the use of low-fee private schools by the poorest in informal settlements, and differentiated demand explains the use of high-fee private schools in formal settlements (Oketch *et al.* 2010).

Pupil school mobility

Children living in urban informal settlements still face serious challenges in accessing free public education. Data collected by the African Population and Health Research Center

Table 2: The most important reason for changing schools (n = 478)

Key reason for changing school	Total	
	No.	Percentage
The school transferred into had better teachers, more-disciplined pupils, and performed well	237	50
The school transferred into was cheaper or provides FPE	120	25
The school transferred into was near or easily accessible to the pupil	45	9
The school transferred from lacked appropriate grade or level	32	7
The transfer was due to relocation of family, pupil expelled from previous school; school on strike	26	5
The transfer was due to peer influence	9	2
The school transferred into had buildings and facilities of good quality	9	2

Source: Oketch et al. (2008).

(APHRC) in two major informal settlements in Nairobi – Korogocho and Viwandani – revealed that 44 per cent (nearly half) of primary-school children in the study sample were enrolled in low-fee 'private' schools (Oketch et al. 2008). It is also apparent that there is high mobility of pupils between schools. Our analysis of pupil mobility was guided by the hypothesis that places in public schools are competitive, so there will be fewer transfers into public schools compared to transfers into private schools in the informal settlement.

School mobility can be driven by supply and demand: the supply of low-fee private schools in the slum areas may be influenced by the demand for these schools and the extent of public investment in the slums (that is, availability of government schools). In spite of having large populations of school-age children, the two slums (Korogocho and Viwandani) had only one school each at the time of this study.

The most frequent reasons given by parents for transferring their child from one school to another were: (1) performance and discipline (as overall); (2) accessibility, and (3) cost/FPE (Table 2).

Pupil school mobility was high among the private schools and among slum residents. Most of the mobility was from private to private or public to private, and not from private to public, among slum residents. The reason for this type of mobility is likely to be that those who move from one private school to another may be searching for better quality. The quality of the slum informal private schools is likely to vary, and this is a likely explanation for the transfers. The number of transfers in the non-slums was fewer, probably because there is adequate supply of public schools to match demand and parents are able to make a choice between public and private schools depending on their disposable income. The analysis concluded that FPE had not significantly altered the slum conditions that would make it impossible for the majority of pupils there to benefit from the policy. This is mainly because the policy failed to address excess demand for primary education and therefore parents kept moving their children from one school to another for reasons cited in Table 2.

Household characteristics and schooling decisions

Household characteristics are an important determinant of schooling decisions. Characteristics such as income and levels of parental education greatly determine whether a child enrols in school, stays in school, learns, and makes progression to higher levels of education. Household schooling decisions, such as the type of school that a child attends, are also influenced by household characteristics. In Africa, studies that have examined the influence of household characteristics on schooling decisions normally differentiate between urban and rural households (see, for example, Handa et al. 2004; Ilon and Moock 1991; Johannes 2005). Rural households are often portrayed as disadvantaged, as having lower income, lower levels of education, and therefore worse schooling decisions and outcomes compared to urban areas. Evidence is, however, showing a high level of disadvantage among households in poor urban neighbourhoods that is influencing schooling decisions in these areas (Ngware et al. 2008a; Oketch et al. 2010).

Households are more likely to enrol their children in primary school if they are richer, residing away from urban informal settlements, are headed by a female, are smaller, live nearer a primary school, and the household head has more education (Ngware et al. 2008a). Children's individual attributes also influence the decision to enrol – for instance, orphans are less likely to be enrolled compared to non-orphans; however, children are treated in the same way with regard to schooling whether they have lost one or both parents. The age of the child is an important consideration in enrolment: older children are more likely to be in school than younger ones.

The analysis also shows how different household and individual attributes motivate decision on the type of school. Households are more inclined to choose a public primary school if they are not residing in informal settlements, are in the lower wealth quintiles, are headed by a female, and have older household heads. The households are more likely to choose a public school as the child becomes older – perhaps to take advantage of the fact that public schools are usually used as national examination centres. These factors are reinforced by the flexibility of private schools, low social capital and networks, and the perceived differences in the quality of education provided by different schools (Ngware et al. 2008a).

Quality of school inputs

The notion of quality of education should go beyond student results and look at the determinants of such results, including provision of teachers, buildings, equipment, and curriculum. Our analysis (Ngware et al. 2008b) examined the input factors and related their quality to the national and international benchmarks in the context of FPE. Benchmarking is important as it provides best practices that enhance the quality of education and learning outcomes.

Table 3 presents a comparison of input indicators and benchmarks set by the Ministry of Education, comparing public *versus* non-public schools; and slums *versus* non-slums. Overall, non-public schools fair better on the selected input benchmarks than public schools in both slums and non-slums. For instance, non-public schools have better pupil–textbook ratios for both slums and non-slums; non-public schools have smaller class sizes in both slums and non-slums; non-public schools also have better pupil–teacher ratios in both slums and non-slums. Meanwhile, both school types have more teaching hours per week in the slums than non-slums. Public schools have better (lower) girls-per-toilet ratio in the slums, while non-public schools have better ratio in the non-slums. It can be concluded that the benchmarks for quality education are not met in all schools in both slums and non-slums.

According to UNESCO (1997), the minimum student classroom space should be 1.5 square metres with single-seater desks, which would translate to 67.5 square metres for a room expected to hold 45 students. The Ministry of Education recommends 45 square metres or about 1 square metre per child in a room with 45 children. Most of the schools studied had student spaces that were below the required benchmark. Government-owned schools had the lowest average student physical space (0.86 m^2). This is mainly due to the large class sizes witnessed after the introduction of FPE. Students in schools owned by private individuals and

Table 3: Benchmarking the quality of primary school inputs attended by pupils in the study sample (n = 83 schools)

Input indicator	Category	Benchmark/ Standards	Observed		Source of Benchmark/ standards
			Slums	Non-slums	
Pupil–textbook ratio	Public schools	2.5	1.7	1.3	Ministry of Education, Kenya
	Non-public schools	2.5	1.6	1.1	Ministry of Education, Kenya
Class size	Public schools	45	50	29	Ministry of Education, Kenya
	Non-public schools	45	22	23	Ministry of Education, Kenya
Pupil–teacher ratio	Public schools	40	47	29	Ministry of Education, Kenya
	Non-public schools	40	27	25	Ministry of Education, Kenya
Buildings (classroom walls)	Public schools	Blocks (stones)	96% blocks	96% blocks	Ministry of Public Works, Kenya
	Non-public schools	Blocks (stones)	95% blocks	95% blocks	Ministry of Public Works, Kenya
Teaching hours per week	Public schools	23	17	8	Ministry of Education
	Non-public schools	23	16	9	–
Pupil – toilet ratio (girls)	Public schools	25	18	20	Ministry of Education
	Non-public schools	25	20	11	Ministry of Education

Source: African Population and Health Research (APHRC) education research dataset.

private religious groups had the largest physical space in a classroom (>5 m^2). Students in schools in informal settlements had among the least student physical space (<1 m^2) – indicating either large class sizes or small classroom space, or both. The main concerns of the classroom physical space include: safety and accessibility to learning; arrangement of furniture; and the teachers' use of physical resources. While public-school student learning space is constrained by the class size, the student learning space in non-government schools is constrained by the classroom size.

Policy implications

Several policy messages emerge from this summary.
- While FPE has led to improved school participation, an unacceptable proportion of pupils from poor households still uses low-fee private schools, not because they prefer to use them, but because they have not been included in the state system due to inadequate

supply. A first step for the government is to find ways of improving the supply of state schools of acceptable standards in the informal settlements, or to incorporate the private providers into the state system.

- Mobility is associated with private schools. Free primary education ought to have reduced the use of private schools, especially among the slum residents who are already disadvantaged. However, parents still search for a 'good' school for their child. Some policy dilemmas to be drawn from the findings of the analysis of pupil mobility include:
  (1) Should all the private schools in the informal settlements be recognised as acceptable and, therefore, incorporated as government schools?
  (2) How do those who run these informal private schools get compensated?
  (3) Would accepting the informal private schools be seen as endorsing 'second class' education, since the structures in these schools are not fit for a school?
  (4) How does the government provide universally free education to pupils who live in the slums who apparently still use low-fee private schools?
- It appears there is already a natural public–private partnership in Kenya's urban education context. How the government can tap into this so that the vulnerable are not left worse off by this natural partnership is a major policy question. Such a partnership targeting urban school quality improvement is one way of mobilising resources for improving quality of education.
- Households that are strongly attracted to and use informal non-public primary schools have distinguishable characteristics. This information is important for demand-driven policies aimed at increasing the use or uptake of free primary education services.
- The existence of systematic patterns of school enrolment and the type of school attended by children from various households demonstrates that even if the intention of the government is to provide public education, equity cannot be attained if demand for education exceeds supply.
- There is a need for the government to expand school infrastructure and employ more teachers in urban settings to cope with the rapid urbanisation, and create opportunities for disadvantaged urban children to access quality education. The aim is to reduce both class sizes and pupil–teacher ratios to the Ministry of Education's benchmarks.
- Finally, education stakeholders go beyond the education sector. Therefore, it is imperative to address the problem of school inputs in a sector-wide approach. For example, provision of school toilet facilities and safe drinking water would benefit from a sector-wide approach with stakeholders from the education, housing, environment, health, water, and local government sub-sectors.

Acknowledgements

This study, including the collection of the data used, has been made possible through a grant from The William and Flora Hewlett Foundation. Several individuals have also helped with the data collection and provided input for this contribution and, while we are not able to list all of them, the following deserve mentioning: Charles Epari and Maurice Mutisya both at APHRC. The findings and views in this contribution are not by association necessarily shared by the funding agency or the individuals listed.

References

Handa, Sudhanshu, Kenneth Simler, and Sarah Harrower (2004) 'Human Capital, Household Welfare, and Children's Schooling in Mozambique', unpublished research report 134, Washington, DC: International Food Policy Research Institute.
Ilon, Lynn and Peter Moock (1991) 'School attributes, household characteristics, and demand for schooling: a case study of rural Peru', *International Review of Education* 37 (4): 429–51.

James, Estelle (1993) 'Why do different countries choose a different public–private mix of educational services?', *Journal of Human Resources* 28: 571–92.

Johannes, Tabi Atemnkeng (2005) 'Household Level Social Capital and Children's Schooling Decision in Cameroon: A Gender Analysis', paper presented at the Regional Conference on Education in West Africa, Dakar, 1–2 November.

Lincove, Jane Arnold (2007) 'Do Private Markets Improve the Quality and Quantity of Primary Schooling in Sub-Saharan Africa?', available at http://www.eddataglobal.org/documents/index.cfm/Private%20Schools%20EdData%20Paper%20%20-%20Lincove.doc?fuseaction=throwpub&ID=79 (retrieved 18 September 2008).

Ngware, Moses, Moses Oketch, and Alex Chika Ezeh (2008a) 'Do Household Characteristics Matter in Schooling Decisions in Urban Kenya?', report WP/37/2008, Nairobi: African Population and Health Research Center.

Ngware, Moses, Moses Oketch, and Alex Chika Ezeh (2008b) 'What Quality of Primary Education are Children in Urban Schools Receiving? Evidence from Nairobi', report WP/39/2008, Nairobi: African Population and Health Research Center.

Oketch, Moses and Caine Rolleston (2007) 'Policies on Free Primary and Secondary Education in East Africa: A Review of the Literature', Create Pathways to Access, *Research Monograph No. 10*, Brighton, UK: University of Sussex.

Oketch, Moses, Maurice Mutisya, Moses Ngware, Alex Chika Ezeh, and Charles Epari (2008) 'Pupil School Mobility in Urban Kenya', report WP/38/2008, Nairobi: African Population and Health Research Center.

Oketch, Moses, Maurice Mutisya, Moses Ngware, and Alex Chika Ezeh (2010) 'Why are there proportionately more poor pupils enrolled in non-state schools in urban Kenya in spite of FPE policy?', *International Journal of Education Development* 30 (1): 23–32.

UNESCO (United Nations Educational, Scientific and Cultural Organization) (1997) 'International Standard Classification of Education ISCED 1997', available at http://www.unesco.org/education/information/nfsunesco/doc/isced_1997.htm (retrieved 30 September 2008).

The evolution of NGO–government relations in education: ActionAid 1972–2009

David Archer

This short contribution provides a brief history, touching on some of the key trends and turning points in ActionAid's education work, and it documents the evolution of the relationship between ActionAid and governments. The story of ActionAid is illustrative in many ways of wider changes in the NGO sector since the early 1970s.

L'évolution des relations entre les ONG et les gouvernements dans le secteur de l'éducation : ActionAid entre 1972 et 2009
Cette courte contribution présente une histoire abrégée et traite de certaines des tendances clés et des moments décisifs observés dans le travail mené par ActionAid dans le secteur de l'éducation. Elle documente par ailleurs l'évolution de la relation entre ActionAid et les gouvernements. L'histoire d'ActionAid illustre à de nombreux égards les changements plus larges survenus dans le secteur des ONG depuis le début des années 1970.

A evolução das relações entre ONG-governo na educação: ActionAid 1972–2009
Esta breve contribuição oferece um pequeno histórico, tocando em algumas das tendências-chave e pontos cruciais no trabalho sobre educação da ActionAid e documenta a evolução da relação entre a ActionAid e os governos. A história da ActionAid é ilustrativa de várias formas das mudanças mais gerais no setor de ONGs desde o início dos anos de 1970.

La evolución de las relaciones entre ONG y gobiernos en el sector educativo: la trayectoria de ActionAid de 1972 a 2009
Este breve ensayo se trata de una revisión histórica del trabajo en el sector educativo de ActionAid resaltando algunos momentos y puntos clave. Además, documenta la evolución de la relación entre ActionAid y distintos gobiernos. Esta historia es en muchos sentidos ilustrativa de los cambios más importantes que se han dado durante los últimos 40 años en las ONG.

Introduction

ActionAid was founded in 1972 in the UK as a small charity that sponsored poor children in India. Today, it is one of the leading international NGOs, with its headquarters in South

Africa and an annual budget of over $150 million. From its early work responding to the immediate needs of sponsored children, it has evolved into a rights-based organisation that links grassroots programmes to national and international campaigning and advocacy work. The driving force in this evolution of ActionAid's education work has been its continuing commitment to the critical analysis of practical experience. This short contribution provides a brief history, touching on some of the key trends and turning points in ActionAid's education work, and it documents the evolution of the relationship between ActionAid and governments. The story of ActionAid is illustrative in many ways of wider changes in the NGO sector since the early 1970s.

1970s: direct help to individual children

ActionAid's initial work in education, begun in 1972, was influenced by the funding mechanism that it used. Short profiles and photos of poor children in India and Kenya were collected and used as a way of putting a human face on poverty. Individuals in the UK became sponsors and were able to see where their money was going and how it was making a difference. Of course, one of the first expectations of the sponsors was that the sponsored children would be able to go to school. So, the money would be spent on school fees, uniforms, and equipment for sponsored children, so that they could go to school and stay in school.

However, within a very short time, ActionAid's fieldworkers expressed concerns that this approach was ineffective and unjust. They were helping one child, but not their brother or sister, or neighbour. It was random and inequitable – but also it was ineffective. ActionAid was helping lots of individual children to access schools, but doing nothing to help the schools themselves – which were often in an appalling state. Even though the sponsors felt happy at giving such direct help, if the school was poor, the children received little education.

1980s: building better schools

By the late 1970s, ActionAid recognised that offering individual assistance to individual children was not cost-effective. Rather, it made more sense to offer help directly to the schools in the poor areas where sponsored children lived. By this time, ActionAid was working in several countries and had a policy of sponsoring large numbers of children in some of the poorest areas of each country. In most cases, the schools in these areas were ramshackle buildings made of mud-brick, letting in little light or air. The most common response was to improve the infrastructure, building modern classrooms that would provide a conducive learning environment. Photos of the new school buildings were tangible, concrete evidence that sponsors' money was directly benefiting the children. ActionAid developed a reputation for building good-quality extensions to government schools at low cost, using local materials and encouraging active community participation.

However, a self-critical internal evaluation of 16 years of building schools in Kenya (Sathyabalan *et al.* 1996) found that ActionAid had no notable impact on school enrolment and no impact on achievement. Indeed, there was even evidence that poor children were more systematically excluded. The key reason for this was the wider policy context. The government was under pressure from the World Bank to limit public spending on education and directly charge all children to go to school. In this climate, school management committees were encouraged to charge 'user fees'. Those schools that had an impressive building felt more confident to raise more fees. Relatively better-off parents and community leaders, who could comfortably afford the fees, invariably dominated school management committees. Most of them had little idea that even a modest fee would have a devastating impact on the poorest children who came from families with little or no cash income. Those who may have been aware of the impact showed little concern and the poorest children ended up excluded from school.

The evaluation in Kenya also offered other insights. In the absence of any other inputs to address the quality of teaching and learning, simply improving the infrastructure of the school did not improve achievement levels. Moreover, some schools in neighbouring areas, where ActionAid did not work, had improved achievement with very-low-cost locally-devised interventions.

This evaluation coincided with other evidence that ActionAid was collecting from many of the areas in various countries where it worked, that showed that many of the poorest children were still not going to school (either as never enrolled or early drop outs). It became clear that the cost of schooling was a major obstacle (Archer *et al.* 2003). There was a range of direct costs that parents had to cover: fees for books, maintenance, or food, as well as the user fees. But there were also indirect and opportunity costs. Poor families depended on their children to work, and sending them to school meant losing part of the household income. Moreover, government schools were often located in the centre of villages and the poorest families often lived a considerable distance away. In one way or another, government schools seemed increasingly inaccessible to the poorest families and reluctant to change. Many ActionAid field workers lamented how bureaucratic the schools were and how unresponsive to local contexts.

Early 1990s: non-formal education

In the light of all this evidence and with an increasing focus on reaching the poorest children, from the early 1990s ActionAid projects began to run 'non-formal education centres' or 'community schools', separated from the formal education system and government constraints. These non-formal education centres would be located in the more remote and poorest communities, using low-cost improvised buildings put up by parents themselves. Local parents were consulted over the location of the centres and became actively involved in every aspect of managing them. They could determine the annual calendar of the school year so that holidays coincided with the peak periods when children needed to work – during harvesting, for example. They could also set the daily timetable so that working children could learn in the morning, afternoon, or evening. This flexibility contrasted dramatically with the rigidly fixed national calendar and timetable of government schools.

While government schools were increasingly being burdened with an overloaded national curriculum (for example, 14 examinable subjects in Kenyan primary schools), these non-formal education centres (run completely independently of government) focused attention on a reduced curriculum that provided children with a core set of skills in reading, writing, and numeracy. While the government schools taught only in the national or officially recognised language, the non-formal education centres would teach in the mother tongue of the children, enabling them to learn more quickly. While government schools depended on text books printed in the capital or imported from other countries, the non-formal education centres could produce locally relevant teaching–learning materials, allowing children to learn to read from materials that dealt with their local environment and local livelihoods. Government schools depended on teacher-centred 'chalk and talk' and traditional rote learning, but these new non-formal education centres could innovate, using child-centred methodologies, making learning stimulating and fun. Most of all, rather than depend on professional teachers who came from the city and were often late or absent, these non-formal education centres could depend on local people who were highly committed and could be trained by ActionAid in a matter of weeks.

From its own evaluations of this work, ActionAid was convinced it was making a difference.[1] The non-formal education centres were reaching the poorest children and often enrolled more girls than boys. In many cases, children learnt rapidly, often reaching the equivalent of fifth-grade primary school within just three years. The centres often had creative teaching and joyful learning environments.

However, in 1996 ActionAid brought together its education staff from around the world to review the experience of running non-formal education centres. Although much of what is narrated above held true, it became clear that there were some fundamental contradictions. Most fundamentally there was a problem with sustainability. ActionAid was running non-formal education centres, but could not continue to do so forever. As an NGO, ActionAid was not a permanent presence in the areas where it worked and, although it could make long-term commitments of up to ten years, an education centre for children cannot be run for just ten years. A new generation of children is continually being born and so, at some point, ActionAid would need to hand over to someone else. The poor communities could not run the centres themselves and charging fees would have been impossible – so there was only one option: to hand over the non-formal education centres to the Ministry of Education. But governments, operating under the strictures of the macro-economic prescriptions of the IMF, had little money to spare. Education budgets were tight and so local and national governments had to invest them carefully. When they saw an affluent international NGO like ActionAid providing education in one area, the local government or district education office would, quite reasonably, decide to invest their own resources in other areas. Over a period of years, this often meant that government investment in education declined in the areas where ActionAid ran non-formal education centres. At the very point that ActionAid wanted to hand over the responsibility for the centres, the government would be less able than ever before to assume that responsibility.

There were many other problems that emerged when ActionAid reviewed the non-formal education work closely. Not only would governments be reluctant to take on the costs of running the non-formal education centres, but they were also unable to do so because the centres did not comply with government regulations. They were not recognised or registered, their infrastructure did not fit with approved requirements, their curriculum was too narrow, and their teachers were not professionals. Moreover, government teachers saw non-formal education teachers as amateurs (distrusting them and seeing them as a direct threat to the teaching profession), meanwhile non-formal education teachers regarded formal school teachers as lazy and bureaucratic. As a result, those children who completed a non-formal education course were often unable to access government schools either because their learning was not recognised or they were not competent in one of the key subjects taught in formal schools (usually the ex-colonial language). Poor children emerged as victims once again.

As the analysis went deeper, it became clear that, unintentionally, ActionAid was absolving governments of their responsibility and was becoming an agent in the privatisation of education for poor children. When ActionAid decided, after ten years, to leave an area, local people would clamour for the organisation to stay. They had no sense of the government having responsibility to provide education and no established relationships that could help them to demand this effectively.

Another element in the equation emerged when ActionAid realised that however many centres it ran, these would only ever be a drop in the ocean. Even the huge national NGO, BRAC (Bangladesh Rural Advancement Centre), in Bangladesh, which ran 35,000 centres at one point, was still covering less than 8 per cent of children in the country. The vast majority of poor children are still in government schools.

Perhaps the final nail in the coffin for non-formal education centres came when ActionAid realised that there was no guarantee of quality. It turned out that some non-formal education centres were good (and these were the ones that everyone would visit), but some were bad. There was rarely any quality control and there was little evidence of coherent planning between NGOs, so clusters of centres would appear in some areas and none in others. It became clear that a more systemic approach was needed and that the real challenge lay in reforming the government system.

Late 1990s: towards a rights-based approach

By 1997, ActionAid had articulated its approach to education as one that involved moving *'from providing to enabling'* (ActionAid 1997). Instead of directly providing education services, ActionAid's role was now to enable communities to demand quality education as a basic right and to enable governments to effectively deliver quality services.

One of the key means by which ActionAid helped people to demand education (and other services) was through using the *Reflect* approach, which linked adult literacy and empowerment. *Reflect* was developed earlier by ActionAid through pilot projects in Bangladesh, El Salvador, and Uganda, between 1993 and 1995. It linked the ideas of Paulo Freire and participatory methodologies of Participatory Rural Appraisal – teaching people to read and write while enabling them to develop a critical analysis of key issues facing their communities and organising to resolve them. *Reflect* became a powerful base for working with rights-based approaches: it helped people access information about their rights and built the communication skills and confidence for them to assert their voices and demand change (see www.reflect-action.org or IDS 2007 for more information on *Reflect*). *Reflect* helped create an active citizenry that could demand improved services from government, including improved schools.

By 1997, ActionAid as a whole committed itself to taking a rights-based approach to development (see ActionAid 1997). The organisation was committed to working with 'rights holders' (especially the poorest and most excluded) and holding 'duty bearers' (the government) to account. ActionAid had learnt a lot from *Reflect* about how to mobilise rights holders and also about how to deliver effective education through its work with non-formal education centres, but the challenge was to share this with government and to mainstream good practices within formal schools. ActionAid had significant evidence of the importance of mother-tongue teaching, of the value of child-centred learning, and of innovations that could help reach various excluded groups like pastoralist children, displaced communities, and street children. But influencing national policy and holding the government to account is not easy. There was little evidence that the national policy of governments could be influenced meaningfully by a single NGO documenting its 'good practice'.

Recognising that any serious engagement with national governments could not be done alone, in 1998 ActionAid developed the *Elimu* campaign. This was focused on strengthening the voices of poor people in education decision making at all levels. It was the first systematic attempt by ActionAid to link local and national mobilisation on education. At the local level, this meant enabling poor people to have a greater say in demanding their right to education and in holding schools to account. At a district level, it meant promoting citizen oversight of the work of district education offices. At a national level, it meant strengthening the voice of civil society, building alliances that would place education reform higher up the domestic political agenda. And at an international level, this meant challenging the dominant role of donors and arguing for more effective, better-coordinated aid.

In preparing the campaign, ActionAid's analysis showed that, through the 1990s, education policy making had been increasingly dominated by bilateral and multilateral donors. With government budgets struggling to pay teacher salaries (and usually over 90 per cent of education budgets being absorbed in this way), the only serious money for reform came from donors, but that money came with conditions and expatriate experts tended to dominate discussions about policy priorities. Typically within this policy process, national civil society rarely had a meaningful say, and the parents of poor children, who most needed the reform, had no voice whatsoever. ActionAid came to see this democratic deficit in education as the fundamental root of all the other problems of access, quality, and equity. The *Elimu* campaign thus became a 'process campaign', where the central focus was to address this crisis in democracy through building strong national campaigns in each country. The precise agenda for educational reform that these coalitions would take up could not be predetermined.

These national coalitions or campaigns grew rapidly, linking different local, national, and international NGOs and reaching out to social movements, parent groups, teacher unions, academics, and human rights organisations. The aim was to build such strong national platforms that no government could ignore them. These platforms could consolidate learning from grassroots experiences about what reforms would be needed to enable government to make education rights a reality.

But there was also a need for similar work internationally. So, in September 1999 ActionAid came together with Oxfam, Education International, and the Global March against Child Labour to co-found the Global Campaign for Education (GCE). This was initially conceived as a short-term campaign to put pressure on governments around the failure to achieve education for all. Ten years had passed since the Jomtien conference where 'Education for All' had been promised, and it was clear that little progress had been made. The GCE demanded that global leaders recognised the crisis in education; it proved effective in getting a much more serious 'Framework for Action' agreed at the World Education Forum in Dakar in April 2000.

But it was clear that pressure would need to be sustained, so the GCE grew, reaching out to many other actors. By the late 2000s, it was able to mobilise people on education in over 120 countries, with over 10 million children actively involved in the week of action in April 2009. Through such campaigns, NGOs are putting pressure on governments, in both rich and poor countries, to deliver on their promises (Macpherson and Tomlinson 2007). In rich countries, the focus is on governments delivering on aid promises. In poor countries, the focus is on governments delivering on the rights embedded in most national constitutions, arguing for increases in allocations to education in domestic budgets and advocating for policy changes (such as the abolition of user fees) which will help to deliver on education rights for all.

A continuing evolution

Since 2000, ActionAid has systematised a rights-based approach to education (see Newman 2007, and www.right-to-education.org). It has done ground-breaking work in challenging the IMF around its use of public-sector wage-bill caps (see Gray *et al.* 2009; Marphatia *et al.* 2007) and innovative work on the links between education and HIV (see Archer and Boler 2008; Hargreaves and Boler 2006). ActionAid has also forged a strategic partnership with Education International and teacher unions in order to focus attention on the importance of professional teachers and the threat presented by the fragmentation of the teaching profession. It engages actively with the international donors and governments in the Education for All Fast Track Initiative, working to ensure greater space is available for civil-society voices at all levels.

In the late 2000s, ActionAid works in 40 countries with an annual budget of over $150 million; the global headquarters has moved from London to Johannesburg, and it has a truly international board and team of directors – making it the largest Southern-led international NGO. Its education work continues to evolve, and the commitment to critical evaluation and learning remains strong. In 2009, a comprehensive formative evaluation looked at how Action-Aid has progressed in assuming a rights-based approach to education (Sayed and Newman 2009). The evaluation concludes that ActionAid works on 'hot issues' and acknowledges the progress made towards mainstreaming rights-based approaches, but also raises new concerns. As ActionAid becomes more sophisticated in policy and campaigning work, there are risks of it becoming too detached from grassroots programme work. As ActionAid challenges governments to deliver on education rights, it also needs to work constructively with governments to make public schools work effectively at local level.

This is the new mantra across ActionAid: it is committed to making government schools and government education systems work more effectively for the poorest people, promoting the concept of 'rights-respecting schools'. It aims to link work with local governments and district education offices to work with national ministries of education and ministries of finance – while maintaining pressure on international institutions and governments in rich countries to play their part. The challenge for the 2010s is to connect programme, policy, and campaigning work at all levels.

Conclusion

Thirty-seven years on from its foundation, ActionAid has moved a long way, and it remains committed to ongoing evolution of its education work. While that evolution sometimes happens in response to changes in the external environment, the most important factor in driving that evolution has been a willingness to take a critical perspective at all times, including on its own experiences. As ActionAid evolves, its relationship with governments also evolves. Sometimes, NGOs taking a rights-based approach are seen by governments as threatening and unwelcome, but when it is done well, it can lead to highly constructive relationships. After all, the rights-based approach is premised on the belief that it is government action, not NGO provision, which will make the difference in securing education for all.

Note

1. Documented in many ActionAid country reports 1995–1998, but not through any external evaluation.

References

ActionAid (1997) 'From Providing to Enabling', internal report from Addis Ababa meeting of education staff across ActionAid in July 1997, London: ActionAid.
Archer, D. and T. Boler (2008) *The Politics of Prevention: A Global Crisis in AIDS and Education*, London: Pluto Press.
Archer, D., J. Adu-Gyamfi, and A. Goyal (2003) 'Global Education Review', London: ActionAid.
Gray, A., A. Marphatia, and D. Archer (2009) 'Education on the Brink', Johannesburg: Global Campaign for Education.
Hargreaves, James and Tania Boler (2006) 'Girl Power: The Impact of Girls' Education on HIV and Sexual Behaviour', *Education and HIV Series 01*, Johannesburg: ActionAid International.
IDS (2007) 'Springs of Participation', Brighton, UK: Institute of Development Studies.
Macpherson, I. and K. Tomlinson (2007) 'Driving the Bus, The Journey of National Education Coalitions', London: Commonwealth Education Fund.
Marphatia, Akanksha A., Rachel Moussié, Anne-Marie Ainger, and David Archer (2007) 'Confronting the Contradictions: The IMF, Wage Bill Gaps and the Case for Teachers', Johannesburg: ActionAid International.

Newman, Kate (2007) 'Education Rights: A Guide for Practitioners and Activists', Johannesburg: Global Campaign for Education and ActionAid.
Sathyabalan, V. (1996) 'Building Better Schools', London: ActionAid.
Sayed, Y. and K. Newman (2009) 'Education Review', London: ActionAid.

Index

ActionAid 4, 5, 139–46; building better schools 1980s 140–1; continuing evolution 144; direct help to children 1970s 140; *Elimu* campaign 143; Global Campaign for Education 144; minimising direct engagement in service provision 5; non-formal education early 1990s 141–3; *Reflect* approach 143; rights-based approach late 1990s 143–4
Afghanistan: Basic Package of Health Services 125; health provision 125–6; Home-Based School 44; Ministry of Public Health 125; studies of the basic package 125
The Afghanistan Reconstruction Trust Fund (ARTF) 116
Africa Network for Education for All (ANCEFA) 36
Africa Population and Health Research Center (APHRC) 133
Aga Khan Foundation 40
Aikman, S. 5, 26–38
Al-Hodeidah Association 117
Alhabadi, R. 91
Archer, D. 5, 139–46
Asian Development Bank 70

Bangladesh Rural Advancement Committee (BRAC) 41, 44, 84, 142; school organisation, curriculum and instruction policies 45
Bano, M. 3, 8, 82–94
Barrios de Pie Movement 97, 102, 104
basic education 2
Basic Education Division (BED) 62; Untrained Teacher Diploma in Basic Education (UTDBE) 64
Basic Education and literacy Working Group 69
basic education systems: Sub-Saharan Africa 13
Batley, R.A.: and Larbi, G.A. 110; and Rose, P. 6, 107–13

Bengali Movement 89
Berry, C. 114–21
BRAC Primary Schools (BPS) 43
Brehlavi school of thought in Pakistan 88
Burgos, R.B. 79
Burkina Faso: CSOs 17–18

Cadre de Concertation en Education de Base (CCEB) 17
Canavan, A. 128
Casely-Hayford, L.: and Hartwell, A. 6, 55–67
Chapman, D.W.: and Miric, S. 50, 53
Chinchilla, N.: and Haas, L. 101
Civil Society Education Funds: Fast-Track Initiative 13
civil society organisations (CSOs): activities in Kenya and Tanzania 22; advocacy and service-delivery roles 3–5; Burkina Faso 17–18; capacities and tensions 19–21; collective action in Kenya 18; education sector involvement 22; engagement, changing dynamics 16–19; government and donor relations 21; Kenya 18–19; limitations in capacity 14; Mali 19; political opportunity structures 14–16; role and mandate confusion 22; roles of 13; Tanzania 17
Commins, S. 9, 122–30, 125
Commonwealth Education Fund 4, 17, 34
Communist Party: India 91
Community Development Committees 118
Community Organized Primary Education (COPE) 42
complementary education: cost-effectiveness 42
Comprehensive Peace Agreement (CPA) 125
Coraggio, J.L. 99
Culpitt, I. 99

Dakar Framework and the Education for All Movement 28

INDEX

Danish International Development Agency (DANIDA) 57
de Gortari, S. 98
Department of Economic Affairs of the Ministry of Finance 70
Department for International Development (DFID) 64, 115
DeStefano, J. 6; and Moore, A.-m.S. 39–54; and Torres, C.A. 9
Development Assistance Committee (DAC): coordination Principle (7) 117; do no harm Principle (8) 119–20; state building Principle (8) 118–19
Development in Practice 2
development programmes: donor-driven 9
Dhaka University 89

Education for All (EFA) 2, 48; 2015 target for 10; educational standard in addition to completion 56; EFA global consensus 37; Fast Track Initiative 144; Global Monitoring Report 7; goals of 27; Nepal 118; non-state providers role in success 10
Education for All Global Monitoring Report (2009) 7
Education International 144
education policy advocacy 33–5
Education Quality for All (EQUALL) 58, 64
Education Quality Improvement through Pedagogy (EQUIP) 32–3; Education and Training Sector Development Programme 36; EQUIP2 case studies *43*; EQUIP2 research 45, 53; Oxfam's exit strategy 33; pedagogical model in Shinyanga 34; The Teacher Education Development and Management Strategy 36
Edwards, M. 29, 37
Elimu Yetu Coalition (EYC) 18

Fast Track Initiative 14
Fenton, W. 127
Filmer, D.: and Pritchett, L. 56
Fragile States Group of the Development Assistance Committee (DAC) 123
Free and Compulsory Universal Basic Education (FCUBE) 57
free primary education: Kenya 131–8
Freire, P. 9, 96
From Poverty to Power (Green) 28

G8 Meeting in Gleneagles 30
Galal, A. 50
Galal framework 50
Ghana: complementary education and non-state actors 57–9; Danish Friendship Association 57; education policy questions 65; Ghanaian Government's Education Strategic Plan 56; NGO operations 65; state and non-state sectors 55–67
Ghana Development Communities Association 58
Ghana Friendship Groups in Denmark 58
Ghana School for Life Programme (SfL) 14, 42, 44, 55; attention to good-quality education 62; comparative advantage 62; enrolment, drop outs, graduation and integration **60**; factors leading to success 59; government assessment 62; Government Education Service 61; governmental collaboration 63; government's own appraisal 62–3; graduate integration to formal education 60; impact study 59; National Education Assessment (NEA) 57; nine-month literacy cycle 61; northern districts educational quality provision 56; performance in comparison to non-members 61; and state provision of basic education 63–5; students completion and retention rated 61
Girl's Education Pilot Project 119
Global Alliance for Vaccines and Immunization 127
Global Campaign for Education 4, 30, 144; Civil Society Education Fund 23; Oxfams' role in formation 28; TEMNETs role in formation 33
Global Fund on AIDS, TB and Malaria 127
Global March against Child Labour 144
government financing: NGO provision 5–6
Gramsci, A. 100
Greenaway, D. 72
Greenway's framework 69

Haas, L.: and Chinchilla, N. 101
Hadith, S.U. 91
Hale, S. 98
Hartwell, A.: and Casely-Hayford, L. 6, 55–67
health: in fragile states 123–8; state and non-state providers 124–5, 127–8
Health and Fragile States Network 128
health provision: Afghanistan 125–6; Southern Sudan 126–7
High Level Forum (HLF) 124
Home-Based School: Afghanistan 44

India: District Institutes of Education and Training (ITIs) 72; Eleventh Plan Approach Paper 71, 75; Kothari Commission review of Education 74; panchayati raj institutions (PRIs) 70; Planning Commission 72–3, 76; Private-aided schools 76; proposed private-public partnership 68; public expenditure in

INDEX

education *74*; public-private partnerships (PPPs) 69–75; *Sarva Shiksha Abhiyan* 74, 78; state as financier 74–5; state as manager 75–7; state as regulator 77–8; Tenth and Eleventh Five Year Plans 69, 74; the Tenth Plan Approach Paper 75; Tenth Plan mid-term appraisal 78
Indian education: state's role 68–81
Indian Education NGO 109
Indian government: strategy for inclusive growth 77
Indian government's Alternative and Innovative Education Programme 109
India's 1990s post-liberalisation boom 73
Industrial Training Institutes (ITIs) 72
International Development Assistance 116–17
International Monetary Fund (IMF) 9, 98
International NGO collaboration: education programming Tanzania *29*
International Non Governmental Organisations (INGOs) 17; diversity and multiplicity with state relationships 35; educational work 30; legitimacy and accountability 30; Mali 19; national education coalition alliance 30; NGO tensions 20; Ngorongoro pastoralist programme 32; UK INGOS 27
International Rescue Committee (IRC) 42
International Women's Day 101

Jalandari, M. 91
Jamaat-i-Islami 88
Jones, L.I. 97; and Torres, C.A. 9, 95–106

Kenya: African Population and Health Research Center 132; children enrolled in private schools *133*; CSOs 18–19; education standards 135; FPE policy implications 136–7; free primary education policy (FPE) 131–8; household characteristics and schooling decisions 134–5; pupil school mobility 133–4; quality of primary school inputs 135–6, *136*; reasons for changing schools *134*
Kenya and Tanzania: universal free primary education 14
Khan, G.A. 85
Korol, C. 102

Larbi, G.A.: and Batley, R.A. 110
LaRocque, N. 71
Latin America: Co-Madres in El Salvador 100; Cooperativa La Juanita 97, 104; Madres de Plaza de Mayo 97, 104; Madres' role in Argentinean civil society 100; memory and social-justice education 95–106; Mothers of the Disappeared in Ciudad Juarez, Mexico 100; Movimento dos Trabalhadores Rurais Sem Terra 101; Red de Mujeres Solidarias (Women's Network of Solidarity) 103; social movements 9; struggle for a voice 96; UNESCO Education for Peace Award 101; Workers Party 98; the Zapatistas 101
Lister, S.: and Nyamugasira, W. 14

Macpherson, I.: and Tomlinson, K. 34
Madni, M. 89
madrasas: orthodox fieldwork in Bangladesh and West Bengal 91
madrasas in South Asia 83; *Aliya madrasa* system 84; Area Intensive Madrasa Modernization Programme 85; Bangladesh Madrasa Education Board 84, 86; curriculum and rigidity of ideology 87; Dar ul Uloom Deoband 86; financial incentives 87–8; Islamic training specialists 92; local context 89–90; Madrasa Nizami 85; Madrasa Reform Programme in Islamabad 86; madrasa schooling language difficulties 88; Nadwa tul Ulama 86; partners in education 82–94; petering out of Urdu as a taught language 90; political will 90–1; *Qoumi madrasas* 84; rigidity of Islamic thought 87; trust in the reformer 88–9; *ulama* ideological commitment 91–2; West Bengal Board of Madrasa Education 84; West Bengal Madrasah Board in Calcutta 86
Make Poverty History Campaign 30
Mali: CSOs 19; INGOs 19; NGOs 19
Marx, K. 96
Menem, C. 98
Millennium Development Goals (MGDs) 2, 56, 115
Ministry of Education (MOE) 43; Access and Participation thematic working group 58; Complementary Basic Education Policy Department 63; Education Strategic Plan 58; MOE / BED study 62
Ministry of Education, Science and Sport (MOESS) 63; Draft Document on Complementary Basic Education 63
Ministry of Human Resource Development 109
Miric, S.: and Chapman, D.W. 50, 53
Moore, A.-m.S. 6; and DeStefano, J. 39–54
Mughal Empire 85
Mulk, N.U. 85
multi-donor budgetary support (MDBS) 64
Multi-Donor Trust Fund in Southern Sudan 123
Mundy, K. 28, 37; *et al* 4, 12–25

INDEX

Naeemi, M. 88–9
Nahual Institute for Global Studies programmes in Central America 97
Nair, P. 88
The National Education Assessment (NEA) 57
national-level reform programme: India 87; Pakistan 87
neo-liberal agenda: privatisation 98–100
neo-liberalism 76, 96, 98; agenda 112; economic policy failure 101; education 99; globalisation 99
New Economic Policy 70
Ngorongoro District 32; misunderstandings between Oxfam and LGA 35
Ngware, M.: and Oketch, M. 7, 131–8
non-governmental organisations (NGOs) 2; Bangladesh 111; education programmes 6; Ghana operations 65; growing availability of development aid 3; INGO tensions 20; Mali 19; NGO-funded schools 15; Northern and Southern NGO tensions 23; as policy advocates 112; school management committees 45; service delivery and advocacy 4; in service provision and advocacy 4; start of education provision 8; strategies to achieve influence 110–12; supporting non-state schooling 46
non-profit organisations (NPOs) supply of education 78
non-state actors: and education delivery and education aid *116*; education delivery in fragile states 114–21
non-state providers (NSPs) 123; Egyptian alternative supply model 51; Haitian reliance 47; management structures 52; post-conflict fragile states 122–30; role in relation to state building 124; schools absorbed by governments 47
non-state provision 2; and aid donors 8; engineering approach 50–1; improvement to education 50–2; organisational approach 51–2; political accountability approach 52
non-state and state provision 41–50
Nyamugasira, W.: and Lister, S. 14

Oketch, M.: and Ngware, M. 7, 131–8
Organisation for Economic Cooperation and Development (OECD) 117
Oxfam: collaboration with LGA 31; Global Campaign for Education 144; Memorandum of Understanding 33; Ngorongoro District 31; Oxfam GB Tanzania 32; pilot project for delivering diverse education 31; Project Coordination Committee 32; Regional Pastoral Programme 31; role in formation of Global Campaign for Education 29; role in Tanzania 4; TENMET policy-advocacy work 34

Pakistan: new Islamic public face 90
Paris declaration pledges of coordination and country ownership 110
pastoralist education 31–2
Poverty Reduction Strategy Papers (PRSPs) 14
Primary Education Development Plans (PEDP) 34
Primary Education Development Programme (PEDII) 109
Pritchett, L.: and Filmer, D. 56
privatisation: neo-liberal agenda 98–100
Programa Nacional de Autogestión para el Desarollo Educativo (PRONADE) 41; government founding 48
public-private partnerships (PPPs): India 69–75

Quality of Education Programme 119

Rabata-ul-Madaris in West Bengal 91
Ramamurti, R. 99
Rose, P. 1–11; and Batley, R. 6, 107–13
Sarva Shiksa Abhiyan (Universalisation of Elementary Education Programme) 109
Save the Children UK 127

The Scanteam evaluation 119
Secondary Education Development Plans (SEDP) 34
Sengupta, M. 70
Senior Secondary School 59
September 11th terrorist attack 8, 83
Shinyanga District partnership: Oxfam and LGA 35
Sikaso region: school enrolment increase 50
social movements: Latin America 9
South Asia: governments and NGOs 107–13
South Asian language development and factions 89
Southern Sudan: Comprehensive Peace Agreement 126; Government of Southern Sudan (GoSS) 126; health provision 126–7; Save the Children UK 127
Southern Sudanese and Khartoum-based conflict 125
Srivastava, P. 7, 68–81
state and non-state provision 41–50
state-non-state collaborations preconditions 46–7
state-non-state relationships 3, **49**

INDEX

Sub-Saharan Africa study 12–25; basic education systems 13; basic statistics *15*; Burkina Faso findings 18; Burkina Faso and Mali national sector plans 15; communication among civil-society 21; faith based organisations 20; Kenya findings 18–19; Kenya and Tanzania national sector plans 15; Mali findings 19; national education-sector plans 16; national educational development 14; national parents' associations 20; private providers and the business community 21; research design 13–14; sector-wide approach (SWAp) 18; Tanzania findings 17; teachers' unions 16
Sudanese People's Liberation Army 125
Sudanese Relief and Rehabilitation Association 126
Tanzania: CSO engagement 17; INGO-state relations 30–5
Tanzania and Kenya: universal free primary education 14
Tanzanian Education Network (TENMET) 17, 33, 35; Education and Training Sector Development Programme 36; Oxfam policy-advocacy work 34; role in formation of Global Campaign for Education 33; Teacher Education Development and Management Strategy 36; validity of civil-society monitoring 35
Teamey, K. 40
Tilak, J.B.G. 74, 75
Tomlinson, K.: and Macpherson, I. 34
Torres, C.A.: and DeStefano, J. 9; and Jones, L.I. 9, 95–106

United Nations Children's Fund (UNICEF) 48, 64
United Nations Educational, Scientific and Cultural Organisation (UNESCO): Education for Peace award 101; Institute of Statistics data 40, 83
United States Agency for International Development (USAID) 48; Educational Quality Improvement Program 39
Universal Basic Education 60
universal free primary education: Kenya and Tanzania 14
Universal Primary Education (UPE) 63, 65
universal state provision: post-colonial ideal 108
US Agency for International Development 115

Wafaq-ul-Madaris Al-Arabia in Pakistan 91
war on terror 88
Welmond, M. 51
West Bengal, Rabata-ul-Madaris 91
World Bank: characterised educational agenda 99; District Primary Education Project 75; standard structural adjustment package 70
World Health Organization (WHO) 108

Yemen Social Fund for Development (YSFD) 116, 120